Being Jewish in America

BEING JEWISH
IN AMERICA
The Modern Experience

ARTHUR HERTZBERG

SCHOCKEN BOOKS • NEW YORK

First published by SCHOCKEN BOOKS 1979

10 9 8 7 6 5 4 3 2 1   78 79 80 81

Copyright © 1979 by Schocken Books Inc.

Library of Congress Cataloging in Publication Data

Hertzberg, Arthur.
Being Jewish in America.

1. Judaism—20th century—Addresses, essays,
lectures. 2. Antisemitism—Addresses, essays,
lectures. 3. Jews in the United States—Politics
and government—Addresses, essays, lectures.
4. Zionism—Addresses, essays, lectures.
5. Israel—Addresses, essays, lectures. I. Title.

BM45.H452   296'.0973   78-54390

Manufactured in the United States of America

To two teachers:

SALO WITTMAYER BARON   א״לי

LOUIS GINZBERG   ל״ז

Contents

III. ZIONISM AND ISRAEL

Being Jewish in America

Preface

A PREFACE IS the hardest part of a book to write because suddenly one must decide whom to thank. That is a manifestly impossible task, because who can answer the question of what he owes to whom? This is especially true in a book of essays written through the years for many journals with the cooperation, always very generous, of a variety of editors.

Some of my intellectual debts are acknowledged in the book, and especially in the newly written introductory essay and in the dedication, but only some. The greatest debt is to my parents. What I learned from them has remained the matrix into which all the other influences have been poured. My father, who wrote in rabbinic Hebrew and in Yiddish, taught me how to write. The finishing touches to that education were put by my first editor, Elliot Cohen, who performed that office for me, as he did for many others, in the sternness of his love for young writers.

The immediate impetus for collecting the essays in this book came from Naomi Levine, now vice-president of New York University and at the time executive director of the American Jewish Congress. No book is ever completed, even one such as this which was half-written in advance, without a crisis or two. My friends Hyman and Ruth Glickstein were particularly helpful and supportive. Through the years, most of these essays have been typed and pored over by Anne Bischoff and Reby Evans. My wife Phyllis has worked on all of them, to their great benefit, and acted as my secretary for some of the earliest.

The choices as to what to include and exclude and how to structure the book were made by Seymour Barofsky, editor-in-chief of Schocken Books, who is an unusual combination of both an editor and a friend.

Some of these essays have been rewritten or adapted from their original versions, but in no case have the meanings been changed.

Precisely because these pieces were written in the very midst of events, it seemed to me that they ought to stand as is, to suggest how one Jew felt and thought as his generation went through turbulent times.

ARTHUR HERTZBERG

October 27, 1978

Introduction

VERY EARLY IN MY CAREER I chose to study history and not theology. This was a conscious decision made when I was very young and long before I could explain it. I thought then that I was abandoning theology because I was unready at nineteen to wrestle with the contradictions between faith and reason, and that I would return to this arena when I was finally able to defend the faith with incontrovertible argument. Now, almost forty years later, it is clear to me that I was then bidding farewell to formal theology permanently, never to return, and not for the reasons which I gave myself in 1940.

The majority of the intellectuals among my friends, even those who like me had grown up within the Jewish tradition, had solved their problems of belief by abandoning religion for some secular ideology, usually some form of Marxism. They were even more sure that they possessed Truth than the most unyielding of orthodox religious believers. My problems were different. I took the Talmud too seriously to be able to displace it as sacred text with *Das Kapital.* If I was to live without question or deviation under the discipline of tasks imposed from above, it seemed to me that believers, such as my parents, who spoke for the Jewish God, had much more right to make such demands than Stalin or Trotsky, in the name of the iron laws of history.

What was growing within me was a temperate skepticism. I knew that I did not possess the keys to the kingdom of heaven, but I had not become such a relativist as to believe that God was dead, that everything was permitted, and that men might choose whatever values they found convenient. I read such humanists as John Dewey and Bertrand Russell in the late 1930s and, despite their high-mindedness, I felt in danger of my life. Their relativism left me with no defense against the right of men to choose fascism. I insisted on believing that some values were indeed higher than

xi

others—never mind the intricacies of philosophical argument—and that some cultures and traditions were nearer to decency and god-liness—never mind the technical theological arguments. It was even clearer to me that cultures and traditions changed and yet they retained, if they had character, a core of recognizable personality.

I thus moved toward history not in order to relativize all values and all traditions, but, on the contrary, to try to find con-tinuity with my ancestors even as I was entering an intellectual and academic world they had always feared as the seductress, "Greek wisdom," and as I was becoming a Zionist, and thus united with Jews whom my own grandfathers had excommunicated a few decades earlier for their secularizing heresies. I could solve the issues of relatedness, of belonging, only if I placed myself in some profound historic current in which all Jews, past and pres-ent, even as they clashed, belonged. That meant that I ceased believing that any of the Jewish ideologies, including my own, was the whole truth. To believe that meant that I had to exclude, and I had to face being excluded. History, I was sure, would not allow any ideology complete victory; else some men would belong to the elect and most others would be damned. Only absolutists, and not even all of them, could delight in such prospects. I could not live with any of that, and I still cannot. I have argued in several of the essays in this volume that believing people must bet their lives on their faith in such a way that they do not rob anyone else of his essential place in the world.

The one thing that I have never doubted or found it neces-sary to "prove" or "explain" is the bald and unique fact of Jewish existence through the ages. A creative remnant has al-ways survived, despite the woes of persecution or the blandish-ments of other cultures and values. That remnant, as I have been at pains to describe many times, has recreated itself in angular, *sui generis* ways in every society to this very day. Perhaps be-cause a rabbi's son is not like all other Jewish children, it was clear to me very early, as a college student, that the Jews would not become an ethnic minority like all others in the United States or a "normal" nation among nations, by creating a Zionist state in the Middle East. I was arguing this point some nine years later in the summer of 1949 in two articles that I wrote (not included in this collection) in *Commentary* from Tel Aviv and Jerusalem, when the war of Israel's independence had not yet ended. Short of the complete disappearance of the Jews, the ineradicability of their uniqueness was something that I knew as fact, past and present. History and not theological abstraction thus provided me with my First Principle: The Jews are different. This "difference" had not been wiped away by liberalism and capitalism in Europe. It persisted in Communist Russia and it had not vanished in New Deal America. Why indeed should anyone want this singular tradition to vanish?

Only the religious believers and the Zionists saw and cared as I did. And yet I did not fit easily into any party or school of thought. I did not ever believe that Zionism in any of its forms could solve all the problems of Jews with the Gentiles or even among ourselves. Since I could count, it was obvious that there were fewer of "us" than there were of "them"—far fewer—and that Jews could never persuade all of "them" to our view of ourselves. Since I could hear and read, it was obvious that we Jews were in large, often bitter, disagreements among ourselves. The Jewish God had neither settled our inner doubts by miraculous sign nor discomfited our enemies by visiting upon Hitler the plagues he had once sent Pharaoh. I thus concluded that, within Jewry itself and as between Jews and Gentiles, untidy arrangements were more likely than ideological victories. Unless we were in the midst of the wars of Gog and Magog, which are the preamble to the coming of the Messiah, even victories are illusory and destructive. The unity of the Jewish people and its relationship to non-Jews could both be maintained only in some realm at once more mysterious and more practical than easily defined, clear-cut categories.

Among Jewish thinkers, I have been closest to Ahad Ha-Am, the central figure of cultural Zionism; to the greatest of the Orthodox Zionist mystics, the first chief rabbi of Palestine, Abraham Isaac Kuk; and increasingly to the founder in America of Conservative Judaism, Solomon Schechter. There are aspects of all three which put me off (the thinly veiled atheism of Ahad Ha-Am, the too-frequent chauvinism of Kuk, and Schechter's pervasive romanticism), but in quite different ways they represent two affirmations: inclusion within the flow of Jewish existence even for viewpoints that they vehemently oppose, and awareness that in the here-and-now world that is given to men we must reduce the tensions. Through Solomon Schechter I was led back to Nachman Krochmal, who remains for me the most profound and significant Jewish thinker of the modern age. Krochmal in his alas! still untranslated *Guide to the Perplexed of Our Time,* written almost a century and a half ago, identified the Jewish experience of God with history, and the uniqueness of Jewry with the regenerative power which has raised them, again and again, from the ashes of decline and destruction.

The theologizing of recent years has left me cold. It has seemed to me for the most part to wander between the shallow and the hysterical. The reigning preoccupations have been Auschwitz and Israel. On theological grounds, it has seemed to me that there is nothing to be said about the Holocaust that was not said after the destruction of the Second Temple, during the Crusades, after the expulsion of the Jews from Spain in 1492, and after the slaughters in Eastern Europe in 1648.

In our day, the "voices of the Holocaust" continue to keen in anger, hurt, and defiance. Such catharsis was necessary, but life insists on moving past purgation. Even a wounded people cannot scream forever, especially if its present reality neither in Zion nor in America is that of a victim. Job may once have been advised to curse God and die, but no one can live in permanent war with Him, or with the rest of mankind.

The theologizing about Israel has been mostly in the key of certainty that the state is the preamble to the redemption promised in the religious tradition. I have never been so certain that I know what God is about, and I become very less certain when I hear such theologies used to validate hard-line politics. I am not persuaded, despite my admiration for Kuk, that the secular life of Israel is in some mysterious way pointing, in the near future, to God's Kingdom on earth. My Zionism regards Israel's creation as a historic necessity of this century, as men have tried to solve problems within their reach. There is an idolatry, it seems to me, in being so sure that we know God's political will. I learned from Maimonides that we really do not know what God is, but only what He is not.

My own particular dialogue with God, with the Jewish past, and with other Jews, especially those who were creating contemporary Israel, has taken place in twentieth-century America. Most of my contemporaries were American born, the children of immigrants. I came here at the age of five in 1926, as part of the very end of East European migration to the United States, which was choked off by the discriminatory Immigration Act of 1924. I was raised in a hasidic home, the home of a *rov,* in which the language remained, to the very end of my parents' lives, Yiddish, soaked in rabbinic allusions. The earliest picture that exists of me, at the age of five arriving in this country, is in the "uniform" of a hasidic child, a black satin *yarmulke* on my head, the sides of which were adorned by long *peot.*

I was to traverse in my lifetime and experience at least two generations of American Jewish acculturation, and I was therefore never so overwhelmed by the great scope that post–World War II America offered as to think that all had been and was well, and would be forever and ever. The immigration laws that closed the doors of America in the 1920s to the Jews of Poland were and remained a very personal disaster. My maternal grandfather and his entire family were told to wait fifteen years for an American visa. I was then the "secretary for English" for the family and was writing letters to the State Department, so I knew the painful details. The quota for Polish Jews was "oversubscribed" for the next fifteen years, and so my grandfather and his family were gassed in a bunker in Lemberg on January 6, 1942, a date that I discovered only recently after thirty years of asking questions of survivors.

I was graduated from college in 1940 just before the American entry into World War II. In that era, bright young Jews were still being advised not to attempt to enter academic careers because the prevalent fierce academic anti-Semitism was very hard to beat. A few years later, after World War II, a new era dawned. Hundreds of thousands of the very people who, at best, could get a job in the 1930s only in government bureaucracies, rocketed to prominence in America. By then, I had read—and already lived through—too much history to be persuaded that the secular Messiah of democracy had now made his appearance, even though I knew that America in the 1950s was the best situation that Jews had ever experienced in the more than two millennia of their Diaspora existence. It was clear to me that an expanding society would need all the talent that it could find, but I had few illusions that the clock of social change would stop once Jews were admitted to the most honorific roles in society. There were others, especially blacks, waiting to bid for a place.

To conceive of what was happening in the 1940s and 1950s in ideological terms as some dawning of a now more spacious doctrine for all America, as the realization here of the heaven on earth of which the Enlightenment had dreamed, seemed to me to be partly true, but largely self-deluding. I did not doubt that Jews would discover that their interests and those of others, both above and below them in the socioeconomic pecking order, did not always converge. In part I thought this was because of my awareness of the politics of Jewish life in Poland in the 1930s, where Jews had been an embattled community which had to think of group interests and group alliances. In part my thinking derived from relativism about ideologies in general, which was prevalent in the philosophy department at Johns Hopkins in the late 1930s, under the influence of Arthur Lovejoy, who invented the history of ideas as a field of study.

Most important, I suspect, was my unquestioned commitment always to the positive inner life of the Jews, to its numinous quality, to the God whose hand was mysteriously present within Jewish history. My contemporaries could pretend to themselves, and very convincingly, that they were fighting against anti-Semitism because they had a profound passion for removing discrimination in America as a whole. In due course, some of the very people who were once so busy laboring for full equality in America that, even in the sight of still-smoking death ovens, they could not be bothered with the struggle for Zionism, were to appear as the paladins of the struggles today for "merit," in conflict with black interests, for very hard positions in the superpower politics between the United States and the Soviet Union, and for Israeli maximalism.

I did not believe in the 1940s, and I do not now believe, that any of these notions represent truth. They were, in all their contradictions, epiphenomena; they are the rationalizations of people whose prime concern, then as now, is their personal success in a successful America. I do not condemn either of these purposes, having served both with a considerable amount of my energies, but my dominant commitment has always been to the Jews, not to ·ny one Jew, and to the Jewish tradition rather than to a newly arisen, untraditional intelligentsia bidding to be the priesthood of either revolution or conservatism.

Jews have survived in history best by accommodation and not by confrontation, unless circumstances were so dire that there was no alternative. We did reach two such impasses in our tragic century, when a few ghettos under Hitler revolted, and when the battle for the Jewish state had to be fought with arms, first against the British and then the Arabs, but we were never at such a point in America, and we certainly are not today. To push for revolution in the 1930s or for "merit" in the 1970s is to sharpen the social conflict. Jews require alliances that are reknit again and again and a continuing restudy of the Jewish self-interest.

My life with the conflicts and problems of modernity has not led me toward any hankering for the old ghetto or any illusions about its simplicity. Leaving the ghetto has produced a new set of problems, especially the erosion of inner life in an open society. Nonetheless, the drive to break down all the political and economic barriers against Jews that could be broken down was a historic necessity and an inevitability. I have experienced the journey from the foreignness of the Galician small town and the "east side" of Baltimore to post–World War II America as the exchange, after substantial gains, of one set of problems for another. Because the journey was never messianic, I never thought that the prices that we were paying in acculturation and surrender of inner identity were to be accounted as minor.

As early as 1911, A. D. Gordon, the great theoretician and founder of Labor Zionism, who himself never visited America, wrote a passionate article addressed to the Jews of Russia. Gordon said to those masses that they might indeed achieve their dreams by going to the "Golden Land"—but, he asked, at what price? He then painted a picture predicting family dislocation, alienation of children from parents, and disrespect for Judaism. I read those words of Gordon in the early 1940s, a generation after they had been written, with a shock of recognition. In the generation since, the period during which I have been writing about Jewish life, the disrespect has disappeared, but Jews themselves have become so acculturated that they identify Jewish life not with the life of the tradition, even secularized as culture, but with political activity and the expression of Jewish group feeling.

The essays in this book represent my outlook through the years on such problems as Israel–Diaspora relations; the links and polarities between Jews and blacks, and Jews and Christians, in America; the relationship of Jews to their own tradition; and how a contemporary Jewish outlook should define itself. By design, the more dated and polemical essays have been excluded, but I am not entirely sure that this has been a correct decision.

I should at least note briefly where I have stood on some of the major controversies of the last two decades. My opposition to the war in Vietnam was a public matter as early as 1964. I knew almost by instinct that the war was bad for America. Within Zionist circles, I was almost the only member of the World Zionist Executive (which I joined late in 1969) to oppose the then-dominant view that support of American objectives in Vietnam would redound to Israel's benefit because America would thus be a more secure ally for embattled small peoples. I was certain that the cause of Israel could only be hurt by identification with a losing war, which was being opposed in the United States by large parts of the moderate political opinion which had traditionally been pro-Zionist.

In 1973–74, when the bulk of the Jewish community was pushing for public confrontation with the Soviet Union through the Jackson Amendment, I was in a small minority which took the view that some reasonable deal, such as an annual emigration figure of close to 40,000 which was being offered by the Russians through the good offices of the White House, should be accepted and that out-and-out confrontation was to be avoided.

In relationship to the Arabs, I have argued in a variety of ways and in many forums, long before the Yom Kippur War of

1973, that time was not on our side, that it could not be bought endlessly, and that accommodations were possible at political prices that reasonable men ought to be willing to pay. I have always known that Arabs, having pride and feeling and injured dignity like all other men and women, would not simply go away and forget about the woes they think that Jews have caused them.

In the arena of American domestic affairs, I have fought for racial integration. Once, in a very melodramatic moment in 1966, when a local election in Englewood, New Jersey, was ripe with racist innuendos, I "forbade" my congregation (as if congregations have ever accepted such rabbinic dicta) to vote for the offending candidates. Nonetheless, I have always seen the black–Jewish encounter as more complicated than either side would have it. On the most difficult continuing issue, that of "merit," I have taken the view that society does indeed owe some generous, and thus unequal, recompense, to all who begin life as the heirs of past deprivations. It is even to the Jewish interest that a black intelligentsia and middle class be fostered. I have held these views in part because I prefer, always, accommodation to legalistic justification for doing battle, but in larger part because I am a Zionist. The demand for Jewish sovereignty in this generation was a form of asking for "affirmative action" on an international scale. Vladimir Jabotinsky, the most maximalist of Zionists, argued this way in 1937 before the Peel Commission: the world owes Jews unequal favorable treatment in this age as recompense for the depth of past deprivation. I cannot be a Zionist and not hear this cry when others utter it.

Russians, Arabs, blacks, liberals, and several successive American administrations—these have all been the targets of the confrontationist temper which has pervaded too much of the Jewish community in the last decade. I have kept arguing that a small people does not need so many opponents. Part of the problem is, I think, that Jews have not yet come to terms with the Holocaust. We keep reenacting in the freedom of the 1970s what we think we should have done in the 1930s—but we are different and so is the world. We have ceased being the "have-nots" of the depression era and are not quite at home with our status as "haves" in the post–World War II era. For that matter, the major figures in the world with whom we are dealing now are also different. Brezhnev is not Stalin; Sadat is not the grand mufti of Jerusalem; and Carter is not Franklin Delano Roosevelt.

There is only one major issue about which I have been thinking for the last thirty years on which my mind has changed. It is the question of Jews and public education. I have been arguing that in the realm of public policy Jews must be less confrontationist and more flexible. In the educational realm, however, which involves the whole question of the transmission of Jewish faith and commitment, I now conclude that, at least in precollege education, Jews must move by choice into greater isolationism.

The Jewish passion for the public school befitted an immigrant generation trying to make its way in American culture and society. It is no longer appropriate to a group which has arrived and which is indeed, as one of the marks of its success, now crowding into the most honorific private schools all over the country. An elite cannot survive this way. It must impart its own ethos and its own sense of worth through educational institutions appropriate to its own self. The American Jewish community will thus have to move toward creating a large network of Jewish private schools in which transmitting Jewish religion and culture are the central and suffusing concern. This mode of education can no longer be left among Jews to the minority, which consists of the bulk of the Orthodox and the more traditional elements among the other groups within Jewry. If the Jewish community is to survive significantly, it cannot happen unless the young are rooted within it very early—and in the open society this means private education.

A prime element of such Jewish schooling will be the link to Israel: to its culture even more than to its problems; to the traditions that resound in its language and the rhythm of its Biblically determined calendar, more than to the modernities, and sometime vulgarities, of its street life.

In the eighteenth century, the climactic element in the education of a gentleman was the "grand tour" of Europe. Among East European Jews the educated classes sent their male children away from home to a yeshivah as their "finishing school." Com-

parably, the experience of Israel must be built into the education
of American Jews, for two paradoxical reasons. Among some of
the young, such a year during their teens will produce an inner
crisis which might result in their choosing to live in Israel: Zionism and Israel will thus be enriched. Most of the students will
choose to live out their lives in the land of their birth. American
Jewry and America as a whole will, hopefully, be enriched by a
new generation whose Jewish sensibility is less politically ethnic
and more culturally and spiritually Brahmin.

American Jews are less confident now because all of our successes added together, both our participation in the drama of
Israel and our interest in world Jewish affairs, have not solved the
recurrent problems of living as a Jew in the modern era.

The State of Israel was, and remains, a miracle of creativity
on the morrow of desolation, and yet, however the "Jewish problem" may be defined, it is as yet unsolved. The majority of Jews
continue to live in the Diaspora and we thus remain, in classic
Zionist terms, an "abnormal people." Israel has added dignity
and survivalist strength to world Jewry and has even almost become its "religion," but erosion and assimilation continue at all
the frightening rates which prevailed before the triumph of Zionism. The American Jewish community is therefore worried about
its own survival. For that matter, the Communist apocalypse, in
which many of my contemporaries believed in the "Popular
Front" days of the 1930s, has neither eradicated anti-Semitism in
the Soviet Union nor allowed room for any kind of Jewish cultural continuity. Russian Jewry remains a problem to itself and
to the conscience of the world.

A generation which began in the 1930s believing in its own
capacity to succeed is less confident now, more aware of problems
than hopeful of their solutions. The Holocaust is, for the first
time now, really on our agenda because the dimension of helplessness, of being swept by forces which we cannot withstand or
control, is now our own mood as we contemplate the world which
we thought we could remake and which we are, at very least,
barely withstanding.

The prevailing mood today is not thus going forward boldly
to new adventure. It is rather one of defending a heritage which

we weakened in the boldness of the ardor of many of my contemporaries for grand solutions. We are beginning to think that
some of the things that we threw out as material that was un-
usable in the building of great new edifices of the future (who
would need tradition, or religion, or memory of the past on a
kibbutz or a *kolkhoz?*) has weakened the fabric of the ancient
dwellings, which are the only things left to keep us warm in the
recurrent storms. We are less concerned about apocalypses than
in living through this week, and perhaps the next, and the next
one after that.

There is thus a "not-quiteness" about the totality of our experience. It is a blend of the heavens we tried, with some success,
to create on this earth; of the vast problems we could not solve;
and of the ghosts we could not send away.

What these essays through the years are about is my sensibility, even as I lived through the era of pain and horror, and of
hope and glory, that the Messiah has a bad habit of not coming
soon. Our greatest labors do bring him a bit closer, but they do
not compel him to descend to earth. What is given to the will and
wisdom of men is to live decently and reasonably. At least, we
should not make the Messiah tarry.

THE JEW AND THE
MODERN WORLD

CHALLENGES OF MODERNITY

1. *Varieties of Jewish Modernity*

To CONFRONT MODERNITY and to define its relationship to tradition is a profoundly difficult act. To be sufficiently interested in the subject to want to discuss it is already positive proof of one's personal involvement and of the essentially autobiographical nature of the question. Certainly in the Jewish realm, whether one lives by choice in a hasidic ghetto as if the world had not changed since the eighteenth century or one chooses a kibbutz in the Galilee, or bourgeois Jewish life on Park Avenue in New York, the critical new element is that choices have been made, quite consciously, even by the traditionalists. Even the ghetto no longer exists unreflectively. It, too, wherever it has been refounded after the Holocaust in Europe, is constructed as an act of defiance and of resistance.

Modernity is the solvent of tradition. Almost invariably the questioning of the older values leads to their rejection, if only because their basis in divine revelation has been undermined. What is most characteristic of modernity in most of its permutations is that after God has been dethroned, or even made to move over in His heaven, men attempt to find some scale of values by which they can live. At the very worst they try to justify their nihilism and find ways of surviving in a complex universe.

Based on a lecture delivered at the University of Denver on May 22, 1975, which appears in Stanley Wagner, ed., *Great Confrontations in Jewish History,* 1977, pp. 125–135.

3

Modernity begins in the Jewish community with Spinoza. I know that there are other theories. For Ben Zion Dinur, the greatest of the Zionist historians, modernity begins with a serious effort to return to the land of promise. Modernity begins after sixteen centuries of passivity—but this is to identify Jewish modernity with the effort to create a State of Israel. For Gershom Scholem the modern age begins with Shabbetai Tzevi, with the radical upsetting of halakhic Judaism by the greatest of pseudo-messianic revolts. Scholem is thus enabled to argue that the breakdown of tradition, the antinomian elements which come into Jewish experience, are home grown, that they are born from within a subterranean tradition of kabbalistic and messianic revolt, and that modernity is thus not an import. These assertions are comforting to Jews who care deeply about Jewish experience and have revolted against Jewish practices, for they can regard themselves as part of the age-old oscillation, the dialectic within Judaism itself, between halakhists and messianic heretics. The bulk of conventional interpretation has been saying for almost two centuries that modernity began with the French and American revolutions with the grant of political equality in two countries between 1789 and 1791, thus creating the paradigm for the as yet uncompleted struggle for the equal citizenship of Jews in the various countries of their births. Here, too, a value judgment is clearly at play. The presumption is that the new age was intended to be the period in which the Jews were to realize a dream of integration into the wider society, and that such an achievement would indeed be the contemporary equivalent of the messianic redemption foretold in Scripture.

Our theme is, however, narrower than the question of what is the hinge on which Jewish history turned to some kind of new experience. Regardless of exactly when the modern era began, it was marked by the appearance of a Jewish type which could not have existed before the last several centuries: a person of Jewish origin who retains some inner connection, if only that of memory, with his Jewishness, who largely or totally abandons both the Jewish faith and the Jewish community but does not convert to another religion. This disbelieving Jew, who has not turned Christian, exists for the first time in Spinoza. He was the first Jew who could have become a college professor; he was, indeed, offered the chair of philosophy at Heidelberg, but turned it down because of his Jewishness. As such, Spinoza is, if not the lineal ancestor, certainly the archetype of several centuries of postreligious Jews who are unwilling to convert to Christianity because they believe it as little as they do Judaism.

Spinoza remained· a Jew by situation, and he was universally identified as "the Jew, Spinoza." For Spinoza the measure of truth was not the revealed will of God. In his *Theological-Political Tractate* he subjected the Bible not merely to literary criticism, pronouncing it to be a patchwork document, but to the much more acid indictment of its morality. Before the bar of Spinoza's universal ethics, the Bible was judged to be the account of a people with, at best, occasional glimmerings of universal reason which can be apprehended by any man who applies himself to cultivating it. This view is still a long journey away from making the needs and desires of individual man into the measure of the good. Spinoza is no relativist, but he has pronounced reason without revelation—indeed, reason as the judge of revelation—to be the standard by which men should live. For rabbis, priests, and even authoritative philosophers he has substituted the individual, meditating on universal truth, even as he polishes lenses in Leyden. This individual is, moreover, rejecting tradition but he has no bad conscience. Such rejection is not a running away for the sake of convenience; it is a form of growth, of rising beyond that which has been inherited. To reject the inherited Jewish tradition is therefore less a trauma than a liberation.

This theme has not been understood by most of those who have dealt with Jewish modernity. Jewish thinkers and historians are themselves usually "good Jews," very much like a whole generation of Hebrew writers who were recently students in the yeshivah who wrote in praise of the tradition, of its warmth and grandeur, with a countertheme of self-accusation for having let go of these treasures. The classic phrase coined in modern Hebrew literature by Micah Joseph Berdichevsky was "the rent in the heart," in which the modernizing Jew looked back upon the warm *shtetl* and said to himself, "How come? For what did I ever leave it?" Most of those who have written about Jewish modernity have thus presumed that it is a tale of guilt and trauma.

Spinoza in the seventeenth century was the paradigm for Marx and Freud in the nineteenth. For them, too, modernity meant a going beyond into some wider category of being within which past narrownesses, and especially the discrete life and practices of the Jewish community, are ended. The young Karl Marx, writing on the Jewish question in 1844 in *Zur Judenfrage,* says the Jew is the proto-capitalist. The way to transcend the Jewish question is to solve the problem of all human society by emancipating the world from both Jews and Christians through the social revolution. In a Socialist society capitalism will be gone, and with it all the tensions that it engenders. Freud maintained that all religions, and therefore especially the Jewish religion, represent an infantilism that man must transcend to be healthy. Religion is the archneurosis; it is the accusing finger of the father.

From Spinoza through Marx and Freud, a new attitude was, thus, fashioned among some Jews (I do not have to point out the parallels to other groups), that it is, oddly enough, to the interest of the most historical of peoples, the Jews, to dynamite history. These great Jewish rebels are antihistorical. For them the past is the enemy. Marx wants to destroy its economic and class structures; Freud wants to destroy everyone's personal past by curing him of it. Whatever may be your group history, it is an authority standing over against you like an avenging angel with its sword unsheathed, and it must be exorcised.

Why is this antihistorical attitude so repetitive among the great "outsiders" who were Jews? I suspect that for Jews modernity begins with the idea, whether conscious or unconscious, that if you can destroy the medieval past of Europe, then Jews and non-Jews will begin all over again on an equal footing. I understand, for instance, why Jews for a century forgave Voltaire for his anti-Semitism and tried to forget it because they found his slogan *écrasez l'infâme* (erase infamy) so congruent with what Jews really wanted. They desired their total emancipation, their entry out of the ghetto into the West, their becoming co-founders of a new Western culture, for the inherited Western tradition was heavily impregnated with the myths and symbols of Christianity. For the Jew truly to enter the world required that the Western past be interred. Posttraditional men could then start together, as equals, to build the new age.

It seems to me that what I have been saying here is the explanation for an uncomfortable fact about Jews in the modern age. It is a fact that there has been an outsize representation of Jews since the beginning of the nineteenth century in every movement of political, social, and cultural revolution. It is pure nonsense to deny the obvious, that significant numbers of Jews were central to the untraditional or antitraditional culture in Weimar Germany in the 1920s, or earlier in Germany in the middle of the nineteenth century in literature (Heine) and politics (Marx), or in the protest in American academe in the late 1960s, in the recent fight against the war in Vietnam, or in Russia in the Politburo of the Bolshevik Revolution. There have always been rather more Jews in all these movements than one would expect, even taking into account the fact that Jews belong to the bourgeois intelligentsia. As a matter of fact, the Jews have chosen to belong to the bourgeois intelligentsia because the bourgeois intelligentsia is the only element in Western society which has a tradition of two or three centuries by now of intellectuals proclaiming: "We are secular, posttraditional, universal." This is true in theory, though of course in practice this bourgeois intelligentsia is seldom totally hospitable to those who want to enter its class and enjoy its privileges.

I have often maintained that an important "Jewish" novel is one that was written about a French *arriviste,* Stendhal's *Le Rouge et le Noir,* in which the young man from the country, arriving in the city, trying to make it* in a posttraditional culture, is really a description of Proust's Swann, or of Sammy Glick in Budd Schulberg's *What Makes Sammy Run?* It is thus understandable why Jews are more comfortable in the United States than in any previous Diaspora. This is the only country which was founded after the Middle Ages were over. There is no medieval past in America. There are no cathedrals in which American presidents were once crowned as kings. One does not drive by some American Notre

---

* This phrase was made famous by Norman Podhoretz in the title of his book, *Making It.*

Dame and say to himself, "Only briefly was this a temple of reason." Handfuls though they were, Jews were around from the colonial beginnings on a plane of equality, as individuals.

Having said something about the rebels and revolutionizers of culture and society who were born Jews and who tried to solve their Jewish problem by creating a new heaven and new earth for all men, let me now turn to the more conventional Jews for whom modernity was something to be coped with less dramatically. Many varieties of modern Jewish thinkers (in the introductory essay to my first book, *The Zionist Idea,* I termed them "the insiders"), produced theories to define what being Jewish means, or can mean, in the new age of Westernized education and in a society that was open to Jews intellectually, in fact, and politically and socially at least in theory.

On this theme, a very important book has been written that hardly anyone has read, although it is available in German and has been translated into Hebrew. It is entitled *Die jüdische Religion im Zeitalter den Emancipation (Jewish Religion in the Era of Emancipation)* by Max Wiener. Max Wiener makes the point that those who were trying to maintain Jewish life after the Emancipation did so in a posthalakhic, postbelieving age. The preservative movements of Jewish modernity, those which wanted to find a reason for continuing some form of separate Jewish life, are thus a set of substitutes for the earlier unquestioning faith in the divinity of the revealed traditions. For these modernists the authority of the tradition was severely damaged, but they attempted to construct some definitions, some reasons, some explanations for remaining Jewish.

Wildly disparate though these survivalist theories are, they can quickly be shown to be, at root, the same. The classical Reform interpretation of the nineteenth century was that Judaism was universal morality; it was ethical monotheism incarnate within the Jewish community, which existed in order to be a light unto the Gentiles. So anywhere in the Western world, he who drives by a building that has inscribed over it "And My House shall be a House of Prayer unto all Peoples" knows instantly that he is at the local Reform temple.

Zionism, at least in some of its forms, is not really different as

a form of modern Jewish self-definition. To assert Jewish nationalism is to believe and act in a manner totally contrary to that of
the antinational, universalist, mid-nineteenth-century Reform Jews.
Yet these two warring ideologies ask the same question and try in
their antithetical ways to fill the same need. Except for the religious
faction, the majority of Zionists, political as well as cultural, are
secularists who begin with the presumption that the Jewish religion
can no longer serve as the basis for Jewish unity and that therefore Jewish survivalist policy has to be founded on some other
premise. For the Zionist that premise is the Jewish nation (unlike
the Reform Jew, for whom it was the Jewish ethical community),
and it is in creating this nation as a modern entity, parallel to the
most advanced of contemporary nations, that Jews will find both
a valid reason for their continued existence and a program for
action. The greatest commandment is no longer to suffer martyr-
dom for the sanctification of the Divine Name, but rather to fight
for the rebuilding of the land. Indeed, the political and social
passivity which was engendered in the Middle Ages and beyond by
religious tradition, as conventionally understood, is now looked
back on as a national sin.

There is, of course, a certain illogic, a kind of remaining
re-echo of the classic assertion of the Jewish religion—that Jews
are God's chosen people—that remains even in these newer ideologies. In all logic it should have been enough to produce as reason
for the survival of Jews in the modern age that Judaism was as
moral a tradition as those of the other great faiths. There was no
logical necessity for early Reform to assert that Jews were, at least
potentially, morally superior to all other men. It should be enough
today for Zionism to envisage a Jewish state which validates its
right to existence simply by being, and need not assert that it is
engaged in a struggle to be more cultured, more literate, more advanced than any other small- or middle-sized country. Nonetheless
almost every one of the movements which try to define Jews in the
modern idiom asserts that Jews have an inherent responsibility to
exemplify for society as a whole the highest possibilities of its most
contemporary ideals. Being Jewish thus becomes a corporate way
not of preserving the past but of being a paradigm for the future,
a "light unto the Gentiles."

The tools of modernity itself, what it regards at one or another point in the last several centuries as being a universal value, are thus used to justify Jewish specificness. When nationalism began to be in fashion in the mid-nineteenth century, Moses Hess asserted that the Biblical-Talmudic Jews were the first national community and that they therefore exemplified the highest form of nationalism. In the twentieth century in the United States ethnicity has become a value with positive associations in the public mind, and so we are now being assured that Jewish ethnicity is at once like everyone else's and that it is more intense and deeply rooted —and thus paradigmatic.

The difficulty with all of these attempts to create an explanation of Jewish specificness in terms of standards and values of the general society is that they lack one fundamental *desideratum*. It is the very nature of humanistic values that the individual is free to move from one group to another; it is the very nature of free inquiry, and for that matter of the changes in intellectual fashion, that these values themselves can be changed. Nowhere in the kind of Jewish modernity which tries to cast the Jew for the role of being the most superb example of the modern, whatever that may be, is there a thundering "you must!" Without it, there can only be personal relativism. Thus, Jewish modernity consists of unstable, highly personalized combinations of fashionable rhetoric, used to express what remains of specific Jewish emotions.

It is precisely because such a response is fragmented and unstable that there are today very few "modern" Jews who do not find themselves reacting, perhaps with envy, when the truck of Lubavitcher hasidim comes around and the young hasidim alight to say very courteously to modern Jews: "Your life should be lived differently by absolute standards; we live the absolute and we invite you to live it with us."

I said above that Zionism was created in part in order to define Jews as a nation in an age which had gone far in disbelieving religion, and I more than hinted that belonging to the Jewish people was no more self-evident than belonging to its religion. In either case, abandonment of one's identity and assimilating to the majority remained an option, and continuing to affirm one's Jewishness, in any definition, remained an act of faith.

There was, however, one aspect of modern Zionism which did, perhaps more subconsciously than consciously, attempt to counter the prevalent relativism of the modern age. This was the Zionist theory of anti-Semitism. Hatred of the Jew was described by both Leo Pinsker and Theodor Herzl as the lasting dislike of the unlike, which could end only if the Jews created a normal nation. Neither Pinsker nor Herzl cared much about Jewish culture, ancient or modern. What they both thought they knew for certain was that anti-Semitism would keep Jews Jewish and propel them to their own nationhood, and that this force existed as an objective reality, regardless of how individual Jews might feel. For the disbelieving Jew, Pinsker and Herzl offered a new concreteness as the foundation of Jewish existence: anti-Semitism.

Jewish modernity is thus the community which once had a tradition concretely its own, which tried a number of universalist explanations of why it had a particular spirit which it wanted to maintain, and wants to continue to maintain, but which concretizes its modern existence around the one set of concerns which all Jews share, which they do not share with anybody else: Jews were recently in Auschwitz and might be candidates for it again. Very deep in our consciousness is that its happening again is not an inconceivable idea. Even if you do not act on it, the most pervasive contemporary view is that the one thing that Jews have in common is a seed of worry, which, regardless of their inner estate, they share. The closest thing to a *kehillah* (a communal structure) that exists in Jewry today are the fundraising campaigns for the needs of Jews all over the world.

What, therefore, is Jewish modernity? It is compounded out of the memories of the past. We would like our children to believe that abandoning Judaism is an act of treason even though we have abandoned much of it ourselves. The old traditions still reverberate, if only semisubliminally. It is the notion that Jews are indeed a very creative and important element in the world, and that if Jews disappeared from the world, the world would fall in. That faith descends from some Biblical ideas about the Holy Land, and Jews, and God, and a covenant as the center of it all. We believe it, or rather we act on it without ever really putting it into words and asking ourselves the question: On what basis do we

half-believe all this? Are we consistent? So we talk it out by prais-
ing Jews as a creative element in culture, a seed of Nobel Prize
winners, and so on and so forth.

Jewish modernity is thus the paradox of some desire lurking
within us to be at one and the same time totally involved in the
society and very seriously barricaded against it. Read *Portnoy's
Complaint,* skipping the excessive vulgarity, and get down to the
real problem of Alexander Portnoy in Philip Roth's novel. His
mother wants him to look and act like an upper-class Gentile, but
come home every Friday night for Shabbat dinner, and to do both
very successfully. This is really not far different from what other
contemporary Jewish mothers want of their children—that they be
totally successful in the Western world and very specifically Jewish. The most popular forms of Jewish modernity seem to want
total openness and a portable barricade, both at the same time.

And so we have the modern Jew, poised somewhere between
the tradition he still affirms, at least emotionally, and not quite
knowing what to do with his modernity. He is desperately involved with his Jewishness, torn by all kinds of inner tensions
which he tries to plaster over or talk out of existence. The modern Jew continues somehow to live out his complex identity in an
age in which there are no clear-cut answers but plenty of problems.

2. The Secularity of Israel's Election

MY GENERATION GREW to maturity in fear of Hitler and in the hope
for Zion. Even the question of God was not very troublesome. In
part this was due to the influence of childhood training. Most of the
people I knew had been brought up identifying the faith in God

Reprinted from *Judaism: A Quarterly Journal of Jewish Life and Thought,*
vol. 13, no. 4 (Fall 1964).

with a commitment to Jewish practices. In my father's house I, for one, had heard much of the Talmud but nothing of philosophical theology. As my friends and I began to question, our problems were minimized, because it appeared to us that the question of God was not really a "Jewish" issue. (I was to discover only ten years later that it was.) Therefore, we could depend, so to speak, on Niebuhr, or even John Dewey, to solve that problem for us. Many of us, perhaps the majority, found in Mordecai M. Kaplan the language of theological pragmatism, in a Jewish recension, with which to talk easily about God as process; M. M. Kaplan helped us to avoid the problem of the evil unfolding before our eyes by making familiar to us the formula of the limited God Who was really not responsible for the wickedness of man. Such notions left some of us uneasy, and I, for one, spent many a Monday morning in M. M. Kaplan's class at the Jewish Theological Seminary shouting in inadequate helplessness against his views. I knew that something was wrong with his outlook, but I was more resentful of it with my heart than I could explain intellectually. However, the truth of the matter was that the whole thing was rather an exercise in theological chess. Everyone in the debate knew that the question of God, certainly as we were posing it, was really a small footnote to a larger discussion within Western thought. We had no personal investment in it.

The real issue was the question of the chosenness of the Jew. There was no counterpart for it, really, even in Christian theology of the modern age. The least orthodox of Christians, like Wieman, still had no doubt that Christianity was a marvelous advance on the paganism that had preceded it, and that the Christian morality continued to be the highest stage of human consciousness. From this it followed that Christians of all persuasions, without being much troubled about the issue, continued to feel comfortable with the premise of their spiritual superiority. Chosenness is a specifically Jewish problem because it was the Jews who entered the modern age wanting to define themselves as an acceptable part of the wider world. In the immediate noise and angers of my seminary years this problem seemed to have been provoked by M. M. Kaplan, and his intellectual enemies talked as if it were entirely a result of his heresies—but a little reading soon disabused me of this. He was

in fact confronting the characteristically Jewish theological problem of the last two centuries. He was the ultimate heir of the major
tradition of modern Jewish theology, which has been not to defend
chosenness but to abandon it.

The process began in disguised form in the thought of Moses
Mendelssohn. The "enlightenment" of Berlin, which clustered
around him, consisted of a number of people most of whom would
have said with Mendelssohn, when he was specifically challenged
to convert to Christianity, that Judaism was the superior faith.
Nonetheless, a cultural inferiority complex is the hallmark of their
thought. Their constant cry was the need to demonstrate to general
opinion that Judaism, too, is a civilized religion and tradition. In
part this was, of course, an inevitable practical necessity in an age
struggling for political emancipation, but this was not the whole of
the story. The greatest minds of the eighteenth century, led by
Voltaire, had succeeded in convincing Europe that the Jews were
the secular equivalent of damned, i.e., that they were culturally
inferior, almost irretrievably so. Attempting to enter an age dominated by such opinions the Jews could only presume that their task
was to prove to themselves as well as to other men that their tradition was not inferior. Cultural apartness, or superiority, was simply not discussable.

Even in the realm of formal theology Mendelssohn's relationship to the idea of the chosenness of the Jew is less than clear-cut.
As is well known, he had declared Judaism to be revealed legisla-
tion binding only upon the Jews. In this he did not differ from the
Talmud. He seemed all the more traditional in that he never surrendered the language of Jewish messianic hopes. Nonetheless Mendelssohn emphasized that Jewish faith, as distinct from practice, is
identical with natural religion, which underlies all of the human traditions and is the common inheritance of all men. This amounted to
a denial of any theological uniqueness of Judaism as a faith. Certainly this was the dominant intent of the so-called science of
Judaism from its very beginning in the work of Leopold Zunz. The
function of modern scholarship was conceived in those circles as a
tool to prove that Jews deserved to be accepted in a world which
they did not wish to criticize in any fundamental way.

Reform Judaism, with its assertion that Judaism has a moral

mission to act as teacher to the world, seems an exception to the rule that modern Jewish theology denies chosenness. It hardly bears repeating that Reform Judaism, in its actual practice, was motivated primarily by the desire to remake Judaism in the image of the majority faith. However, even on the level of theology the doctrine of the mission of Israel is not as unequivocal as it appears on the surface. This idea usually appears not as the claim of the Jews to be a unique and transcendent element, a mystery, in the world. In a well-known summary of classic Reform Judaism, Kaufmann Kohler's *Jewish Theology,* the Jewish moral mission is argued as a propensity of the Jews for morality, a vocation like that of the Greeks for art. Particular vocations blending harmoniously with other vocations into the founding and the maintenance of culture is, no doubt, an attractive doctrine. Vocations may indeed be distinct and unique, but this is clearly not the doctrine of the election of Israel. Israel is here imagined as playing one instrument in a symphony; it is not confronting the world as the eternal "other."

This theory of vocations underwent a further refinement in nineteenth-century Jewish theology. There were men to be found among the early reformers who did indeed believe that Judaism was morally superior to Christianity. Nonetheless, even though a man like Kohler is to be numbered among them, the real weight of theological modernity was in the opposite direction. Claude Montefiore devoted himself to proving that there was a substantial identity between Jewish and Christian ethics. He was consciously defending Judaism against the charge that it was inferior to the Christian ethic of love, but his defense amounted to the assertion that Judaism and Christianity are parallel variants of the same tradition.

The true heirs of Montefiore on this point were Franz Rosenzweig and Martin Buber. In different ways the most important of contemporary Jewish theologians developed the thesis of the two dispensations, i.e., that it was the divine intention to appoint Judaism for the Jews and Christianity for the Christians. It follows that these two faiths coexist as correctives of one another, and that the true religious situation is one of equality. Despite those who have hurled Rosenzweig and Buber against Mordecai Kaplan, it is clear that on chosenness, the only point that really matters for modern

Jewish theology, they are in agreement. Whatever may be the differences in terminology, all three are really saying that Judaism is the truth for Jews and that other truths are equally valid for other men.

Jewish theological discussion from Mendelssohn to the present has, therefore, especially in the hands of the formal theologians, really amounted to the step-by-step abandonment of the doctrine of the election of Israel.

But the doctrine has persisted. It has obviously persisted among those who remain Orthodox in religion. It is to be found as the central affirmation of Nahman Krochmal, but he as well as the Orthodox had little influence on Jewish theology in the nineteenth century. The paradox is that this idea of chosenness, which has been exiled by the theologians, has maintained itself in nontheological circles.

To be sure, the doctrine of the election of Israel was not surrendered even among the theologians without a fight. S. D. Luzzatto early in the nineteenth century understood the problem very clearly, and he understood what was happening to Jewish thought at the very dawn of the age of Emancipation. Luzzatto confronted the bulk of his contemporaries, who were rushing toward Western culture, by insisting that there was eternal conflict between the world of the Greeks and the outlook of the Hebrews. Greek and Hebrew identity did not represent twin vocations; on the contrary, the Jews remained in battle for the integrity of their souls and for the salvation of the world, which could come ultimately only through the agency of their divinely appointed values.

The true heirs of Luzzatto as religious critics of the West in the name of Judaism were Jewish political and social revolutionaries who for the most part were operating outside the Jewish community. In the circle of Saint-Simon, for example, there were, as is well known, a number of young Jews. In their writings there is a religious passion for a new spiritual and political world. The brothers Péreire, and also Eichthal, insisted that they were especially fit to create it, and that they were particularly responsible for such an endeavor because this was their destiny as Jews. This kind of motivation is apparent in the young Moses Hess, even in his purely

Socialist days two decades before he turned Zionist. Arnold Ruge called him, and not as a compliment, "Rabbi Moses," because Hess was inspired not by dialectic "laws" or general revolutionary fervor, but by a messianic vision and a sense of destiny which he derived from his Jewish identity. Certainly this is the content of Hess's Zionism. It was from this perspective that he criticized both conventional German Jewish respectability of his time and the world of the bourgeoisie as a whole.

The propensity of Jews for revolutionary movements in the nineteenth century has often been discussed. The conventional interpretation has centered on the woes of the Jews in that age. The revolutionary Jews are imagined as trying to cure these woes by joining the effort to create a new order. The situation recurs in the twentieth century. It was evident, for example, in the high incidence of Jews among the makers of the Russian Revolution. In that situation the usual explanation seems to be particularly pat: the Jews had no rights in Russia and, therefore, the young joined the revolutionary party. We have thus tended to discount the Jewish messianic fervor of many of the young revolutionaries, couched as it often was in terms of their sense of responsibility as Jews to lead toward a better world. It has unfairly been discounted as verbiage because the revolutionary youth was secular, and it was outside the Jewish community.

The sense of cultural alienation of which Luzzatto spoke was inherited not only by revolutionaries but also by intellectuals. These, too, were primarily younger Jews outside the Jewish establishments of their day. Two apostates, Heine and Disraeli, are the archetypical examples of the breed. They knew that which the bourgeois Jew and his theologians were trying to forget—that at his root the Jew is an outsider in a world he did not make. The line from them to Kafka is quite direct, and the literary heirs of Kafka in America today are, as one would expect, a group of Jewish intellectuals who are secular, outside the Jewish community and possessed of very little Jewish learning. They are, therefore, in the mind of the Jewish establishment of today, clearly irrelevant to the history of Judaism. These intellectuals do retain, however, the consciousness of spiritual otherness; this is allied with a messianic discontent with the world. Both states of the spirit derive from a dim but fundamental knowledge that what these men are is rooted in the fact that they are Jews. This consciousness is the sense of being set apart, cursed—and elected.

The great merit of Charles Péguy is that when he saw the quintessence of such a Jew—politically in rebellion against the world and spiritually alien to it—in the person of Bernard Lazare, he recognized him for what he was: a major theological figure, a contemporary prophet of Israel. Lazare knew that he had no community with the respectable. He defined his own community of the elect: "And who are we? We, the intellectuals, the proletarians, and the poor people of Israel. Is not this enough?"

These reflections help to make sense out of one of the surprising intellectual interchanges at the beginning of this century. Ahad Ha-am wrote a stinging, passionate essay on Claude Montefiore's work on the New Testament. Montefiore, the believer, saw little difference between Jewish and Christian ethics. Ahad Ha-am, the agnostic, answered:

A Jew may be a liberal of liberals without forgetting that Judaism was born in a corner and has always lived in a corner, aloof from the great world, which has never understood it and therefore hates it. So it was before the rise of Christianity, and so it has remained ever since. History has not yet satisfactorily explained how it came about that a tiny nation in a corner of Asia produced a unique religious and ethical outlook, which, though it has had so profound an influence on the rest of the world, has yet remained so foreign to the rest of the world, and to this day has been unable either to master it or to be mastered by it. This is a historical phenomenon to which, despite many attempted answers, we must still attach a note of interrogation. But every true Jew, be he orthodox or liberal, feels in the depths of his being that there is something in the spirit of our people—though we do not know what it is—which has prevented us from following the rest of the world along the beaten path, has led to our producing this Judaism of ours, and has kept us and our Judaism "in a corner" to this day, because we cannot abandon the distinctive outlook on which Judaism is based. Let those who still have this feeling remain within the fold: let those who have lost it go elsewhere. There is no room here for compromise.

Such a declaration is no isolated phenomenon. It comes to the fore in our time in the thought of an even more secular figure, David Ben-Gurion:

> My concept of the Messianic ideal and vision is not a metaphysical one, but a social-cultural-moral one. . . . I believe in our moral and intellectual superiority, in our capacity to serve as a model for the redemption of the human race. This belief of mine is based on my knowledge of the Jewish people, and not on some mystic faith; "the glory of the Divine Presence" is within us, in our hearts, and not outside us.

Ben-Gurion's insistence on Western *aliyah* has always frightened those who want to be comfortable in their Western Bashan—and his radical definition of a Zionist repeats Ahad Ha-am's challenge: "There is no room here for compromise."

Obviously, Ben-Gurion is no racist asserting the idea of Jewish biological superiority. What he exemplifies is Jewish messianic consciousness, which he, like Ahad Ha-am, can no longer explain, but both know that it persists. Modern Jewish theology has been no help to them, because it abandoned the task of explanation long ago.

The doctrine of Jewish chosenness therefore exists, but not primarily among the theologians. Perhaps this is what is wrong with contemporary Jewish theology. Perhaps I should have gone twenty-five years ago for light not to the theologians but to the secular Jews. Perhaps Ben-Gurion is really the heir of Jewish spirituality in contemporary context, as the theologians are not. At least he is asserting chosenness and the need of the Jewish community as a whole to stand in rebellion against the world. Perhaps this is what Rav Kook meant when he said that in our time God is using the secular Jewish movements for divine ends. Perhaps the secularists are holier than they know, and the theologians—but I shall not finish that sentence.

3. The Condition of Jewish Belief

THE ESSENCE OF Judaism is the affirmation that the Jews are the chosen people; all else is commentary.

Whether the Jews are indeed the chosen people is a matter for faith. It cannot be demonstrated by argument. In the Bible, and ever since, history has been invoked to "prove" this claim—that Jewish experience, in all its grandeur and in all the depths of its suffering, can be explained only on the presumption that it is the record of the hand of God writing, mysteriously, in human events. It is, of course, possible to argue against this thesis. It can be said that the exodus from Egypt was an insignificant incident involving a paltry band of slaves who then wrote myths about it, and that Auschwitz was but another instance of man's well-known capacity for murdering other men. It is possible to deny that any particular element in the history of the Jews is really unique, and to maintain that the whole of it, despite its obvious singularity, is only a tissue of accidents. But this is not the way the Jewish faith views the history of the Jews.

But why the Jews? In the eyes of faith Jewish chosenness means that the Jews do not know why God chose them (Deut. 7:6–13); they claim no special privilege, except perhaps the somber one of suffering uniquely, of being judged by God, by the harshest standards (Amos 3:1–2; 9:7–10). What chosenness does mean to the faithful is that what has happened and continues to happen to Jews is at the very center of the meaning of human existence.

This assertion of chosenness is, of course, scandalous. It has been under attack from the very beginning of the encounter between the Jews and the West. The roots of modern racism are indeed to be found in this confrontation; those roots, however, are

Reprinted from "The State of Jewish Belief: A Symposium," in *Commentary*, vol. 42, no. 2 (August 1966).

not in Judaism but in the Greek tradition. It is the enemies of the Jews who have used racist arguments against them.

For the Greeks and the Romans, the Jews were the most troublesome of all the peoples they encountered. The Jews persisted in believing that even high, philosophical paganism was wrong and blasphemous. They were preeminent in refusing to accept the Hellenistic notion that "barbarians"—i.e., non-Greeks—could enter culture only if they adopted the Greek outlook. Greek and Roman anti-Semites responded by attacking the apartness of the Jews as misanthropy and by repeatedly charging that these people were bad by nature. This notion recurred in the more anti-Semitic extravagances of the New Testament and of medieval Christian theology. The Jews rejected Jesus, so the argument has gone, because they were evil by nature. The immediate forerunner of contemporary racism is in the attack mounted on the Marranos after the sixteenth century in the name of "purity of blood"—the notion that converts of Jewish ancestry could not escape the "taint" of their origins.

Jews have never understood the doctrine of the election of Israel as having anything to do with inherent biological superiority. They have always known that it is a religious category, not a racial one. What is new in the modern age is that Jews themselves have now joined the attack. Modernity brought with it the construction of an entirely new set of desires by Jews, and "chosenness," with all that it implies, has stood in the way of the new purposes.

The great commandment of the classic Jewish tradition was that the Jews should be "a people dwelling apart," that the community of the faithful should live in some detachment from the world around them. The dominant enterprise of the Jews in the last two centuries has been to achieve their complete emancipation. They have been laboring to establish the proposition that both what they are and what they believe belong in the same realm as the other faiths and communities of Western man. Obviously, the belief in "chosenness" and the practice of apartness stand in the way; it has seemed necessary that all obstacles to "integration" should be removed. Modern Jews have been at great pains to prove that they are really "just like everybody else." Indeed, there has even been an element of homeopathic magic in their eagerness to play down their own doctrine of "chosenness." It is as though they were saying: "Let us stop talking about our being radically different on religious grounds, and our enemies will be moved to stop attacking us as a radically dangerous race."

This has not worked. It has not worked as a counter to Jew-hatred, because no matter what Jews may say or do they continue to be a visibly unique element in the world. The man of faith sees the divine choice ("and you shall be unto Me a singular people") finding, and even pursuing, those who would deny it. They must affirm it, inevitably, through their lives. The only people some modern Jews have ever convinced that Jews are "like everybody else" is themselves. Both their friends and their enemies outside the Jewish community have known that this is not so. Balaam has always seen what the descendants of Moses would pretend does not exist.

The modern attempt to deny "chosenness" has failed just as clearly to answer the crucial question that it raises internally within Jewry: If Judaism represents a slightly different variant of the conventional Western outlook, why should the peculiar Diaspora which is its bearer remain in being? The conventional rhetoric of religious and cultural pluralism is really no answer. If the observance of Passover is indeed the affirmation of a commitment to the freeing of all the oppressed, then perhaps the money spent on matzah this year and the energies put into innumerable Seder observances should have been spent in Harlem or in Hong Kong. If the rituals of Judaism are devised by man to symbolize his values, why can he not freely change or abandon these symbols? If man's values are of his own devising, why can he not change these values and abandon the community that represented earlier stages of his moral outlook? If the meaning of Judaism is that it commands its believers to labor for social progress, why must the believer prefer for himself the Jewish community in America today to the community of the black dispossessed in Watts in Los Angeles?

There can be only one answer to this order of question. The Jewish faith is of lasting importance, and it is an ultimate sin to abandon it, *only* if it be conceived as divinely ordained; else what men have made they can unmake and the communities into which they were born are mere accidents. From this perspective there is no distinction between the moral laws of Judaism and the ritual commandments. Contemporary Jewish religious apologetics cannot really barricade itself behind a distinction between a divinely ordained moral law and man-made ritual. The notion that God did indeed command Samuel to hack Agag to pieces before Him in Gilgal is far more repugnant than the belief that He really cares whether I wear a suit consisting of both linen and flax. The theological difficulty is the same in both cases. We are, therefore, quite properly asked to explain by what principle one can affirm revelation and yet deny some of the commandments and much of the outlook of the sacred texts in which that revelation is presumed to be recorded.

The plain truth is that there is no clear dogmatic answer, and all the attempts that have been made in the last two centuries to provide one are more dangerous than leaving the question open. This is not unprecedented in Jewish theological thinking. Job was troubled by the question of God's justice. His friends suggested elaborate "answers" by which they justified the ways of God, but the author of the book was more impressed by the notion that the justice of God is a mystery which men can understand in part, but only in part. Rabbi Akiba was troubled by the question of man's responsibility in the face of God's omnipotence, and Akiba's famous resolution ("all is foreseen but free will is granted") amounted to saying that man must live with this paradox, and that the content of much of his religious life is to wrestle with the mystery both in life and theory. Both Job and Akiba found that all the possible answers, including the one of denying God for the sake of logic and making an end of the problem, were shallower and more wounding than living with the question.

The crucial problem that confronts Jewish theology in our age can best be stated in a paradox comparable to the one with which Rabbi Akiba defined his dilemma. We must say: "God exists and He has revealed Himself to man through the sacred texts of the Jewish tradition, and yet the individual must be free to make his choices as to what he will affirm as value and what rituals he will obey as representing, for him, authentic commandment."

The commitment of the man of faith to the tradition is under persisting challenge. The contemporary historical disciplines are more of a problem to him than modern science. Our growing knowledge of the physical universe can only call into question literalist versions of the cosmology of the Bible or its miracles, but the essential religious assertion that there is a God who made the world is perhaps less out of fashion among men of science today than it was two generations ago. The "warfare of science and religion" has not been ended by an armistice and peace treaty, but the whole subject no longer seems important to either side. What continues to be troubling is the fundamental relativism about all the actions and all the faiths of man which is the prevailing temper of intellectual life. No one dares to discuss values in our day on the basis of the older premise that, quite apart from any utilitarian considerations, some values are better than others and some spiritual outlooks are of higher estate than any available alternates.

But is Judaism indeed a higher value, or a higher complex of values, than any possible contemporary alternate? The very form in which the question has been posed implies a relativistic scale which presumes that all outlooks must be judged in the mode of comparative cultural and religious anthropolgy. The defense of an idea is to prove that it is more acceptable than some other idea, as democracy is more acceptable, at least to democrats, than Fascism. Judaism cannot possibly be explained or defended within such a context. Stated abstractly, as a set of moral concerns about human dignity and freedom, social progress and peace, there is nothing to distinguish Jewish ideas from conventional Western ones, or even from the moral content of some, if not all, of the high religions. (I would except the non-Biblical ones because their fundamental notion of man's immediate life as incidental leads to quite different moral conclusions from the Biblical ones.)

This does not, however, end the question of the unique significance of Judaism. It is too easy to say that the Jews remain, or ought to remain, an elite on the battle line for the realization of these values. This is a humanist concept which is subject to the criticism that some other group might be arising to become the true contemporary elite. Such leadership cadres have arisen within society as a whole in the past and they will, of course, continue to do so. The Jewish faith and community cannot be asked at every specific moment in time to prove in argument, even to itself, that it is a more significant leadership than the one in fashion at the moment. What Jewish experience does prove is that the Jews have consistently played an astonishing role in the world. This does not mean that Judaism has had its purposes or self-definition clear in every age. Some centuries have been periods of waiting and even of confusion, in which the best the Jews could do was simply to maintain the community and the living tie with their past heritage. I think that this is such an age—of waiting, of looking for answers rather than of being able to give them.

In the moral realm Judaism does have, even in this age in which its distinctive accents are muted, one continuing great idea to suggest: its faith in the Messiah. For the last two thousand years there has been a continuing polarity within Judaism between the persisting main body of the faithful and recurring challenges arising among them in the name of an immediate messianism. Viewed from the perspective of continuing Jewish experience, there is a straight line from Jesus to Shabbetai Tzevi to Karl Marx and Leon Trotsky. In all of these various permutations men have arisen out of the soil of Judaism to announce the messianic age as near at hand and immediately achievable, and toward that end they or their disciples have offered up the existence of the Jewish community. Making an end of it has been regarded as a necessary preamble to some dawning "end of days." To inter Judaism, with thanks, as a superseded stage on the way to a greater new world has been regarded by all kinds of radical messianists not as treason but as a heroic moral act. But the Messiah has not yet come. The world is as yet unredeemed and all the various visions of a realized eschatology, both religious and secular, have obviously been premature. Faithful Jews have taken the risk in every generation of rejecting the notion that the end of days is really now announced. Their faithfulness has preserved Judaism in its proper attitude of waiting—and of being the soil out of which the Messiah will yet come, in a form we cannot imagine. Judaism will continue to breed those who would reject it for seemingly broader visions. The man of faith must believe that such messianists, too, play some role in the divine plan, but the faithful must remain just that—faithful.

We cannot derive, and it is even dangerous to attempt to

derive, from classic Judaism a specific and precise political and social outlook, except in the broadest terms. Believing Jews are forbidden to hate or to oppress other men; they can therefore not be totalitarians in politics. Nothing is clearer than that they must oppose the antireligious element of communism, but there is absolutely no reason to say that only the capitalist economic order is acceptable from the perspective of Judaism. What Judaism can do for the individual Jew is to permeate him with the total feel of the tradition and then leave him to make his own personal choices in the realm of men's immediate actions. Many Jews remember, as I do, a grandmother who said often about some matters, out of the very depths of her being, that "a Jew doesn't do this." As political and social doctrine this may seem imprecise, but one who is not alien to the inherited Jewish experience finds this standard both precise and most exquisitely moral.

It should be clear by now from the drift of my argument that I regard any question about Judaism as the "one true religion" as irrelevant in the form in which it is put. Classical Judaism believes that the many faiths of man all play a role in the divine scheme. What Judaism does contend is that its divinely appointed role is uniquely its own, and that the appointment is both its task and its destiny.

In the age of waiting there is really one task for Jews as a continuing community of believers. It is to eschew theological or ideological definitions of Judaism, which are particularly impossible in a period of general intellectual confusion and uncertainty, and to turn to the two things Jews can do: to reforge the link of personal knowledge and experience of the inherited Jewish learning, and to maintain the Jewish community in being as a distinctive entity. We shall not necessarily succeed with all Jews, and we shall perhaps fail even more today than we have in the past, but must persevere in the effort.

It is not only Jews who know that the Messiah has not yet come; the world knows it too. Advanced Christians are confronting the unredeemed world. As they sit amid the rubble of all the shattered hopes, including their own theological ones, advanced Christians are hoping to redeem the world by a new devotion to Jesus. This is a very "Jewish" stance, for we Jews have been in the business of living through and beyond tangible and intangible exiles and disasters from the very beginning of our experience. We know that all is never lost—but, for that matter, that all is never won, either. In the age of the concentration camps and of the re-creation of a Jewish commonwealth in Israel we have known both the greatest despair and historic comfort.

To be a Jew means to believe, and to wait.

4. After Emancipation: Jewish Politics and Culture

IN THE LAST two centuries, mankind has been living in a revolutionary era. Jewish destiny and fate have been intimately identified with this era of revolution in all its permutations, whether it was the bourgeois revolutions that continued across Europe in the nineteenth century, or the Socialist and Communist revolutions which were announced in the nineteenth century and realized in the twentieth. The reason for this Jewish identification with the age of revolution is simple: it was the new age, rather than the old, which brought the Jew, at least in legal theory, if not always completely in practice, equality as a right.

The position and politics of the Jew in the modern era have, therefore, been identified with the era of revolution and with revolutionary forces, and anti-Jewish forces, those which have been against Jews or against their new position in society, have been lumped together as the forces of counterrevolution. Thus a very simple equation grew up which became almost the historic faith of the modern Jew: to think that the Jew had no political or cultural

Opening paper, American Jewish Congress Dialogue, in Jerusalem, July 31, 1972, printed in *Congress Bi-Weekly,* vol. 40, no. 6 (March 30, 1973).

enemies on the left; that the revolution in its various permutations was by and large to be regarded as his friend, and that his enemies were the counterrevolutionaries.

I would like to submit, as my very first thesis, that recent Jewish historical studies—what have been called "the new Jewish historiography," some of it written in Jerusalem by Shmuel Ettinger, Jacob Katz, Edmund Silberner, and Uri Tal; some of it written in the United States by several people, including myself—have produced a kind of counterthesis. The counterthesis is that we have misperceived the relationship of Jews to the forces of revolution, and that the truth is that the doctrinaire left never emancipated the Jews; that is, that those elements within the revolutionary forces of modernity which imagined a new heaven on earth created by political means were elements which, very often, if not always, could imagine this new society rejecting Jews as harmful and obnoxious and even excluding them.

For now I will content myself with one quotation from Voltaire. Voltaire, the great apostle of the idea of human liberty, human freedom, and human equality, writes this about Jews in the climactic essay of his life on the subject (and he is not writing about Biblical Jews; he is writing about the Jews whom he does not want to include in his new society): "The Persians and the Scythians are a thousand times more reasonable. They [the Jews] are all of them born with raging fanaticism in their hearts, just as the Bretons and the Germans are born with blond hair. I would not be in the least bit surprised if this people would not some day become deadly to the human race."

This is not Rosenberg in *The Myth of the 20th Century*. This is Voltaire. And as Silberner has established in a very thorough book, *West European Socialism and the Jewish Question,** the most doctrinaire of the nineteenth-century Socialists, quite a list of them, generally tended to be anti-Semitic. What they consistently maintained was that it was possible to create a new world within which the Jew was not a co-founder but an alien miasma, and that that world could be created only by defending oneself against the possibility of Jewish infection. And from that to the epithet

---

* The book exists in Hebrew and in German, but there is no English translation.

"irretrievably cosmopolitan" the line is fairly direct; Voltaire, Proudhon, and Fourier are the direct ancestors, along with Karl Marx, of the contemporary left-wing attack upon the very nature of the Jew as being hostile to the new world-to-be-born.

It is a firm conclusion of the new Jewish historiography that the Jew as such was never emancipated. The forces of modernity which were willing to give him freedom insisted that freedom itself was a mechanism to make the Jew over. His best friends regarded the Jew in the ghetto as beneath contempt. Such people as Dohm and Grégoire in the 1780s, the forerunners of the emancipation of the Jews, were also the great spearbearers of the argument that the existing Jews were bad. The reason for emancipating them was that they would thus unlearn their evil ways, abandon their nonsensical traditions and become just like the Gentiles. The existing Jew in his concreteness was thus never accepted, not even by the very people who were willing to give him equality. They accepted only the Jew who was yet to be created. Kafka's "K" in *The Trial* is never called a Jew and yet: to stand before the bar of judgment charged with unknown crimes, waiting to plead guilty to the charges, if only someone would tell the defendant what they were, this is a searing aspect of Jewish modernity.

This is modernity in its emancipating activity, confronting the Jew with the proposition "you haven't quite done it well enough yet."

If this is true, then the problems of Jewish modernity have been the problems of the inevitable tension between an ongoing Jewish existence of some kind—the sheer existence of Jews that carries with it something, or a lot of their uniqueness; something, or a lot of their singularity; something, or a lot of their own particular affirmations and outlooks and ways of being—and a world which emancipated only the mythical Jew who was yet to become.

Despite the paradoxes and contradictions, there has been a modern Jewish policy that has imagined that if the new, revolutionary world were indeed created (whatever revolution might be in fashion at the moment), the Jewish problem, along with the uniqueness of the Jew, would disappear, and the Jew would become one of the new co-makers of the Brave New World. This faith has failed. It is meet and right to say in Jerusalem that the deepest contribution of Zionism to the political understanding of Jews in the twentieth century is the insight that means which solve general political problems do not necessarily solve Jewish problems.

Lilienblum and Pinsker, and then Herzl after them, recognized that university students could make pogroms; that anti-Semitism was a phenomenon which had become naturalized into the modern, post-Christian revolutionary world; that this world, too, could exclude Jews. They therefore announced that Jews could not leave their political destiny in the hands of movements which would, supposedly, incidentally solve the Jewish problem.

I would therefore suggest that we begin by asking ourselves the question: What are "for real" Jewish politics in our time?

Whatever wisdom we can gain from the immediate past suggests that the Jew is not permanently an ally of the political left. Jews should be equally suspicious of the move to the right that is now being urged on them by some Jewish spokesmen for the new conservatism. In recent memory the political right in France, led by De Gaulle, had a brief romance with Israel and the Jews, but De Gaulle soon settled France's problems in Algeria and turned toward the Arab world, with nasty words and hostile policies as a parting present for Israel and the Jews. I have no great faith that De Gaulle's American counterparts are a more secure ally for the Jewish people. They are now pro-Israel, in part as a way of being anti-Russian and in part in order to express opposition to the New Left in domestic politics. Such purposes are not the sure and certain foundation of a pro-Israel policy, through thick and thin.

It seems to me that Jewish politics is indeed the politics of self-interest, but it is the politics of Jewish self-interest in a world within which we do have a stake both in social stability and in progress, both in order and in reform. It seems to me that Jewish politics has to be the politics today of our own specificity, but it is a specificity which can make of its allies not permanent allies and can deal only in a frequent reassessment of its options.

In the second place, important as political action is for the Jewish people, it is no substitute for spirit and culture. Theodor Herzl invented the idea that it was possible to have Jewish politics without Jewish culture. That is what *The Jewish State* is all about. Herzl recognized that modern anti-Semitism had created, inevitably, a specific Jewish politics of Jewish national need and Jewish national destiny. But he was testy, angry, and bored, almost to the very end of his life, with the notion of Jewish cultural specificity.

Those historians of Zionism who have tried to make him over into a more pious cultural Zionist have been rewriting Herzl in the image of their own desire rather than accurately depicting the late nineteenth-century Central European, Budapest–Viennese–by-way-of-Paris intellectual who saw clearly that in the political world Jews had to act with an eye to their own interests and to finding allies as they could, in accordance with their own vision of what they had to do—but who had no clear-cut sense of Jewish culture at all.

The great paradox of Jewish modernity is that there is a far greater consensus in Jewish politics than there is in Jewish culture. For at least a century, Jews have been united, or very nearly united, only in the defense of Jewish rights. So it is with the American Jews of today, who are organized as a community primarily in the defense of Israel. That is the lowest common denominator, the active principle, the actual premise of Jewish unity.

But this politics has not necessarily translated itself into any really serious action in the field of culture. True, Israel itself represents in its own culture an attempt to create a national culture on the basis of the tradition, in line with it and yet different from it. And yet it is an open secret that that attempt is in process and has far from succeeded, and that its most serious problems, the problems of the *Kulturkampf,* are still in the future. In the United States and in the rest of the Diaspora, nothing is clearer than that Jews are politically "Jewish" and culturally quite seriously assimilated, and that there is no definition of a Jewish cultural modernity to tide us over or to root us in this modern era.

Jews in Israel are at least aware that they have a cultural and spiritual problem waiting for them while their major attentions are diverted elsewhere. The Diaspora, and especially American Jews, are peculiarly less conscious of the problem. Since their political lives are spent in the general society, as citizens of the United States or some other country, their Jewish "island within," their spiritual lives, as it were, is in what they do in pro-Israel political and fund-raising activities. These are now the primary *mitzvot,* the acts of identification with specifically Jewish needs and ideals.

In the United States Jewish politics has *become* Jewish culture, has become the content of American Jewish life to a very great degree, and in some of my blacker moments I imagine "American Jewish" as a kind of sitting in the stadium, watching Israel, cheering it, being pleased with it, etc. I would like to suggest that we Americans face the problem of Jewish cultural definition in the post-Emancipation, postrevolutionary era—the problem of what is the thing to which we are loyal. What is the tradition that unites us? What in heaven's name would American Jews do the day after Mr. Sadat sends his foreign minister to meet Mr. Eban and Mrs. Meir? What would happen after Mr. Brezhnev let all the Jews out of Russia? What would the content of American Jewish life then be? These are very pointed and very serious questions.

JEWS, CHRISTIANS, ANTI-SEMITISM, AND THE HOLOCAUST

5. Anti-Semitism and Jewish Uniqueness: Ancient and Contemporary

ONE OF THE FIRST scholarly tasks that was ever set before me was given me some twenty years ago by my great teacher, Levi Ginzberg. He asked me to translate into English the famous lecture that he had given in 1930, when he came as visitor to the Hebrew University to inaugurate the chair in Talmudic Studies. He there propounded the thesis that the changing patterns of Talmudic law cannot be understood unless they are seen against the background of changing social and economic circumstances and of the new political situations to which they were responding. This thesis has by now become so accepted that it amounts to a cliché, but when it was first stated it amounted to a revolution.

To understand anti-Semitism means to deal not in abstractions

---

First given as a lecture in Hebrew on February 8, 1971, at the President's House in Jerusalem, and then presented, in revised form, as the eleventh annual B. G. Rudolph Lecture in Judaica Studies, Syracuse University, April 11, 1973.

but in the concrete reality of the encounters and difficulties between Jews and Gentiles. Only by paying precise attention to the
facts, by seeing them as they are and not as some preconceived
abstractions would have us interpret them, can we arrive at gen-
eralizations that rest solidly on foundations of truth.

This subject, anti-Semitism, is not an antiseptic one. No matter
where it is raised and no matter who talks about anti-Semitism,
it is a matter that cannot be dealt with with the usual poses, or even
realities, of scholarly objectivity. Anti-Semitism has been the single
most disastrous phenomenon of the twentieth century, and of many
earlier centuries, and we continue to participate, as Jews and as
human beings, in the very conflicts from which we are trying to
stand back in order to understand. Our senses of our own identity,
our religious and political positions at this very moment and for
the future, are deeply involved in our estimate of anti-Semitism.
All of us can bear important witness to this subject out of the
reality of our lives.

I do not at the outset want to use the word "anti-Semitism" at
all because the term itself has, at the very least, the connotation
that the conflict or conflicts in question are of a different order
than all other quarrels between communities and people. This may
indeed be true of the contemporary difficulties between Jews and
others, but we can arrive at such a judgment only later, on the
basis of analysis, and not *a priori*.

One basic distinction must, however, be made between anti-
Semitism and group conflict. The French and the Germans were
engaged for centuries in wars and lasting antipathies; so were the
Christians and the Moslems. These are conflicts of a different order
than the age-old problems between Jews and Gentiles. The difference is, in essence, that group conflicts are battles between people
who regard themselves as species of the same genus, and who
really expect that at the end of the battle each of the contestants
will essentially remain and be the same. Anti-Semitism presup-
poses that the Jews are radically other. Its purpose has usually
been the attempt to remove them utterly from the scene of the
battle, by expulsion or forced segregation, by pogroms or ultimately by death camps. This distinction between anti-Semitism and
group conflict has been obscured in our century by the tragic reality

that many of the more usual conflicts even among Gentile powers have, in the age of ideologies, acquired new, demonic dimensions. Otherwise kindly men can still in our day make distinctions between murder and the shooting of their political enemies. The destruction of the kulaks by the Russian Revolution had been foreshadowed by the guillotines of the Terror during the French Revolution. Modern ideological conflicts have tended to become religious wars, with inquisitions and demons to be fought, and have thus begun to approximate the age-old problems between Jews and Gentiles. Nevertheless, the Cold War rhetoric of the 1950s has receded, and the major contestants in the battle between democracy and communism are talking less and less in ideological terms and more and more in the language of old-fashioned power accommodations. The recent movement of international politics has been away from ideologies and toward return to group conflict as the only tolerable limit for disagreement among people and communities. It is clear, at first glance, that this tendency has not yet redefined "the Jewish question," but there are signs that some change has been taking place here, too.

There is no need to describe even with minimum precision the major current conflicts between Jews and Gentiles. Let us merely list them, without suggesting that there is any order of priority in the listing. Clearly, there is serious conflict, not merely between Israel and the neighboring Arab states, but between the Jewish world as a whole and the Arab world over the very creation and continued existence of the State of Israel. This quarrel has occasioned the use by Arab propagandists of such anti-Semitic tracts as the "Protocols of the Elders of Zion," and the language of jihad has been used. Nonetheless, not all of the Moslem people have been actively involved in this quarrel, and it is becoming apparent that Arabs are at least having to admit to themselves, even in public, that the State of Israel is a fact, though they no doubt continue to harbor the hope that the day may yet arrive when this fact will be no more.

Another major conflict involves all of the Jewish communities of the world in battle with the Soviet Union. Part of this quarrel is in the fact that the Soviet Union has been and remains the chief supporter of the Arabs against Israel. More pointedly, the repres-

sion of Jewish religious and cultural life in Russia and the denial
of permission for Jews who want to emigrate is at this moment, by
Jewish choice, a major international issue.

A third quarrel involves Jews with the New Left. From the
perspective of these political circles the existence of Israel is a
retrograde phenomenon. It is supported by the United States,
which is for the New Left the major source of evil in the world,
and the very existence of Israel stands in the way of the triumph
in the Middle East of those Arab forces which the New Left identi-
fies as the proper representative of their favorite cliché, the Third
World. Part of the anger of the New Left is directed not only at
Israel but also at the Jews of the world. Having provided so many
of the battalions which have fought in our century for internation-
alism, the New Left now finds that Jews are involved in the parochial task of supporting a specifically Jewish country in its insistence on its right to be just that.

In the fourth place, the involvement of the Jews of the world
in Israel, especially in its most heightened form after May 1967,
has been attacked in circles other than those of the New Left. In
the Soviet Union and elsewhere in Communist Eastern Europe,
though not everywhere, Jews continue to be accused of Zionism,
that "ism" of harboring a primary loyalty to their Jewish identity
and to the State of Israel. Comparable sentiments were expressed
in some church circles in the United States which sided and continue to side with the Arabs.

In the fifth place, an older alliance in the United States between
Jews and blacks, which lasted into the mid-1960s, has disintegrated
in recent years. It has been widely noted that those positions in
American society which blacks want, because they are seemingly
attainable, are very often occupied by Jews; that Jews are major
landlords and storekeepers in the black ghetto; and that, in general,
the vision of a society of individuals with opportunity equal to
their merit is comfortable for Jews but discomforting for blacks.
They are demanding unequal opportunities as "recompense" for
their past deprivations, and much of this price is at the moment
being paid by Jews. Some of the rhetoric of this quarrel, too, is
couched in the language of old-fashioned anti-Semitism, but there

are also newer additions of supposed identification of Black Panthers with the Arab and Third World enemies of Israel.

This, in major outline, is an inventory and sketch of the most important contemporary attacks on Jews by their enemies. It of course needs to be remembered that all is far from well on the South American continent, and that there the Catholic church is still dominated by prelates who belong to the older traditions of Christian anti-Semitism. Even in that region, however, Arab communities resident in the region, refugee Nazis, and left-wing forces are the more disturbing part of the picture.

What therefore comes immediately and unmistakably to our eyes from this list is two facts, of the most profound importance: the issues between Jews and Gentiles have little or nothing to do with the age-old quarrel between Jews and Christians. It may be argued, as some do and will, that the current issues are but contemporary secularizations of that older quarrel, but it is undeniable that the overt battle lines are quite different. For that matter, Communists, spokesmen of the New Left, and blacks are all former Christians (or Jews), but this is certainly not true of Arabs. It is too bold an assertion to maintain that Chrisian anti-Semitism is now irrelevant, but it is clear that if Jews were at peace as a people with all our secular enemies, what remains of Christian hatred would not worry us overly much.

The second obvious observation is that at the center of almost all the quarrels in which Jews are involved today stand the existence of the State of Israel, the support that it draws from all the Jews of the world, and the emotions that it evokes among them. This question is crucial to all of the current battles that I have mentioned except the one between Jews and blacks in America, and even there it plays a minor role of some importance. Here, too, it might be argued that the contemporary angers are but retranslations of older hatreds. Did not Haman once say that the Jews were a peculiar people, spread out in all the world, which behaved in different modes from that of all others? This definition of the justification for anti-Semitism has been termed in contemporary social theory "the dislike of the unlike." Pinsker and Herzl, the founders of modern Zionism, held this view, for they saw anti-

Semitism as a rational phenomenon, as the hatred of the world for
the "eternal minority" and the "eternal stranger." The creation of
a Jewish state was proposed as a cure for this disease, by making
the Jews a host somewhere in the world in a country of their own.
In theory, therefore, the existence of the State of Israel should be
making an end of anti-Semitism. That its very existence and all
the relationships with world Jewry that this existence involves are
now at the center of the conflict requires explanation.

It is possible to complicate the question even more. As conflicts with other groups have become sharper, the Christian church
has been the only major contestant with Jews which has been willing and often eager during the last few decades to come to some
kind of accommodation. This has involved most of its major
branches, though, to be sure, the Orthodox have been less willing
than either the Protestants or the Catholics. The marked Christian willingness to issue statements against anti-Semitism has been,
of course, largely rooted in the guilt of their silence during the
Holocaust. It is true that in not a single one of these declarations
has the dream of the church to proselytize the Jews ever been abandoned. Indeed, in the very first meeting after the Holocaust, when
the Protestants gathered in Amsterdam in 1946, the still-smoking
death ovens did not stop them from saying that the highest testimony of their contrition for the murders and the sign of their love
for Jews was to continue to bring them the greatest gift in their
possession, salvation through the founder of their religion. Nonetheless, even on this most sensitive of issues, the Christian mission,
there is today in actual fact large accommodation in practice. In
my own personal experience in the United States, in 1959 a public
Jewish protest in the form of an article that I wrote in one of the
Christian journals led almost immediately to the abolition of a
bureau of Christian Mission to Jews that had long existed in the
central body of American Protestantism, the National Council of
Churches. Much more vehement and powerful protests by the
most responsible Jewish bodies in America and elsewhere in the
world have had no comparable success in breaking the ongoing
alliance between powerful elements in international Christianity
and anti-Israel opinion and activity. The reality of our present
relationship with the highest bodies of Christianity is that there

are no difficulties on all those issues such as race and poverty on which we are prepared to behave as an international religious community, "just like them." Official Christianity continues to deplore older forms of theological anti-Semitism, and is even willing to remove them from its textbooks. The stumbling block, the rock on which the new unity breaks, is the singularity as religious phenomenon and the intensity as present policy of the Jewish involvement in Israel.

Here too, as in almost all the other conflicts today, Israel and Zionism are the crucial issues. There is something more here than a rationalization of the Christian missionary relationship to the Arab world and the desire of various communions to protect their stakes in "holy places." Mid-nineteenth-century Reform Judaism was already responding, at its very birth, to the Christian question which suggested that the Jewish religion in the era of Emancipation had to abandon its peculiar identity, as exemplified particularly in its national hopes and longing for the land of its ancestors. The question had been asked very pointedly, even earlier, by Napoleon at the Sanhedrin that he called together to assure him, among other things, that the Jews of his empire had no patriotism now and in the future for Eretz Yisrael. At the very dawn of the era of Emancipation, in the first debate about Jews in the French revolutionary parliament in September 1789, a liberal deputy from Paris, Clermont-Tonnerre, pronounced the famous sentence: "To Jews as individuals, everything; to Jews as a distinct community, nothing." It is in the light of this past, rooted very deeply in the beginnings and in the whole movement of the new encounter between Jews and Gentiles in the modern era, that we can perhaps begin to understand the paradox that all of the anti-Jewish movements of this day, including the overt attacks from Christian quarters, are divorced from religious motifs, and that their central target is the great endeavor of Jews really to behave like conventional modern men in a national state of their own.

There have been generations of argument and bitter exchanges about whether there was a "social compact" as part of the legal emancipation of the Jews under which the Jews agreed to give up every element of their own ethos and disappear as individuals into the wider society. No such formal social compact ever existed, but it is impossible to study the century of battle for Jewish rights on the European continent without concurring that an informal agreement of this nature largely did exist. The best friends of the Jews, those who obtained equal rights for them, expected that Jews would disappear or at the very least become completely inconspicuous. They did not anticipate the kind of Jews who would, even in some new form, make unique and singular demands on society.

It is this last point that has never been clear to Jews themselves. The reigning presumption in all the schools of Jewish thought and action in the modern era, including classic Zionism of the political kind, has been the notion that Jews must now cease being *sui generis,* and that their becoming "just like everybody else" could indeed be realized in life. I would indeed now suggest, as the second premise on which to base an understanding of contemporary anti-Semitism, that the whole movement of Jewish history since the beginning of the era of Emancipation has therefore had as its purpose such a reordering, such a "normalization" of the relationship between Jews and their environment so as to make an end of anti-Semitism. In the most hopeful dreams of those Jews who fought for equal rights and acceptance in Gentile societies, their purpose was to help bring about a new society, a new age of heaven-on-this-earth, for the modern era was conceived at a time when man could, and would, remake his immediate world into the messianic era. These were the most ecstatic visions of love and brotherhood. In prosaic daily life, what Jews wanted to achieve was sufficient equality and likeness to others to become species of the same genus as all other individuals or groups, so that the difficulties would become the normal day-to-day problems among equals. Knowing full well that in their most recent ghetto forms Jews appeared to be radically different, every version of emancipatory thinking, including all the major theories of Zionism, accepted the proposition that Jews had to change in important ways in order to enter the modern world as full equals. The presumption is that once this occurred anti-Semitism would be over.

As is well known this did not work out as planned, for anti-Semitism did not disappear in the nineteenth century. On the contrary, it attacked Jews with renewed fury, and its targets were not only alien Jews still mostly in the ghetto, such as those of Czarist

Russia, but also very Westernized and fashionable ones, the "new men" such as the Rothschilds and Captain Dreyfus. It is nonetheless superficial to interpret Jewish reaction to the pogroms of 1881 in Russia and to the Dreyfus Affair as a turning away from dreams of emancipation and equality in the Gentile world to a renewed, somber awareness that the hatred between Jacob and Esau was unavoidable and eternal. Great as was the shock that these events administered, they did not destroy the peculiarly modern Jewish faith that somewhere, in some attainable situation, through some more exact reordering of the identity of the Jew and of the society in which he was to live, Jews would become species of the same genus as other men and anti-Semitism would end.

In the twentieth century each of the major options offered by the era of the Emancipation has not only been attempted, it has even been realized at very nearly its optimum. The West European dream of the personal emancipation of the individual in a society in which, in legal theory, group and tradition did not matter and whatever remained of such loyalties was a private matter, was realized under the most favorable circumstances in the United States around 1960. Communism stunted the opportunity that it afforded for Jews to have complete equality as a national minority among the many in Russia, but for at least a decade in the 1920s until the mid-1930s it seemed that a Yiddish-speaking national culture of great range was being fostered, and it has been said that only the paranoia of Stalin made an end of this success. The normalcy of the State of Israel since its creation, including the re-creation of Jewish military capacity, has been apparent for all to see. The whole drive of Israeli statesmanship, from the beginning of Israel's independence to this very day, has been to change the relations between Israel and its Arab neighbors into one of normal recognition and acceptance. While not forgetting that Israel's creation owed something to the claim that Jews were making on the bad conscience of the anti-Semitic world, Israeli statesmanship has wanted to move away from the presumption that this state remains special, a unique creation of the United Nations and therefore uniquely bound by its tutelage and its decisions.

Only in relation to the Jews of the world has Israel continued to insist on emphasizing ever more throughout the years of its

existence that it holds a unique relationship and special responsibilities—and it is this relationship which is under special attack. In
reverse, very little of Jewish religion and culture and of the integrity
of the Jewish family remains in the Soviet Union, and nonetheless
an otherwise unparalleled connection remains between this community and a country outside the borders of Russia. All of the
studies of the American Jewish community showed that the opposition to intermarriage had dropped in a few short years among
American Jews from over 80 percent to half that, and that most
of those still opposed were over forty-five, that is, preponderantly
the children of immigrants who retain ties to Jewish religion and
culture. Nonetheless, the connection with Israel is overwhelmingly
strong in all segments of the American Jewish community. The
conclusion is simple and inescapable: the very secular, "like-all-
the-nations" State of Israel has become the contemporary equivalent of the older Jewish religion; that is, the loyalty that it evokes
throughout the Jewish world is the contemporary factor of Jewish
uniqueness and Jewish distinctiveness. This is the contemporary
embodiment of "their ways are different from those of all other
people."

This relationship to Israel is not a factor evoked primarily by
anti-Semitism, of either the older, theological kind or the newer,
racial and economic conflict between Jews and some of their
neighbors. On the contrary, at the very height of its power and
integration into the American community, before Jewish–black
relations had deteriorated seriously and at a time when *aliyah* was
at its lowest ebb, the American Jewish community in 1967, and
even more in 1973, supported Israel with a vehemence that aston-
ished itself. It was an assertion of their contemporary Jewish ethos.

To say this with pride requires that we remember that it is
precisely this kind of Jewish self-assertion which our enemies have
attacked repeatedly since near the beginning of our history. Hellenistic anti-Semites found us unsocial because we would not eat
or drink with others or be hospitable to their gods; Christian ones
found that we were the one community that rejected the "new
light" for all mankind; contemporary ones see us as a peculiar
international sociopolitical entity. In utter honesty we have been
all of these things, and we continue to be them, in secularized

forms. I, for one, even harbor the hope that the persistence of this uniqueness will yet lead within the Jewish world to some revival of the spirit—but let us at least understand that the quarrel with our enemies is about the recurring uniqueness of world Jewry. We do not widely differ from some of our critics on the actual facts. The quarrel is about moral judgment, about the value of what we are and whether our Jewishness fits into some vision of human society as a whole.

My third, and concluding, premise about the understanding of contemporary anti-Semitism is that if the Israel-centered relationships are the equivalent of the older Jewish religious uniqueness, the economic profile of Jews, not as forced by anti-Semitism but as willed by Jews themselves, is the contemporary equivalent of the ghetto.

From the very beginning of the era of the Emancipation, indeed even as a preamble to it, in the thinking of such men as Naftali Tzevi Weisel, the restratification of the Jews into a "normal" economy, in which they engaged in all the pursuits, was propounded as necessary to the true integration of Jews into the larger society. What this meant in actual practice was a series of repeated attempts on most of the continents to create a class of Jewish farmers and to foster, in many places, Jewish artisans and Jewish industrial proletariat. This has met with substantial success in Israel, though even here there are signs that the older, Ashkenazi element of the Zionist resettlement is moving away from the farm and from physical labor toward becoming a white-collar elite. In the two great Jewish Diasporas, those in the Soviet Union and in the United States, it has been crystal clear in the last half century that the movement of Jews has been away from proletarian pursuits, away from direct involvement in primary production, and toward fighting their way into the intellectual, scientific, professional, and managerial elite. Again, it is an untrue cliché to say that this happened as a direct result of existing anti-Semitism. Precisely because the movements in the United States and in the Soviet Union have been in reverse, they provide us with comparative material and enable us to see what has actually happened. In the United States, the Jews began as a depressed, immigrant proletariat in sweatshops in a few pursuits, largely in the needle trades. There was no real bar to their spreading out horizontally into other industries, such as steel and coal, which were hungry in the early decades of the century for any kind of labor; those who chose to farm were even assured of large subsidies from the fund created by Baron de Hirsch. Nonetheless, Jews chose to remain in the largest American cities and to do battle with economic anti-Semitism for upward mobility into those pursuits which required maximum education and, at least in some of them, brought Jews closer to the very center of intellectual, business, and political life. It was not anti-Semitism which has created in the United States the marked and radical otherness of the economy of Jews from the rest of the country. On the contrary, several generations of Jews have fought their way successfully toward this otherness.

In the Soviet Union, the more than fifty years since the Bolshevik Revolution have been marked by a reverse phenomenon. Jews began as a major element of the revolutionary elite. They were prominent at the very center of power, in the early central committees of the Communist party, in diplomacy, in the press, and in every other pursuit which required training of the mind and the capacity to adjust rapidly to changing situations. In the early decades of the Bolshevik era, when admission to universities was available by and large on the basis of merit, Jews preferred that avenue to self-realization to settling on the farm in Birobidjan or in the Crimea, or going to work, except as project engineers, on the great new dams and power stations being built in the "five-year plans." The point and thrust of Soviet anti-Jewish policy has been in the last two decades the removal of Jews from their most prominent place in the elite and their proletarianization, especially through the denial of places in the universities to which their merit entitled them. Even those Jews in Russia who have no Jewish survivalist sentiments of any kind continue to fight against this and to refuse to accept the notion that they must be "normalized." Such a battle between the Jews and the reigning majority in society is not new in Russia, nor unprecedented. *Numerus clausus* was the slogan of Polish anti-Semites between the two wars, and their announced purpose, too, was to make the Jews of Poland into a "normal" economic element.

There is considerable truth in the explanation which argues

that Jews moved in the modern era into certain kinds of capitalist pursuits, into the free professions, and into the intellectual world because the kind of economic experience that had been forced on them by the ghetto predisposed them to such endeavors; because persisting anti-Semitism excluded them from pursuits except those which depended on highly personal, easily transportable skills; and because the inherited Jewish tradition laid great emphasis on the culture of the mind. I am not persuaded by these explanations. It is simply not true that Jews have had in their medieval and early modern past a continuing distance from physical labor and a continuing pervasive intellectuality. Whatever else the hasidic phenomenon might have been, it was certainly at its origins anti-intellectual. The rich Jewish businessman did exist, but as the pervasive expression of Jewish economic endeavor he is a myth of Karl Marx and Werner Sombart. We need not enter into these vexing issues in order to establish the point that is necessary for our argument. There can be absolutely no doubt that throughout the modern era Jews have had ample and recurring opportunity to turn proletarian and become economically "normal." It was to go in the reverse direction, away from primary production and toward the contemporary secular "priesthood" of intellectuals, managers, and technocrats—those figures who were first recognized as a "priesthood" by Saint-Simon in the early years of the nineteenth century—that Jews have fought against their enemies in every modern society.

Economic and social integration into a new society of equals, to settle in as individuals throughout all the countries of their dispersion, has been the other, non-Zionist dream of Jewish modernity. Feudal and guild societies denied Jews this opportunity, and so "the career open to talent" promised by the liberal revolution found its most devoted partisans among Jews. It is not accidental that counterrevolutionary forces such as the royalists in France in the nineteenth century, or new groups now bidding for a place in the sun such as the blacks in America today, should center their attack on Jews. Let it also be remembered, however, that men of the social and political left, not all of whom can be termed vulgar anti-Semites, insisted throughout the nineteenth century and into our own that Jews must enter proletarian pursuits in order to be truly emancipated and that their refusal to do this in any great numbers meant that they were insisting on a "priestly" —or demonic—role in society.

There are many obvious answers to such demands and such attacks. It is clear, at the very least, that every group in society must not behave exactly like every other group. We even know by now that the notion of physical labor as the only guarantee of personal virtue is a romantic myth. For the purpose of our present analysis it is enough to assert the undeniable, that there was Jewish drive and will and choice in the creation of the otherness of Jews in the open society, and that, indeed, the more open the society has been, the more "other" Jews have become.

We must now, inevitably, confront the question of meaning and of interpretation. I am completely persuaded that contemporary anti-Semitism, even of the most immediate secular kind, is rooted psychologically and emotionally in many centuries of training given to Western men by the Christian church. Let me be even more forthright: I know that to emphasize the secular and the non-Christian in modern anti-Semitism is often disturbing, because it seems to provide too easy an absolution of Christians for their past. Let me also admit that the anti-Semitism of the past has had a major hand in fashioning the intellectual stereotypes of the dangerous alien in all its forms, with which the Jews have had to contend in new guises in the modern era. What I am leaning against in this paper is a premise that was enunciated most clearly by Sartre and has been morally comfortable and comforting to generations of Jews in the last two centuries—that whatever is peculiar and attacked, in the case of Jews, is a creation of anti-Semitism, and that is therefore chargeable entirely to the account of negative, external circumstances. Quite apart from the facts, there is an enormous inherent difficulty with such a premise, for it contains inevitably a negative estimate of the inherited Jewish culture. This must be judged by such thinking as a response to a stunted life, and such attitudes toward anti-Semitism involve the presumption that true freedom for the Jews means that they should and will cease being specifically Jewish. My immediate difficulties with this thesis are not moral or theoretical; they are rather that such explanations do not fit the facts of the modern era.

Whatever might be true about medieval Jewry and the anti-Semitism that it faced, the national peculiarities of contemporary Israel as the center of a world Jewish community and the socio-economic peculiarities of world Jewry are not disfigured responses to Jew-hatred. Anti-Semitism, ancient and modern, has had something to do with this history, but the essence of its meaning is not that what we have been doing is forced on us, but rather that it is willed by Jews. This people of ours is a peculiar people in the modern era not only because the greatest of tragedies, the Holocaust, has happened to us, but because the whole direction of our activity has been, by choice, toward creating a worldwide society of our own like no other. If contemporary anti-Semitism is a re-echo in the rhetoric and conflicts of this day of the age-old Gentile impatience with our otherness, the will and passion with which we have created this otherness again is our own contemporary version of the ancient voice which once echoed in our ears commanding us to be "unto Me a peculiar people among the peoples."

Jews engage in the discussion of anti-Semitism for more than purely theoretical purposes. We keep retesting the temperature of the waters in which we must swim and the indices of our own strength to survive, because these are everyday matters of the most profound and personal concern. Here we enter a realm that is beyond historical description and analysis in an attempt to see beyond the present. On the simplest level, we know already that wherever the position of Jews in society has become relatively "normal," anti-Semitism has indeed ceased and group conflict has taken its place. For example, the political policy of Willy Brandt, former chancellor of West Germany, was less pro-Jewish and pro-Israel than that of his predecessors whose personal pasts were far more questionable. I have no doubt that when he publishes his diaries there will be recurrent entries about his feeling that it is possible to differ strongly with the contemporary policy and needs of the Jewish people and to regard that as a conflict among present equals rather than as anti-Semitism. I sometimes wonder whether King Hussein looks across the Jordan through the binoculars of an anti-Semite or those of a ruler whose very personal existence depends, in some measure, on the goodwill of a far more powerful and advanced society across the way. What inheres in these examples is that, especially since 1967, a substantial amount of "normalization" has indeed taken place in the image of Israel as a state and society. It ceased in those glorious days being the symbol of a haven of the weak and the persecuted; the countermyth, of superhuman strength (which owed something to old anti-Semitic ideas and notions about the Jews as both very weak and powerfully demonic), has by now also receded. Certainly political peace in the region, which now seems a possibility, will help translate anti-Semitism into group conflict.

On the other hand, the ingathering of the exiles seems still a far-off dream. The peculiarity of Jewish inner relationship will long remain, and only the most doctrinaire of classic Zionists would argue that the Diaspora will soon either come to Israel or disappear entirely. We may be living in a period of "time lag," that is, in an era in which the normalization promised by Zionism and the end of anti-Semitism that will come with it is not around the corner in this immediate generation. The Zionist "End of Days" will come in, let us say, a century or so. I am prepared to believe that it will, and I certainly think that it should. Nonetheless, I wonder whether those voices which are already being raised, even in Israel, about the nature of our contemporary Jewish culture will not continue to insist in future generations with ever greater vehemence that to be either Belgium or Switzerland in the Middle East is not what being Jewish is all about.

In the immediate present I have another suspicion. Every study in recent years of economic pursuits and intellectual level in advanced societies tends to establish not that Jews are becoming more like Gentiles, but that Gentiles are becoming more like Jews. For example, there are ever fewer people in primary education in the United States as a whole nowadays and, proportionately, ever more in the colleges. The best projections for the end of the century are that in America as a whole about 4 percent of the labor force will be engaged in physical labor and about 80 percent of the young will be receiving a college education—but this is precisely the present profile, to the decimal point, of American Jews. On the global scale, societies are beginning to have to deal with one another much more flexibly than on the nineteenth-century presumption that all political identities are determined by nation-states. Indeed, some of the most pernicious things that have happened in recent years, such as the tragedies during the partition of India and the horror of the Nigeria–Biafra conflict, have resulted from attempts to avoid the living together of different peoples. The very same General Charles de Gaulle who objected to the loyalties of French Jews to Israel tried to evoke such loyalties to France among French Canadians.

Nonetheless, it would be far too hopeful to imagine that anti-Semitism will soon end. It will clearly persist to the degree to which Jews remain a unique entity in the world, and I do not think that we Jews are really prepared completely to surrender our distinctiveness even in the days of the Messiah. At least, so I read the ancient Midrash which insisted that the commandments which were given specifically to Jews would not end even in the apocalyptic era. Our internal Jewish problem remains the giving of content to this uniqueness. The larger and more searing question is whether, in the century that has witnessed Auschwitz, which has now secularized almost completely its conflicts with Jews, new definitions of human society as a whole are indeed arising.

At root, the question of anti-Semitism remains not one of Jewish behavior, now balanced between its own uniqueness and accommodation with the world, but of the Gentile conceptions of society. So far the ancient Greek notion that "barbarians" must become Hellenized to be accepted—that no radically dissenting group can be allowed to maintain itself—has dominated in the Western world. This is the age-old social principle from which anti-Semitism has sprung. This "Hellenistic" vision is now questionable, both morally and in its practical capacity to deal with the future. In the next century, as East and West encounter each other, many unlike communities will have to live together in decent peace or the world will be in the deepest trouble. Anti-Semitism is indeed now indicative of the basic, persisting *hubris* of the West. Jews can survive anti-Semitism, but can the West survive its persisting nature?

Jewish history has always been an interweaving of what we

are and what we have learned from the environment, of what we
have fought for and of the attacks that we have resisted. So it is
today. The journey is not yet ended, for the Messiah has not come
—but, like all of my ancestors, I hear his footsteps.

6. *To Believe—and to Wait*

PERHAPS IT IS IMPRUDENT and even presumptuous for a Jew to
comment on the current debate within Christianity on the mission
of the church to the Jews. The issues that have been raised in this
debate must, however, concern him, if only because the validity of
Judaism as a faith and the present estate, both spiritual and tem-
poral, of the Jewish community are once again under analysis
from Christian perspective.

To say the obvious and expected first, Jews cannot but prefer
Reinhold Niebuhr's proposal (which represents a position not far
different from that which Paul Tillich is known to have held) that
there be theological coexistence between Judaism and Christianity
till the end of time. Nonetheless, one must agree with Niebuhr's
critic, George E. Sweazey ("Are Jews Intended to be Christians?"
in *The Christian Century,* April 29, 1959), that coexistence would
represent a theological revolution. Sweazey's assertion that since
New Testament times the Jews have always been a, if not *the,*
prime target of Christian proselytism seems undeniable. Nor can
it be gainsaid that, on Sweazey's premises, proselytism is an in-
tegral element of that evangelism which is the "Great Commission" of the church, and that to excise it by making theological
peace with Judaism would call all Christian evangelism into question. Sweazey thus appears as the defender of classical Christian

---

Reprinted from *The Christian Century,* vol. 76, no. 37 (September 16,
1959).

theology against a radical new proposal. In his approach to the Jews he seems to walk consciously and resolutely on the highroad marked out by his Christian ancestors through the centuries; he believes that he brings them the higher truth which has come to replace and indeed fulfill what he considers the partial truth of Judaism.

Such a classicist no doubt expects the Jew also to react in the ancient way: to debate about all the Biblical texts that have so often been a Jewish-Christian battleground and to argue against the truth and divinity of the Christian revelation. In the medieval age, a Christian classicist would agree, the discussion could never reach its fullest stature on either side; for Christians too often vitiated the spiritual power of their case and mission by invoking force, and Jews, even if they might have wished to proselyte for their faith, were debarred from doing so. Hence a twentieth-century Christian like Mr. Sweazey is, to his credit, very insistent on the responsibility of the missioner today to recognize the equal rights of Jews in our democratic society and to labor, in Christian love, for their complete religious liberty. By the inherent logic of this acceptance of freedom, such a Christian undoubtedly would welcome free competition with a Jewish missionary movement, which is possible in the democratic world today. This indeed is the "answer" of some Jews to Christian evangelism: they are proposing a new departure for Jewry, something which has been foreign to it for at least as long as Christianity has dominated the West; i.e., campaigns are being announced for conversions to Judaism.

Obviously the debate between Sweazey and Niebuhr arises in part at least from the situation in America and the Western world today. So does the movement for Jewish missionary activity; such an undertaking would have been unimaginable in medieval times, in a world dominated by papal power, or in John Calvin's Geneva. The twentieth-century Christian-Jewish encounter cannot therefore be understood in purely theological terms. Sweazey knows as well as Niebuhr that the church and those whom it would convert—and those who would convert it—all live in history. Perhaps we can discuss the meaning of both Christian and Jewish faith better after a journey through the complexities of the present. Perhaps it will then appear that a revived Christian mission to the Jews will involve Christianity in problems that cannot be solved in the way Mr. Sweazey suggests: by a self-denying effort to end all mention of Christ in Rotary Club invocations and to reduce the large presence of Christian forms in the public schools.

With varying degrees of precision, Mr. Sweazey seems to know several things about the present condition of the Jews in America which predispose him to believe that Christian proselytism among them is a real possibility. The most prominent of his arguments is that "many Jews in America scarcely have a religion," that "even those who cherish a strong sense of the Judaic tradition often seem to hold it as a sort of super-intense patriotism, without personal awareness of the God or the religious teachings of their forefathers." Second, he is aware that American Jewry has not yet conquered the last frontier, namely, full personal and social acceptance by a society which politely but thoroughly practices exclusion of the Jew. This awareness is implicit in Mr. Sweazey's suggestion that "friendship is important" and in his emphasis on the fact that 98 percent of Christians with a Jewish background indicated in a questionnaire study that they had begun to "look toward Christ because of friendship with a church member." Mr. Sweazey also alludes to the discomfort caused Jews by Christian observances in the public schools and the like. He suggests that in approaching the Jews "churches can do more to encourage better inter-group relations, not primarily to make a straighter highway for the Lord but simply because of the self-sufficient value of good feeling and appreciation. Christians must be encouraged to discountenance prejudice against Jews wherever it appears."

Sweazey's awareness of these sensitive areas in American Jewish experience prompt him to a generalization which appears to make him slightly uncomfortable. What he is saying is that the strength of Christianity in Jewish-Christian encounter is Christendom; i.e., the fact that American society is primarily Christian and that even in this tolerant age a religious minority like the Jewish continues to feel the pressure of the overwhelming majority in many forms. But Sweazey points out that the conversion of Jews to Christianity out of their desire for betterment of their personal status in society would represent the equivalent of "rice Christianity," and clearly that is not what any sensitive or committed Christian desires.

As Mr. Sweazey emphasizes, those who would undertake to evangelize American Jews have something to offer which (in their view) is much more religiously valid and exciting. Large numbers of Jews, they say, have no real religious convictions, only group loyalties and a sense of involvement in the history and destiny of their people; they are therefore ripe for the true spiritual experience which Christianity can give them. The premises on which this central point rests can be questioned on several grounds. Statistically, the rate of synagogue affiliation has risen dramatically since World War II. By now (1959), at least three-fifths of all American Jews belong to some synagogue. (See the present writer's article on religion in the *American Jewish Yearbook, 1958.*) At least another fifth is in the broad sense identified with the synagogue, and, more significantly still, probably almost nine out of ten Jewish children in America receive some training in the Jewish religious school. An elaborate study of this question (see the *New York Times,* May 29, 1959) confirms this fact, indeed shows that in the last decade religious school attendance has risen at a higher rate in Jewry than in any other American religious group.

While Jewish leaders differ in opinion as to the quality of the religious revival that these figures betoken, there can be no doubt that this is not the record of a group in flight from its religious moorings. A generation ago American Jews behaved primarily like an ethnic minority; today the religious organizations are the central and stabilizing institutions of Jewish life. Granted that this religious identification is to some degree merely the formal expression of secularism and group loyalty, is Judaism's situation essentially different from that of the major Christian denominations?

The various churches are consistently examining themselves as overly secularized ethnic and class temples of "togetherness." For example, Roswell P. Barnes emphasized before the General Assembly of the National Council of Churches of Christ in 1957 (of which body he was then associate general secretary) that the statistical evidences of growth in church membership were not "adequate criteria for judging religious values or the influence of the churches in society." Dr. Barnes urged that organized Christianity slough off all standards of institutional success and look for leadership to saints and thinkers rather than to organizers.

Leading rabbis would echo these words—indeed have done so. They too know that the swift growth of synagogue membership involves them in the same danger of becoming merely "organization men," and they too are trying to use the opportunity of this moment to teach their people faith in the God of Abraham. In sum, American Jews do not look to the church down the street as the bearer of a pure faith, undefiled by what is wrong with contemporary America—if only because its minister is quite likely, and his bishop or presiding elder is almost certain, to be telling all who will listen that the struggle for piety is as hard a fight among Christians as among Jews. There can be camaraderie in this battle, but there is no overwhelming evidence that it is more nearly won at one end of the street than at the other.

Clearly, American Jewry is today no more disintegrating because of its internal ills than is American Christendom. Like Christianity, Judaism is self-consciously and proudly at home in this free society of ours and it resents any implications, no matter how subtly put, that it is looked on by others as a communion to be destroyed. Being human, Jews will be suspicious of the proffered embraces of a Protestantism that may be trying to convert them through love, using honey rather than vinegar tactics. They will tend to brood again on the horror of the nazi years, when the Munks, the Bonhöffers and the Berggravs, who stood as Christians for decency, were not the sole spokesmen of Christianity; for there were Christian chaplains with the nazi armies and, unlike the Communists, the nazis were never formally excommunicated by any of the historic Christian denominations.

Jews will contemplate the pronounced anti-Zionism of many church circles and note that every single state that has arisen in Africa and Asia since World War II—even Nasser's Egypt, which is anti-Christian—has found almost unqualified support in organized Christianity, except Israel. This is not the place to enter into the merits or assess the moral guilt of those issues. But one fact is plain: an aggressive Christian mission to Jewry can only break open the scars of these wounds and stir up the bitter passions of yesterday. The possibility of Jewish-Christian cooperation and symbiosis, which is a chief glory of America, will be lessened if not destroyed.

Nor can a Protestantism missionizing among Jews expect the Roman Catholics to maintain a benevolent silence. By its very momentum, such an effort will soon, if not immediately, turn into a broader attempt to convert all Americans to Protestantism. Catholics have certainly read the many statements of recent years that South America is the great Protestant hope. They know that they are often regarded in Protestant circles exactly as Mr. Sweazey regards Jews; i.e., as being Catholics because of their Irish, Italian, or Spanish ethnic memories, but a people bereft of true religion. It will take no imagination for Catholics to react to a Protestant mission to the Jews, conceived as an effort to dissolve the Jewish community, by closing whatever roads are open between them and other Christians. The America that we know would then be at an end.

These reflections lead to a consideration of the two great turning points in the life of Christianity in our generation: the radical change in the nature of its encounter with Eastern faiths and the trend toward Christian reunion that is symbolized by the ecumenical movement. A Christianity that must rethink its relationship to its traditional mission fields and that is seriously attempting to reunite is clearly so changed that this change must affect, and be affected by, the Jewish-Christian encounter.

In 1953 S. C. Carpenter could write, in the widely read Penguin volume *Christianity,* that "others are either ignorant of what is happening or strangely blind to the significance of the fact that Asia and Africa are gradually becoming Christian." Dr. Carpenter's confidence in Christianity's success is not shared by Edmund Perry, who writes in his 1958 volume *The Gospel in Dispute:*

> For the first time in its entire history the Christian faith is on the brink of a decisive encounter with the other major religious systems of the world which are now determined to define the encounter in their own terms. . . . The missionary inroads of Christian faith into these other religions have been made by an of-

fensive church against defensive religions. Henceforth the Church has to meet a counteroffensive by the other religions, for there is a resurgence of vitality especially in Hinduism, Buddhism, and Islam, and this resurgence is characterized by a feverish missionary zeal which puts the Church on the defensive. . . . No contemporary devotee of any one of these older faiths is willing to think of his faith as a preliminary faith which should give way to or lead into Christianity. . . . From his point of view, Christians' claims to exclusive truth and grace in the Gospel are the same fabric as the attitude of racial and cultural superiority which characterized the political and economic domination of Asia and Africa by the white man.

Today therefore, for the first time in its history, Christianity is in a "Jewish situation." Judaism has been marked from its beginning by a tension between the universal and the particular, between God who speaks to and about all men and the incarnation of that faith in the particular destiny and needs of the children of Abraham, Isaac, and Jacob, who are its bearers. Christianity appeared in the world announcing itself as the universalism of Judaism, incarnate in the Messiah who had come, and stripped of any particular reference to Jew or Greek. But today Christianity is the religion of the West and primarily of whites. It remains, of course, a gospel addressed to all men; and yet it cannot but know that, in the here and now, it is solidly rooted in one geographical area and in one cultural organism.

A Jew does not have the right to suggest to Christianity how it shall solve its own basic dilemmas on the contemporary scene. He does, however, have both the right and the duty to speak about the meaning of Christian evangelism for the future of America in its life-and-death struggle for the minds of men in the non-Christian world. America as a whole and all that it stands for will go down to defeat and disaster if our age is made into a new seventeenth century, a time of "wars of religion." The peoples of Asia and Africa will respond to our American leadership only if what we offer as a counterfaith to communism is not Christianity or even Judeo-Christianity, but rather the greatest of all American values: the vision of a world order in which all men serve side by side and help each other to be true to themselves, to their own hopes and aspirations.

Let me add that in the next century American society and indeed the whole Western world will inevitably tend to become pluralist in a much more complex way than ever before. A few years ago America took the first step toward opening the door of immigration to Asiatics and Africans by assigning modest quotas to that part of the world. And now it has admitted Hawaii to statehood. That means that more and more Buddhists, Hindus, and Moslems will come to our shores, because America cannot be true either to itself or to its responsibilities if it refuses them entry. The pluralism of our society will therefore have to take on a different cast. No longer will it be merely Jewish-Christian or religious-secular. Our society will have to devise a framework in which religions essentially foreign to each other will be able to meet in the common marketplace of an America which is steadily becoming a microcosm of all humanity. A revived Christian evangelism reasserting its "Great Commission" to convert, and hence to dissolve, all other faiths will not only embarrass America before the world; it will undercut our foreign policy and lend new fuel to the appeal of communism in the East.

But what of the "Great Commission"? A classicizing Christian like Mr. Sweazey might share every one of my fears and yet declare, "God helping me, I can do no other." Assuredly the social consequences of a faith cannot always be allowed to determine its expression. But on the other hand it is obvious that American society and the world need theologies that are at once true to themselves and yet make possible a reasonable peace among religions.

No one who believes in a divine revelation can possibly be satisfied with the easy answer that every one of the great religions has some good in it and that all are therefore equally valid. If this be true, then idolatry and paganism have had some uses, for they certainly produced great aesthetic values, at very least in ancient Greece. I for one am not much happier with the Niebuhr-Tillich idea (which Franz Rosenzweig prefigured) that Judaism and Christianity are both aspects of a larger revelation and that they exist to correct and supplement each other. Being a classicizing

Jew, I stand with classicizing Christians like George Sweazey in insisting that these two faiths cannot both be ultimately right. If Christianity is God's true revelation of Himself, then clearly I, the Jew, am living in the greatest error, for I continue to reject the "highest light" that God has vouchsafed. But the converse is also possible: If Judaism is true, then the Christian has arrogated to himself the claim of being the true Israel, made a man into God, and falsely proclaimed the Law to be abrogated. For classicists like George Sweazey and myself, there is no escape from living in the gravest danger, for each has bet his life and his salvation on one of these two possibilities.

How then can we refrain from trying to convert each other? How can we seriously propose to live in peace?

It seems to me that the clue to an answer is to be found in the very ecumenical movement within which Mr. Sweazey is laboring. The Eastern Orthodox Church is part of the World Council of Chuches, though it is known not to have surrendered one iota of its conviction that other bodies with which it is sitting are not true churches.

Several rationales for such cooperation in the ecumenical movement have been suggested, with particular emphasis on the fact that each church remains free and, indeed, commissioned by its own light to convert members of other denominations. It is nontheless clear, at least to an outside observer like myself, that the meaning of ecumenicity is in the ultimate sense eschatological. It represents a largely unspoken acceptance of the premise that the church is likely to remain divided on matters of faith and to live with this division; that the historic denominations will, despite some normal traffic across the various lines, not engage in an all-out attempt to destroy each other; and that the question of which of the many churches is Christ's true church will be left for the judgment of God at the end of time. If this be not the inherent meaning of ecumenicity, then the Protestant response to Pope John's recent call for a council of churches makes no sense. What Protestantism asks as the price for attending such a meeting is acceptance by the Roman Catholic communion of the idea that Protestants have a right to the danger of living outside the authority of Peter's successor, until God shall judge between them.

I can only propose to Christianity as a whole and to Protestantism in particular that this premise on which it is refounding modern Christianity, and this demand that it is making of the Roman Catholics, be applied in the relationship of all religions in the modern world, both East and West. Let us stand separately for our various truths. Let us stand together for the peace of society. Let us not do to one another that which is hateful to any of us. And let us await the judgment of God.

7. A Generation Later

ANGER. Anger at the world which let the Holocaust happen. Anger at the Western tradition with its pretenses at civility and the rotten endemic reality of its Jew-hatred. But, above all, anger at myself. I was young when it all happened and said to myself, "Who am I to scream?" So I was silent.

Not shame, except my own. I am not ashamed that the Jews for the most part went helplessly to their own murder. It was not their duty to make it easier for me to forgive myself for surviving. They thought then that what was happening was a worldwide pogrom, which most could survive by making themselves as inconspicuous as possible. So most of these Jews had no "honor" in the Western sense—but what can such a remark possibly mean? Was it dishonorable for our ancestors to survive pogroms by hiding? Is it more honorable to fight, in uniform, in such fields of honor as Vietnam—or even, much as I still cannot make myself care about the Germans, to firebomb Dresden? Let those survivors who would justify their own existence, or their flight while leaving behind others dear to them, deal in honor. That is their problem, not mine.

Reprinted from *Midstream,* vol. 16, no. 6, June/July 1970.

Not pride. This, too, would be impertinent, even more impertinent than the shame. What entitles me to feel any identity with Janusz Korczak, who refused to let the children of his Children's Home go to their deaths alone and so he went with them? Would I have imitated him—or for that matter would I have behaved like the rabbi in Lemberg who refused to take refuge in the palace of the archbishop and left it to be with his community, to be shot by the Nazis as soon as he walked out the door? Pride in the presumption that I might have behaved that way? Perhaps, but I do not know and I hope that I shall never know. Korczak and Rabbi Levine and countless thousands died the way they died for themselves and for God and not to make me feel better or to be proud to be a Jew. I do not have to face even the memory of their destiny because it is not likely ever to be my own. What I must face is my real situation, which has been fashioned in part by what has happened to them. But these events are not its paradigm.

No shaking of my fist at God. The Holocaust is a shattering horror not alone because so many were murdered. It is shattering because we did not believe that the world of "progress" was capable of such destruction. The Jews of the first century did not believe that the Temple could be destroyed. Job did not believe that God would let a righteous man suffer. I have never been able to explain to myself, let alone to a mother, why her child should already be blind and on the way to dying of cancer in a children's ward at the hospital. The difference between Hitler and the Crusaders was primarily a matter of technical efficiency. Is it the technology of murder, which became "modern" and "advanced," rather than the intent of Jew-hatred, which was not remarkably different, that now creates a theological problem? Let contemporaries speak of the "death of God" in Auschwitz, as the medievals implored Him to manifest His presence and end His wrathful absence and His unconcern. All this is rhetoric with which we plaster over our horror and try to find a way of asserting that in some addition, in a mathematics that is beyond our ken, these fragments of life, memory, and jagged edges of pain, the pain of others as well as our own, do add up. Perhaps they do. All I know is that there is no other way of living without believing this—or going mad. Auschwitz can be thought about but not by theologians. It cannot be "explained." It cannot, I think, be felt again even by those who once were there. It happened. Even this happening did not stop the world, or even the lives of those who survived. Perhaps it should have made an end of the world, but it did not and it is now a generation later. The question cannot be how or why the world can go on, for it does. It can only be how different it is now because Auschwitz happened.

Not guilt. I did not die at Auschwitz nor did I survive it. As a statement of fact this is obvious, but I say it nonetheless because I am tired of the impertinent metaphors among the novelists and theologians who play-act with this theme. They must, for men must cope as best they can with the memory of their own or other people's helplessness. I am not guilty for not having been at Auschwitz because those who were not would not have chosen it and had I been in Poland in 1939 it would have been chosen for me, too. My own personal survival was an accident, because my family made the choice in the very last week of the validity of their American visa to come to the United States in 1926. Most of my contemporaries, the children born in Galacia in the years after World War I, were murdered in the 1940s, and a few survived, but their history is not my history and I bear no burden because of the accidents which made theirs different. Men are guilty only of the things they choose and not even of the horrors that are chosen for them or those they do not share. There is guilt in the Holocaust, the pain of those who think they traded too much in the camps for their own survival—but of that let no man who was not there dare speak or even think—and the lasting, sometimes forgotten but always present ache of those who lived those years in Baltimore or Belfast and forever ask themselves whether they did enough. The second guilt can be brooded on, to become the content of a lifetime of "spiritual nobility," but such brooding is a fake. It does not help the dead and it only abstracts one from the choices that must be made by the living.

Only loss—and anger, always anger. The anger is easiest to describe because it is always there, not so much by itself as suffusing every other theme and every train of thought. I learned too young that evil can triumph, that prayer is not heard, and that those whom I thought were powerful were not. This is, of course, a realization that is part of the somber dignity of growing up, but I think that this knowledge gave my generation a shock that children get when they are orphaned by the wanton murder of their parents. Some anger always remains, directed at one's self. Such children may confront this anger and even conquer it, at least in their conscious being, but it never really goes entirely away. Aunts and uncles and cousins may rally to their side. They may even create warm new families of their own and bring distant relatives who were of the same world as their parents into closer contact in an often frenzied desire to replace the loss. Such orphans can make do, perhaps even quite creatively and with dazzling energy, but what has been denied to the individual child by the death of his parents when he was very young are the normal stages of learning from them, loving them, and separating from them. Even for those whose parents were alive, what was burned in the gas ovens were our parents.

I know, of course, that Polish Jewry in the 1930s was not a museum of kaftans and hasidic conventicles. All of our Jewish modernity, and much of that of the world as a whole, had arisen within it and was being passionately maintained by partisans of many persuasions. The revolution, socialism, Zionism, Yiddishist natonalism, Esperanto, Polish patriotism—the list parallels all the permutations of life and thought in the twentieth century. This community was not very ancient, for Jews had come to Poland from more Western regions in Europe and perhaps some from Southern Russia only in relatively recent centuries, but these were the heirs of the learning and the passion of all the centuries of Ashkenazi Jewry. This community in the last two decades of its existence was poor, embattled, and rent by internal strife. By its own earlier standards it was losing some of its verve and authenticity—but many parents have bad times, grow older, and have trouble with each other and with a hostile world. In the 1930s the spiritual capital of Zionism was more nearly in Warsaw than in its diplomatic center in London or its Palestinian capital of Tel Aviv. The center of Yiddish was in Vilna and of hasidism in whatever town in Poland in which your rebbe resided. Classic rabbinic learning had its headquarters in innumerable yeshivot in

Poland and Lithuania. The more modern Jewish scholarship was cultivated primarily in Germany, but increasingly the scholars involved had received their basic training in their native Eastern Europe. The center of the Westernized forms of the Jewish religion were in Germany, notably in Frankfurt. On the eve of the advent of Hitler every single aspect of the Jewish spirit, except perhaps the kibbutz movement, derived its basic inspiration from European Jewry and, for the most part, from the Polish community.

In my teens, even after the advent of Hitler, I still imagined that I would return to Poland for part of my education. I was already too "modern" to think that I could fit with my young uncles, who were not much older than myself, in the court of the rebbe of Belz, but I expected that I could visit this world, and not as a tourist. Was I not the grandson and namesake of the childhood teacher of the Belzer rebbe? Was not my maternal grandfather one of the pillars of the rebbe's empire? I never got there. What remains of Belz was replanted after the Holocaust in Jerusalem and I never go to the city without visiting the yeshivah on Agrippas Street, but it is not the same. Young hasidic yeshivah students, the age of my own children, and even their teachers who are almost all of the postwar generation, can neither link me to the past of my family nor release me from it.

But the trip to Poland that never was had purposes which looked beyond the visit to the world of my grandfather. I was no more than fifteen when I realized that I had gone the route of several generations of predecessors among the children of the deepest Polish and Lithuanian Jewish orthodoxy, that is, I had moved toward Zionism, a love of Hebrew and of Yiddish, and an eclectic love of the forms and content of the Jewish tradition. I could clearly locate myself within the Jewish modernity for which such figures as Ahad Ha-am and Sholem Aleichem spoke. In breaks between doing my high school homework and the serious business of continuing to study Talmud I read such "moderns" to help my self-understanding. No one else in my high school class, even though it was largely Jewish, had such problems. For that matter, neither did anyone in my Talmud class. In both of these circles the choices had been made very early. The best of my high school contemporaries were on their way to teaching sociology at Harvard and becoming marginal Jews. My fellow Talmudists would soon be leading figures in English-speaking orthodoxy. I was on the way to neither of these paths, and most of those who then felt as I did were not in Baltimore, or even in New York, but in Poland.

In 1938 my father wrote to Moses Schorr, the head of the modern rabbinical school in Warsaw (its students were ex-yeshivah students who had chosen to become "Westernized") to explore the possibility of my coming to study there. He wrote back in ornate Hebrew that the "time was not ripe" for an American youngster to come to Warsaw. I knew as I read that letter that there were disasters to come. I knew it even more as my parents redoubled their efforts in the winter of 1938–39 to get some of my mother's family out of Lemberg. I watched the letters come that winter, with their tales of an "American quota" oversubscribed for a decade, and I fantasized of becoming powerful among the *goyim* so that I could save my brethren—but why did I not then go screaming at the front doors of the State Department?

There were those of my generation who thought that New York's Lower East Side was the capital of Jewish authenticity in the United States. I knew that it was a colony of Polish Jewry. Indeed, much as I was coming to despise T. S. Eliot for his dislike of Jews, I could understand why he, in particular, had to go to England to find the sources of a tradition which, in all its resonances, was hardly present in Saint Louis or even in Boston. It was tradition that was the key to his problem, at least as I understood it; it was certainly the essence of my own. One can choose to lose one's identity in a new world and glory in the fact that the past can be made not to matter. Alternatively, one can assert the dogma and practices of a religious faith anywhere. An identity compounded of history and memory could hardly exist without living relationship to an older community. Warsaw, Vilna, and Lemberg were, inevitably, my Oxford and Canterbury, not only in what remained unchanged there but also in the very variety of all the clashing newer forms of Jewish experience which abounded in those cities. I knew that what I had to learn could not really be imparted to me by those, of whatever age, who had reconstituted bits of these experiences in the United States. I was, myself, such a transplantation. American Jewish intellectuals of European provenance were, even in the mind of the fifteen-year-old, more colleagues than teachers. They, too, were children away from home, perhaps even brilliant children like Joseph in Egypt preparing the way for the rescue of his family from famine in Canaan, but children, nonetheless. They were clearly even more alien than I to the American scene and much more plagued by the question of where was their home. These were unanswered questions in New York, and I did not need others to help me define them. I knew rationally very early that these were questions in Warsaw, too, but in some part of myself, probably that part of me which remains the child of five who was blessed by his grandfather in the railroad station in Lemberg when we left for the United States, I continued to believe that in Poland I would find certainties and affirmation—or at very least contemporaries whose uncertainties were like my own.

I think I became a Zionist because I never got to Lemberg. It was, of course, clear to me in my college years in the late 1930s that the Jews had to get out of Europe and that the only door that might possibly be pried open was that of Palestine. I had no doubt that a more interesting, and more rooted, Jewish life was arising in Palestine than we were creating in America. By 1943, when I began to know that the disaster to European Jewry was enormous, I also knew, without ever saying it in words, that the community which involved so many of my emotions could not possibly be anything near the same when the war ended. I could never go home again, not because I had become radically different, as I had, but because home would at best be a semihabitable ruin. And so there began a curious, but I suspect not atypical, inner dialogue between myself and Tel Aviv.

Those who had created that great city gloried in its newness; I went to it for the first time before the guns stopped firing in 1949 in search of the very Eastern Europe against which its newness was a rebellion. It is surely no accident that to this day the majority of Israelis prefer Tel Aviv, and most Jews from the Diaspora infinitely prefer Jerusalem. I understand with my head that contemporary Israel represents that Jewish modernity which alone is likely to survive, and therefore I huddle next to it. I know that eclectic Jews like myself can live with their eclecticism much more easily in a land of their own than in the Diaspora, and that knowledge is the recurrent demand on me for *aliyah*—but it is a demand that reason makes more than emotion. I can find Jewish modernity enough on any one day wherever I may be; I need only to look at myself. It is the older resonances that I cannot find in all their perhaps imaginary fullness in Baltimore or New York. And so I keep going to Jerusalem in search of Lemberg.

Since 1967, I go again and again to the Wall. The only time that it does me any good, on the deepest level, is late at night when the Wall is practically deserted. I can then turn my back upon the newly paved plaza, forget that this Wall is now disfigured by its uses as a tourist attraction or even as a national monument, and say some Psalms for the souls of all those who deserved better than to die in Auschwitz and who deserved more than I to stand in this place. Sometimes I even dare imagine that I am trying to carry on for them, but I instantly banish the thought as another example of arrogance and impertinence parading as deep feeling. What can it possibly mean that one's own life, even at its most committed, also bears the content and meaning of other lives, especially of the lives of martyrs? I suppose that what it does mean is that the orphan, whether he wants to or not, must become the head of his house.

Israel is one of the children of Eastern Europe; it is the creation of the rebellious child who left because he found the ancestral home intolerable. American Jewry in its overwhelming mass descends from those who left that home not because they willed some new beginning but because there was not enough food to go around. Both communities presumed that Jewish Poland would remain. We are what is left after the Holocaust and we huddle together, but I wonder what the relationships within the Jewish world would be today if Warsaw and Lemberg as they existed in 1939 had survived the war. Is it such a foregone conclusion that contemporary Israel would be the place to which Western Jews, and even Israelis themselves, would always look for Jewish inspiration? Would not many of the young in New York, and even in Tel Aviv, now go to Jewish Vilna and to Warsaw, or to the villages in the Carpathians in search of all the resonances of their Jewish selves?

On the surface of events the generation of which I am part has been astonishingly energetic and creative. In America we have fought our way to the very center of the economy and of society and we have established the visible presence of organized Jewish life everywhere. The State of Israel is largely a creation of the same generation, of those who were young enough to fight in 1948. It might thus be said that, as before in Jewish history, catastrophe has evoked redoubled energies among those who survived. I do not believe this. It is true on the level of tangible achievement, and in Israel it is even true that some new heart and new spirit, some serious new beginning, is appearing. My own closest friends in America are just now able to think again of the Holocaust, for in our deepest being we have been stunned. The very frenzy of our success, indeed even our great endeavors for Israel, have been forms of shouting down the brooding horror. It is, however, not merely twenty-five years later; it is a generation later. What is hurting now, and what is helping as well, is the coming to their own adulthood of our children. They look to us to represent the past, having resolved our own relationship to it, and we can no longer fail them by avoiding the question of the Holocaust in ourselves.

For two decades I did not move beyond the feeling of being the last, not of the just, but of the East Europeans. You cannot, however, be a parent and be an epigone; your children ask insistently that you help them make sense of their own world in the light of the sense that you have made of yours. To such questions no rational answers can be given. Perhaps it is only age and the passage of time that has helped. I have no better ideology than I possessed twenty years ago, but for me the gloom lifts somewhat as I look at the young. In their eyes we are not orphans but parents, and such we must be.

Jeremiah knew this when the first great disaster hit our people with the destruction of the Temple in 586 B.C. He advised the exiles: "Take wives and beget sons and daughters, and take wives for your sons and give your daughters to husbands that they may bear sons and daughters." How much I wish, no longer for myself but for the young, that they could become themselves by knowing Tevye in the flesh—and how inadequate I feel at the task of handing on as living experience to the next generation some part of that which I briefly learned from him. I have taught my own children some Yiddish so they can talk with their grandfather and with all the grandfathers who went up in flame, and Hebrew, not to order a taxi at Lod Airport, but to read the works of their rabbinic ancestors. In the words themselves there is memory and in teaching them the words I hand on something—and with every word I not only weep for Vilna and for Warsaw and for Lemberg; I try to call them back to life.

THE AMERICAN EXPERIENCE

JEWISH LIFE

8. Celebrating Jewish New York

I WAS FIVE years old when my family brought me to America and all I spoke was Yiddish. In elementary school they taught us to sing "land of the pilgrims' pride, land where my fathers died," and I knew enough to understand that my fathers hadn't died here at all. My teachers' fathers had, but certainly not mine.

Forty years later the words in this patriotic hymn still troubled me—until I came across a response by Maimonides to a question by Obadiah the proselyte nearly eight hundred years ago. Some time around the year 1180 Obadiah asked, "How can I, who was not born a Jew but who accepted the faith, recite the morning prayer, which begins with 'Blessed art Thou, O Lord our God and God of our fathers, God of Abraham, Isaac, and Jacob,' when these are not my ancestors?" Maimonides answered, "They are your ancestors; they are your fathers because you accepted their tradition." Suddenly I realized that this was, after all, the land where my fathers died, because this was the country and this the city that I had embraced. And I understood the passion Jews feel for America and for New York.

During the course of two thousand years, Jews have coexisted with other races and religions and ethnic groups everywhere in the world. In America, Jews have not merely coexisted with other

Reprinted from *Congress Monthly,* vol. 43, no. 6 (June 1976), based on a speech given at Gracie Mansion, May 3, 1976.

people in a strange land; here we were founders as well as sons. Thus, it is possible to write a lengthy history of the Jews of London, but the history of London itself could be written without the Jews. You cannot, however, write the history of New York or of the United States without citing what Jews did, along with many other people, to shape the ethos and form the essential character of the country and its largest city. You cannot understand America as a place in which Jews have been allowed to live reasonably well without persecution. You can only understand the meaning of America and the role of New York if you accept the idea that New York is not merely a great Irish, Italian or Puerto Rican, or black city; New York is also a great Jewish city. New York is all of these things together, and it is out of the interrelationship of all these "cities" that there comes the unique spirit which is American.

But there is something else, more obvious but less perceived. There is something about New York which has given rise to a pluralism within Jewish life that never before existed. What has happened is that a certain spirit of American live-and-let-live—a pragmatism that is beyond theology and outside ideology—has made it possible for all kinds of Jews—Orthodox and Reform, Conservative and Reconstructionist, Zionist and Bundist, atheist and hasid—to live together not only in one city but in one community. That a tour of Jewish New York can in the same morning visit Temple Emanu-El on Fifth Avenue and the installations of the Satmar rebbe in Williamsburgh—and that such a tour can be organized by the American Jewish Congress, which is in debate with both institutions on a number of issues—that this can happen is in itself part of what New York is all about.

Ir va-Em be-Yisroel, a city and a mother in Israel. The city did not need to be Jerusalem or Safed. This was the name given throughout the ages to such places as the Shushan of Mordecai and Esther, where the Purim drama took place, the Cairo in which Maimonides was doctor to Saladin, or even a small and obscure town such as Miedzeboz, in which the Baal Shem Tov, the founder of hasidim, lived and taught. True, Jews always remembered Zion, but what they had in the here and now were cities and towns out of which they made centers of their tradition and living wells of Jewish spirit and learning.

In size and in freedom, the greatest Jewish community that has ever existed in all of history is the one in New York. It has also become, especially in the last century, a center of Jewish creativity and learning beyond compare. There is no aspect of Jewish life in America or in the world which has not affected New York or been shaped by it. In the modern era New York is thus, par excellence, a mother city for world Jewry. Within its boundaries, young as it is—a mere three centuries or so, a stripling by comparison to London, Paris, and, of course, to Jerusalem—New York contains the evidence of the most important contributions of America to the Jews and of the Jews to America. The early Sephardic cemeteries of colonial days remind us that here the battle for Jewish equality was very nearly won even before the American Revolution. There were Jewish burghers of the city, helping to mount guard as equals with all the rest, long before that was possible anywhere in Europe. Indeed, as the distinguished American historian Richard Morris has said, the evidence of the near equality of Jews in colonial New York and of the freedom that they attained with the American Revolution was cited in Europe as the proof that such things could exist even there.

The immigrant Jewish ghetto on the Lower East Side is largely no more, for even the *Jewish Daily Forward,* the last of the major Jewish dailies, has moved from its old building on East Broadway and the buildings on Second Avenue now seldom house Yiddish plays. The cut and thrust of all the parties and all the theologies have moved to other realms of America. Nonetheless, to know something about the Jews of New York is to remember that the dreamers of that ghetto deeply affected American life as a whole.

The radicals and social reformers became themselves, or through their children, among the critical founders of the New Deal. Those in that ghetto who refused to be assimilated in the "melting pot" defended their own culture and identity by creating for America the theory of cultural pluralism. The children of Spanish Harlem or the very Lower East Side who are receiving at the expense of the City of New York bicultural education are the heirs of a battle fought and not easily won by Jewish immigrants who preceded them to New York.

In art, in music, in literature—and for that matter in restaurants —New York is a cultural microcosm of the whole world and the heir to much of its spiritual treasure. Here are the great museums and libraries not only of the United States but of many other countries. This is equally true of New York's Jewish components. The greatest collection of Jewish manuscripts in the world is in the library of the Jewish Theological Seminary at Morningside Heights. The great surviving Jewish library which enshrines the memory of East European Jewry is at YIVO on East 86th Street. The New York Public Library has the best collection of Jewish books of any public library in the world, except perhaps the British Museum in London. Not a day goes by without an exhibition of Jewish art at one or the other of the Jewish museums or, for that matter, the general ones.

It is true that the concept of New York itself has now to be understood in broader terms. For New York is more than the five boroughs; it is even more than the metropolitan area, for which the cultural and intellectual institutions of the city are a resource freely used. New York is both a training ground and a concept. It is dear to many millions who have spent the critical and formative years of their lives within the spirit of this great and unique city. It is certainly true of almost the whole of American Jewry, most of whose ancestors came to the U.S. through its port and learned from New York's hospitality that America was not Czarist Russia. It is true to this day that all Jewish learning and creativity in the U.S. are inconceivable without the resources and the institutions of New York City.

Above all, New York is a transforming agent, a source of hope and a cause of celebration for all the Jewish people of the world. New York has meant, especially in this century, that the Jews are a community to be reckoned with, that they are part of the shaping of national and world policy, and that here in New York there is a community which is a force in the land. To the Jews silenced in Odessa or persecuted in Damascus, and even to the whole of modern Israel—and to our American Jewish brothers in the smaller communities of this free land—there is always the knowledge that the authentic voice with which the Jewish community thinks and feels, its protective compassion and its free will, will be demonstrated in New York, and will be heard all over the world.

The Jews' love of the City of New York and what it stands for should be understood, then, as a commitment to the one place in the whole of our Diaspora experience in which we have been at home. We are part of the action, functioning with one another as citizens in an American way which is yet very deeply and recognizably Jewish. And I am very glad that we are in the house of the mayor of New York, who belongs to that tradition which we celebrate.

9. American Jewish Experience:

An Interpretation

THE CELEBRATION OF the bicentenary of the American Revolution has produced its own Jewish cliché: the Jewish community in the United States is even older than the Republic. We were again being reminded that there were Marranos on Columbus's ships and that the first boatload of twenty-three Jews sailed into the New York harbor of Peter Stuyvesant in 1654, only to find that even those pioneer Sephardim had been preceded by one Polish Jew, Jacob Bar Simson.

The Touro Synagogue in Newport, Rhode Island, stands as living testimony to the presence of Jews in the colonial era, for it was to this congregation, among others, that Washington wrote his famous letter pledging the United States of America to "give to bigotry no sanction."

Reprinted from *Jewish Chronicle,* London, September 3, 1976.

Nonetheless, if there had been no Jews at all in the United States from the very beginnings of its history to the period after the Civil War, the history of America would have been very little different. American Jewish history is a paradox. The pioneering handful of the first two centuries, largely cut off as they were from their European brethren, were of profound importance to Jewish history and of very little account to the history of the United States. The much more foreign mass migration that came between the Civil War and World War I (1865–1914) seemed much more "Jewish," much more inward looking in its immigrant ghettos, and yet this group was a critical factor in the transformation of the United States from its agrarian, provincial, and Anglo-Saxon past to its technological, internationalist, and pluralist present.

There were no Jews among the framers of the Declaration of Independence, nor of the Constitution of the United States. Indeed, the disestablishment of religion by the American Constitution was an act which did not primarily contemplate Jews or even Catholics. Those who wrote the first amendment to the constitution, which decreed the separation of church and state, intended it as an act to make peace among the warring Protestant factions.

Jewish peddlers were of some economic importance in mid-nineteenth-century America, and some of them who traded across the battle lines during the Civil War got into trouble with General Ulysses S. Grant, who issued an order singling them out, thus provoking an incident which he never completely lived down. Nonetheless, the fortunes of the Civil War turned on forces to which the Jews then in the United States, who numbered perhaps fifty thousand at the time of the Civil War, were largely an exotic footnote.

Those early American Jews did matter to Jewish history. In the debates which began in earnest again in France and Germany in the 1770s about giving Jews more rights, the usual argument advanced by their enemies was that Jews were incapable of being educated into becoming proper Westerners. "Foreignness" and "usury" were supposed to be in their blood. The friends of the Jews repeatedly cited those in the American colonies for refutation of such charges. In the New World Jews were being treated as equals, or very nearly as equals, and they were behaving with complete civic responsibility. Here Jews were bearing arms and voting in elections without scandalizing their neighbors or subverting society. Those Jews in the new country were "proof" that conduct could be altered by freedom and that Jews were indeed "worthy" of better treatment. Men of goodwill in Europe thus saw in the United States the laboratory which justified their emancipationist thinking for all of Jewry.

That equality was granted and was successful in the United States was a source of even greater hope to the Jews themselves, who in their masses in Europe had not yet been given even the most basic of freedoms. That is why, even more than the supposed economic opportunity of "streets that were paved with gold," the United States was a messianic symbol for more than a century for oppressed Jews. Millions emigrated to its shores, but those who remained behind hoped that what America represented would soon happen in their own country.

On the other hand American reality until, at very least, the beginning of the twentieth century was culturally Anglo-Saxon, Christian imperialist. To be accepted in America meant to assimilate to the dominant norms, and this the first two waves of Jewish immigration—the colonial in the eighteenth century and the Central European in the middle of the nineteenth century—did very rapidly. They accepted the "social compact" that in return for political and economic freedom as individuals Jews would indeed take care of their own through a network of charity institutions, but they would not call into question any part of the structure or values of American society.

The America of today has its most immediate roots in the American Civil War of 1861–65. Here the decision was made by force of arms that the future direction of the country would be industrial and technological, toward the growth of big cities and toward rapid conquest of the western half of the country. This turning required vast numbers of new immigrants, and some thirty-five million came between 1865 and 1914. Such numbers were not available from Western and Northern Europe, and so they were provided largely from the central, southern, and eastern parts of the continent. Very nearly three million of those immigrants were Jewish, and they came overwhelmingly from the most alien of cultural contexts, the Yiddish-speaking Pale of Settlement in Czarist Russia.

The whole of this immigration radically altered the shape of the United States. It is too shallow to say, as Oscar Handlin once pronounced, that the history of the United States as a whole is that of immigration. The earliest waves of immigration before the Civil War first created the largely Protestant Anglo-Saxon image of the United States, and those that came in the next century either conformed to that image or fought it, like the Irish, with scant success. The "melting pot," which meant the demand to conform to Anglo-Saxon norms, was challenged successfully only after the beginning of the twentieth century, when this quite un-Western, newest and largest mass migration resisted total acculturation. The self-definition of America thus changed, and in this turning point Jews were significant in numbers and even more significant in the people and the ideas that they provided for several radical reformulations of American existence as a whole.

We are thus confronted by a paradox: the most "American" waves of Jewish immigration, the earliest ones in the first two centuries of American life, meant least to America; the "least" American, the most scandalously foreign East Europeans, have had a major influence in transforming America as a whole.

To cite a few examples: the inner religious life of American Jewry had largely been remade to conform to Protestant congregational norms by 1880. The census of synagogues in that year showed 206 organized congregations in the United States, of which 200 were Reformed. Twenty years later this was no longer true, for hundreds of Yiddish-speaking synagogues and conventicles were to be found in the immigrant quarters of all of America's big cities. What has remained from that transformation is that Jewish religion in America ceased needing to seem respectable in Gentile eyes. It accepted upon itself the burden and the dignity of its own singularities. The Sunday morning service was very prevalent in Jewish congregations in 1880. It has by now died even in Reform congregations everywhere in the United States.

In a more complicated way Zionism in the United States has represented a comparable development. It was opposed in its earliest years and even into the 1930s and 1940s by the bulk of the descendants of the earlier waves of Jewish immigration. For them, as for Edwin Montagu of the British cabinet which issued the Balfour Declaration, this called into question that their national identity, which such Jews wanted to believe was that of Americans of the Jewish religious persuasion. To be a Zionist was to be guilty of "dual loyalty," that is, of having communal loyalties which expressed themselves in political terms which were other than those which could be accepted by a conventional American. True, the earliest Zionists could point to the Irish in America who continued to hate Great Britain with the passion that they had brought with them from the Old Sod, or even to the admiration of the Midwesterners of German extraction for the Kaiser's Germany. Nonetheless, the dominant attitude in the United States in the earliest years of the twentieth century was still the notion expressed by the presidents of those years, William Howard Taft and Theodore Roosevelt, that "hyphenated Americans" were bad Americans. The Zionists, who were in their overwhelming masses East European Jews, nonetheless persevered in the American political arena and succeeded in getting America as a whole to accept the notion that respectable special-interest groups were formed not only on the basis of domestic concerns (e.g., labor, oil interests, or farmers) but also out of communal and foreign policy commitments. The charge of dual loyalty did not stick in America because the Zionists refused to knuckle under to it and they thus broke ground in the United States for all kinds of dissenters from the supposed American consensus. The young people who refused to serve in the Vietnam War owe rather more than any of them will ever realize to Yiddish-speaking Zionists.

Part of the post-1882 immigration has recently been described admirably by Irving Howe in *World of Our Fathers,* an account which centers on the Yiddishist-Socialist elements among the newcomers. Socialism and a labor movement existed in the United States before Jewish workers arrived in large numbers, but no historian of labor and of reform in the United States can now write about these forces without paying particular and large attention to the Jews. It is not so much a question of important individuals as Samuel Gompers, the first president of the AFL, or of Sidney Hillman and David Dubinsky of the needle trades. What is more important is that for nearly two generations Jewish workers, dominating the manufacture of clothing, produced a model of union discipline and union organization, as well as an example of class consciousness. The reformist political programs of the Jewish unions, from a reduction of working hours to many programs of social welfare, became the platform of American labor as a whole and a major component of Franklin Delano Roosevelt's New Deal.

In the cultural realm there was no specifically Jewish culture in the United States before the East European immigration. The Central European wave which came in the mid-nineteenth century was German speaking, and expressed itself in that language. In many places Jews were even the founders of German theaters and literary societies. It was in the "Lower East Sides" of New York and half a dozen major cities that theaters, newspapers and the total culture lived for a generation or more in a specifically Jewish language—in Yiddish—in the tonalities of a specific Jewish voice. One hears no echo today in American speech of the Iberian dialects of some of the colonial Jews, or of the German of the Central Europeans, but one need only drive through New York, or watch TV for two or three hours anywhere in the United States, to hear, even if sometimes slightly vulgarized, the re-echoes of the Yiddish of Delancey Street of the early 1900s. This culture has entered into the mainstream of American experience, and many of the best-sellers of this very day are being written in nostalgic reevocation of it—and those books are being read by America as a whole. The South, the West, and the Boston of the Brahmins are all regions on which important schools of American literature are grounded. In our time, Malamud, Bellow, Howe, and I. B. Singer (who remembers Warsaw directly) have made of the world of the Yiddish-speaking immigrants a valid and coequal "region" of American experience.

In sum, therefore, the newest migration insisted on its own life. Even as it acculturated to America, it continued to do battle for a number of values which were its own. This newest migration insisted on its own religion, its own politics, its own vision of a more just America, and on the right of its own group culture to equal respect in America. These insistences were not one-generational phenomena, for even the present generation, which has mostly forgotten its Yiddish and has become quite Westernized in its manners, nonetheless clearly represents a uniquely different element in America as a whole. American Jewry's credentials to be an indissoluble part of America are nevertheless less questioned today than ever before.

It was not accidental that by the early years of the twentieth century young American Jews of the newest immigration, such as Horace Kallen and Mordecai Kaplan, were defining a new image of America not as the melting pot but as culturally pluralist. As a matter of fact, the practice of other groups (Italian, French, etc.) never equaled either the theories of cultural pluralism or the intensity of the performances of Jews in maintaining their group identity. For all of the hand-wringing about the rates of erosion and intermarriage in the United States—and the problems are very serious indeed—the American Jewish community of East European extraction is the only minority in America as a whole which has survived by choice effectively now into the fourth generation of recognizable cultural and political difference in the United States.

At the beginning of the third century of the history of the United States of America the country and society of today remember their first historic century as historic past of a simple, pastoral, heroic age. Their direct links are with the country which began to be defined in the second century of American existence. In that century the Tevyes were crucial to the development of the United States as a whole. The hope for the third century of American life is that the United States, with Jews as a continuing creative force, will make a seminal contribution to justice within its own borders and to decency within the world as a whole.

10. The Present Casts a Dark Shadow

WILL THE JEWS continue to exist in America? Any estimate of the situation based on an unillusioned look at the American Jewish past and at contemporary sociological evidence must answer flatly—no.

It is a myth that there is any real continuity to Jewish history in America. I challenge the historians of B'nai B'rith, now engaged in celebrating the memory of the founding fathers of the order 120 years ago, to produce a genealogical study of the families of these worthies. If the majority of their descendants are still in the Jewish community, I, for one, would be pleasantly surprised.

My own researches through the years into the early histories of several of the old American congregations have pointed to the opposite conclusion. A few years ago we celebrated the 300th anniversary of the coming of the Jews to the United States. At that time curiosity impelled me to take a look at the list of Jewish dignitaries, a committee of fifty important figures from all over the country, who headed the celebration of the 250th anniversary, a half-century before. Even a cursory glance at that list showed that a substantial proportion of their families, perhaps a majority, were no longer in the Jewish fold. There are a few exceptions. Some notable Sephardic families in New York, Philadelphia, and a few other places still continue the tradition. By the very weight of larger numbers many of the German Jewish settlers who came to America in the middle of the nineteenth century are still evident as Jews in their descendants. But it is an open secret that by the fourth and fifth generations (i.e., the present ones) the rate of falling away from them is very great indeed. In reality, the contemporary American Jewish community is not the culmination of the three centuries of Jewish experience in the United States; it is in

Reprinted from *Jewish Heritage,* vol. 6, no. 3 (Winter 1963–64).

many senses a fresh beginning, representing the East European Jews who arrived in this country in great numbers after 1882. That immigration is now beginning its fourth generation. What the second and third generation represent is writ large in the institutions that have been created, especially in the last twenty-five years. This is a high-water mark, from which we are now beginning to recede.

The crucial sociological evidence is in the rate of intermarriage, what we know about the Jewish affiliations of young people now in college, the decline of the Jewish birthrate, and a realistic look at the so-called religious revival of the past decade. Everyone has been saying until very recently, with some pride and satisfaction, that there is less intermarriage among Jews than within any other group in America. The figure that is oft quoted is less than 10 percent. We now know that this is a delusion. The figure is true if you add the marriages of the parents and the grandparents and those of the young people now marrying; but what is crucial to any projection of the future is only the marriage of the present generation. All competent studies of intermarriage from this group alone add up to an estimate of between 15 and 20 percent. The vast majority of the children of these marriages, on the evidence available, are lost to the Jewish community even in those cases where there has been formal conversion by the non-Jewish partner.

The most recent studies of our young people at college are even more frightening, especially since almost all Jewish children over seventeen go to college. A rule of thumb seems to be that the more prestigifying a college is, the more likely it is that a number approaching half of the Jewish students on campus are on their way out of their religious commitment. Some of this is no doubt youthful bravado, and many of the college atheists will in due course be presidents of sisterhoods. Nonetheless, the flight at college betokens a thinness of Jewish knowledge and emotion that bodes ill for the quality of the Jewish life in the next couple of generations.

There is also the falling Jewish birthrate. Every study that has ever been made shows without exception that the Jews have by far the lowest birthrate of any subgroup in America. It is likely that Jewish births do not replace Jewish deaths. When added to the factor of attrition inherent in a rising rate of intermarriage, the figure of perhaps three million Jews in the beginning of the next century is more likely than the present five and one-half millions.

What of the vaunted religious revival? Certain things are indeed better, but there can be no doubt that we are not in the midst of a new birth of piety. Synagogue building and belonging have been in recent years a form of acculturation on the American scene. I am not at all sure, however, that America itself operates in terms of religious subgroups. Other subgroups are coming to the fore. It is almost a rule that what the most urban Jews are doing in one generation reflects what the whole country is going to do in the next; for example, the economic profile of America as a whole, with its shift away from the farm and even blue-collar occupations, is ever more an approximation of that of the Jews for the last several generations. The drift of the Jewish young away from Jewish activity into liberal politics, art centers, and enjoyment of their parents' money probably foreshadows what the newer segment of the middle class will be doing soon in place of church belonging, if they are not already.

The sociological problem is, however, not the most important. The essential crisis is the crisis of faith. It has in reality remained the same since Jewish modernity began two centuries ago. Some Jews have barricaded the door against the outside world. The conviction that pervades certain parts of Jerusalem and of Brooklyn has been that any trace of Westernization ultimately leads to disintegration. On the other end of the spectrum, the radical Zionists have really accepted the same diagnosis. In the Diaspora, in their view, Jews and Judaism cannot survive the end of the ghetto and of its form of faith. Such Zionists have argued that territorial concentration was now indispensable to Jewish survival, for those who would choose to live outside the land would disappear in fairly short order. The majority of the Jews of the world have refused to follow the demanding path of either of these two alternatives in favor of some middle position balanced between the claims of traditional Jewish faith and the counterattraction of modern materialism, doubt, and heresy. As ways of belief our contemporary sects have failed, without exception, to produce either an answer that compels the perplexed to believe or a source of emotional power that touches their hearts. The middle positions are comfortable; in the long run they have not comforted or inspired. The needle has been stuck for a long time now in the groove marked "modern Jewish religious thought." The music that has been coming out is at best nostalgic; at worst, repetitive and irrelevant.

Will there be Jewish survival? On the basis of present trends I can only repeat that the answer must be in the negative. History, sociology, and the emptiness of contemporary Jewish religion all point in the same unhappy direction. Why then go on?

I cannot answer for others. For myself, I keep working at the business of being a Jew simply because I must. I have no pat theological formulas to offer, even to myself. There are no rose-colored glasses through which I can look to assure myself that I am part of a successful enterprise. I am sustained against despair in the first place by a belief in the importance of rebellious creative minorities —of a saving remnant. I do not know how much of Judaism or of the Jewish community will remain some generations hence. It is my task to see to it that there is more rather than less; it is my faith that what there may be will be put by God to use.

Ultimate solutions are not given to men. We can only maintain the tradition of Jewish learning; we can hope that those who follow after us will continue to care; we can pray that God has not taken us on this long journey through the centuries that Judaism might die in these United States in a hundred years or so. If it does, I must labor that some Jews should still be left to carry the tradition from these shores and replant it.

What does the future hold for Jewish Americans?

11. Jewish Education Must Be
Religious Education

THE VERY FIRST session of the National Conference on Jewish Education took place in New York two years ago. It included representatives of such diverse tendencies as the Orthodox parochial schools and the Reform Sunday schools. The major intellectual achievement of the gathering was a new definition of the aims and purposes of Jewish education that was embodied in something called "A Charter of the Rights of the Jewish Child," which was adopted unanimously and, by that fact alone, acquired great significance. Here at last was a common denominator on which all those most interested in Jewish education were prepared to agree. But in whose image was it proposed to fashion the new Jew?

The first point of the "Charter" defines the tangible content of Jewish education as "an accurate knowledge and sympathetic understanding of the life, the labors, the ideals, the struggles, and the achievements of the Jewish people from the beginnings of their history to the present day." In the next paragraph the kind of Jewish emotional allegiance to be instilled in the child is equated with "a feeling of belonging to the community," and "an understanding of his oneness with his fellow Jews, in the United States, in Israel, and in every corner of the world." The fourth point, trying to dispel any suspicions of parochialism, asserts that such an education will strengthen the child "in commitment to democracy as the way of life most in accord with Jewish teaching, and will awaken in him a deep sense of kinship with all mankind."

A close reading of the Conference resolutions reveals an im-

Adapted from *Commentary,* vol. 15, no. 5 (May 1953).

plicit estimate of the "real" Jewish situation in America, which is seen as a perpetual confrontation with anti-Semitism, actual and potential. It follows of necessity that Jewish authenticity and maturity are attained when the Jew is able to cope successfully with a non-Jewish world that is at best neutral and not infrequently hostile. The conferees insisted that participation in Jewish group culture would give the child an island to which he could safely retire when threatened by the "outside" world. This reasoning was clothed in the language of progressive education, sprinkled with such terms as "growth," "freedom," and "self-realization." One got the impression that Jewish education was a department of preventive psychotherapy.

But the "Charter of Rights of the Jewish Child" is interesting for more than what it explicitly says. Equally revealing is what is never mentioned. The Lord of Hosts, for instance. In a subsidiary resolution the term *mitzvot* is translated as "virtues and responsibilities," which is a neat way of avoiding the stark, demanding ring of the word "commandments." The covenant is no longer with the Almighty to whom all Israel once pledged at Sinai: "We will do and we will hear"; it consists rather in a sense of emotional closeness to other Jews.

Nor are parents given much importance in the "Charter." They are mentioned only once in an auxiliary resolution, and even then only in passing. It is the community as a whole, the national organizations and the fund-raising and fund-disbursing bodies, that are exhorted to take a greater interest in Jewish education. And the need stressed is the need for properly trained and adequately paid teachers and more professionally staffed supervisory bureaus. From this, one might gather that the best educational structure was the one that gave a free hand to the professional educators, without interference from parents. They were to sit back with nothing more to do than pay the necessary bills. The experts would take care of everything else.

This kind of thinking is, among other things, a startling indication of the pervasive influence of the community-organization-*cum*-trained-professional approach to all Jewish problems. Large-scale philanthropy doubtless functions best when a managing group of executives plus functional technicians stand between the individual "lay" Jew—defined chiefly as fund-contributor and -raiser—and the recipient. But that education, and particularly Jewish education, can dispense largely with the father-child relationship is a novel hypothesis. One wonders about what kind of person this American-Jew-as-father is who can be so blithely bypassed. And is he really the American Jew as he really feels about himself and his child as a Jew—or only a myth born of the community professionals' contempt for, and suspicion of, the "layman"?

The image of the father hovering over the discussions of the Conference was the second-generation Jew who was a "good Jew" —after a certain fashion. He was active in Jewish affairs, including, one hopes, the synagogue, possessed of enough Jewish instruction not to commit any glaring blunders at a service or public function that required the pronunciation of some Hebrew. (Such errors were, however, not irredeemable in the case of those who had "good Jewish hearts," which they proved by devoted labor for such causes as Welfare Funds and the United Jewish Appeal.) A "good Jew" was of necessity concerned for the fair name of his people; he not only lived by high civic standards but also had at his fingertips the answer to any question about the Jewish attitude to Jesus, and he could also prove, with citations, the depth and range of the Jewish Contribution to Civilization. As a "good American" he was active on behalf of the Red Cross and did not cut himself off from American culture by staying home evenings to read Faulkner or Proust (or the Bible) instead of attending dinners where he could shake hands with movie stars in the interest of "better understanding."

What the Conference proposed, in effect, as a valid educational aim, was to produce future generations of American Jews in this image. And one could understand why none of the Conference's resolutions called upon parents to assume any large personal obligations in the educational process; that would have made no more sense than a sculptor's asking his model to help him carve or model the figure he was working on. The parent was to be passive, the educator was to use his art—and lo! the generations would run smoothly on.

In terms of the pure logic of its position, this new Jewish education does not necessarily require a Jewish teacher. A trained group-worker of any background, provided he be sympathetic to "minority" culture and loyalties, could conceivably do as well. He might, indeed, be even more effective than a Jewish teacher, who would probably be encumbered by his own unresolved inner conflicts; the non-Jewish teacher could more calmly approach the task of making Jewish children sympathetic to the evaporating Jewish past and at the same time well-adjusted and secure. It is only in the dimension of faith that it is obligatory for a Jewish adult to confront a Jewish child in a dialogue across the desk of the classroom or the table at home—in which dialogue the child is taught to hear that the Lord is One, and to recognize Him as the God of Abraham, Isaac, and Jacob, and to recognize himself as the Son of the Covenant with Him.

The Conference's approach assumes that the major Jewish adjustments to the American milieu have already been made, that in the main they are adequate, and that for the foreseeable future the American Jew will not change in any significant respect. All this is highly questionable. The American Jew is not yet completely formed, he is still in transition; and, indeed, precisely the very features of his spiritual physiognomy that the new education proposes to enshrine are those most characteristic of a generation in transition.

These features doubtless do exist, but to believe that their sum provides us with a true picture of the American Jew is superficial. There is more to him than the fact that he has Yiddish-speaking grandparents and wants not to hate himself or be hated for it. Being human, he wonders about the ultimate meaning of life and seeks for some faith and purpose with which to face his death. Being contemporary, he is plagued by a sense of helplessness and futility. Being Jewish, he is confronted by the experiences of the last twenty years more sharply than ever with a sense of peculiar destiny. It is in all of these respects that the American Jew most seriously needs to come to terms with himself. To ignore the most personal—and hence most cosmic—feelings of the contemporary Jew means, when translated into educational theory and practice, to cut him off from just those sources of the Jewish heritage that might help him grapple with his loneliness, his demon, and his God.

It can be maintained, perhaps with some truth, that the recent marked increase of metaphysical and theological discussion among Jews reflects the mood only of some intellectuals. Certainly the laity, precisely because they are not articulate, cannot produce and are not producing a fluent verbalization of their own needs. Nevertheless, the very history of Jewish education in America bears witness to an intensified, continuous *religious* seeking on the part of the "average" Jew. Let us consider, for example, the associations evoked by such words as *kaddish, yizkor,* and bar mitzvah. Even the most casual reader of the writings of the educators will have become aware of these terms as the *bêtes noires* of Jewish education. They recur again and again as the symbols of that intellectual and spiritual poverty on the part of parents against which the educators fight in the name of some other, more grandiose ideal. But though the champions of Yiddishism, socialism, Hebraism, and humanism have hacked away vigorously and untiringly, these hydra heads have always sprung up again with what have been—to them, the ideologists—ever more frightening visages. Insistently, the parents have urged these words, and the *religion-centered* training of the young that they imply, upon the most diverse schools of Jewish education, including the most revolutionary secular and the most anti-traditional Reform.

And through the years all statistical studies have shown the increasing predominance of the synagogue school over all other forms of Jewish education. More revealing still is the recent growth of the movement for parochial schools. Between 1940 and 1951 the proportion of children attending such institutions in New York City has risen from 8 to 23 percent of the entire attendance at Jewish schools. Nor is this phenomenon restricted to New York. Recently, indeed, the Conservative movement put itself on record as favoring such schools for at least an initial four years of training, and maximalist voices are being raised in favor of a similar policy even among the Reform. Almost all the existing parochial schools are very Orthodox in their teaching—notoriously more Orthodox than most of the homes from which the children come.

Thus, today, a significant number of American Jews show a willingness to abandon even that most precious of democratic institutions, the public school. Can anything be more indicative of the

strength of religious motives behind the interest in Jewish education now felt in the Jewish community?

Countless teachers can bear witness to expressions of this interest that are often bizarre. Is there a Jewish schoolmaster anywhere
who has not heard unnumbered times the parental admonition,
"Don't make my child too religious," followed usually by, "I don't
want him to grow up to be a rabbi"? Nonetheless these same parents illogically continue to ask the Jewish school to produce, by
some miracle, *religious* Jews. The basic problem of Jewish education in America is whether this miracle is possible. Can a valid and
worthwhile school be created for children whose parents are
muddled in their beliefs, to be run by educators who are rather
certain of their doubts?

We must take heed, nevertheless, not to be stampeded into
solutions by the intensity of the need and the difficulty of the problem. That some, for example, long for the spiritual wholeness of
their piously Orthodox parents or grandparents does not necessarily
validate an Orthodox education for their children—not unless they
themselves really believe in, and live by, the literal Revelation of
the sacred writings. Orthodox behavior by parents and teachers
who do not really believe, no matter how thoroughly it is acted out,
is hardly likely to be effective, for children have an unerring sense
for the real values of their elders. They will soon discover that they
have been put into a make-believe world created solely for their
conditioning. Deprived of real spiritual relations with their play-
acting parents and teachers, they will end up by resenting the traditionalism so carefully cultivated for their sake.

Nor is it really possible as yet to found the Jewish religious
school on new and clear affirmations of faith. It is true that the
present condition of the Jew clearly demands a new spiritual impulse. A strong current of some kind of pietism would solve many
problems—that of education among them—for it would give content
and vision to Jewish life. The very intensity of the need should
make one suspicious, however, of a too ready acceptance of any
of the budding schools of theological thought; at this stage, they
are more a reflection of the presence of religious seeking than a
guide on the road toward the faith being sought. To at least one

observer, neo-hasidism seems too laden with nostalgia, neo-Ortho-
doxy too obviously descended from its Christian counterpart, and
Jewish existentialism too alien and individualistic for any of them,
alone or in combination, to answer our contemporary quest for a
Jewish faith. These new religious movements have as yet hardly
made a major impression on the mass of American Jews and,
therefore, a widely compelling educational program cannot be
founded on them. There is no escape from dealing with our time
as it really is. It is an age to which the Word has not yet been
spoken, but which, in its deepest soul, is waiting for it.

The contemporary task of Jewish education is at once more
modest and more difficult than the cultivation of well-balanced individuals or convinced partisans of one or another doctrine. Its
function is to fight a holding action in order *to keep alive the skills
and content of tradition so that the fire of illumination will have a
Jewish bush on which to flame.* If the school is to be successful in
this, it has to do two things: the content of its curriculum must provide an adequate seed-ground for a future religious revival in the
grand manner; and this content must be susceptible of being taught,
with complete intellectual honesty, out of a wide variety of Jewish
conviction.

The basic tensions of Judaism through the ages have been
between Bible, and Midrash, between Halakhah and Aggadah, between the *mitzvah* and its rationalizations or philosophic justifica-
tions. The more fixed and stable of the two poles has always
been the sacred writings and practices as over against the changing and individualistic commentaries with which they have been
surrounded.

Let the major content of Jewish education then be the great
texts of the tradition beginning with Bible and Talmud. Since we
want the young to find their homes in this inheritance, let the emphasis of the school be on a thorough knowledge of the Hebrew
of the classic ages. It is quite irrelevant whether the children in the
Jewish school ever learn to chat a bit in the argot of Israel (they
can acquire that themselves quite easily later on, if they are so
minded) provided most can understand the *Humash* in the original,
and some can read the less complicated medieval classics for edifi-
cation and even pleasure.

It is also not of great importance that the young be taught any considerable amount of Jewish history, the present end-all and be-all of too many curricula. Even to serve the purposes of Jewish apologetics and to generate pride in one's group and ancestry, a collection of names and facts is a questionable tool. The present history textbooks in our religious schools fail dismally to give a notion of the sweep and content of the Jewish experience. This attempt had best be saved, in any case, for the late high school, college, and adult reading of the students; they will by then already have had a firsthand confrontation with the thoughts of our greatest spirits. A page of Hillel in the original must precede by many years the nearly exact dates of his career, and at least an attempt at reading Judah Halevi before we face the thirteen-year-old with his strange name in a Sunday school textbook, followed by the rather mystifying explanation that he was a medieval Jewish philosopher and poet.

Along with the classical texts we must also teach the young the manner in which *all* the *mitzvot* are to be observed. Although true, it is no fair counterargument to maintain that some *mitzvot* have fallen into almost complete disuse, or are incomprehensible, and that most are not practiced at home. There is warrant in the Jewish past for the teaching of even those aspects of the Law that have no practical relevance. Have not the technical details of the service of the Temple been studied by Jews since the Exile? And this was no waste of spiritual energy or a mere exercise in archaeology. Without two millennia of such studies, and the prayers for the restoration of Zion which accompanied them, there would be no Israel today. There are other examples—i.e., the growing importance of the ceremony of the First Fruits—of how customs and practices kept in suspended animation by the activity of the school have now been lately revived.

It does not really matter that the very teaching of such skills in the performance of the *mitzvot* will create problems at home. Parents are not really so set in their disregard of the tradition that anything they themselves do not practice becomes out of question in the Jewish school. Certainly strains will be caused, but what of it? That is the very nature of an age of religious uncertainty and the inescapable burden we must bear. We have not yet enough common convictions to write a Shulhan Arukh for this day, but we at least can give the young all the material out of which they may, in their time perhaps, write one.

The kind of Jewish education envisaged here will certainly face the same problem that all our modern Jewish schools now face: the whys and wherefores that the children confront us with. At this point we must act with an honest and candid intellectual tentativeness. Here, too, there is warrant in the tradition itself. Even the greatest teachers of the classic past often said to their students that they were not sure of their own understanding of aspects of the Bible or Talmud, and they made hesitant suggestions "according to the poverty of their own understanding." By all means let that plurality of convictions obtain that now characterizes American Jewry, but these convictions should not be taught as dogmas to the exclusion of the actual content of tradition. Teachers and parents should give their explanations in terms of "the poverty of their understanding" when explanations are required, but let it be admitted and emphasized on all sides, particularly to the children, that such formulas are personal and subordinate to the texts and experiences themselves. Without making a virtue of spiritual uncertainty, will there not perhaps result from such candor an honest relation between the young and their elders as they join in the deepening of their Jewish knowledge and their search for a personal faith?

Along such a path the Jewish school can again assume its real function—that of speaking in mature accents of mature things. Of what these "mature things" are we no longer have the clear and strong idea our forefathers had. Instead we are turned and spun by winds of fashionable doctrine. Under the circumstances, about the best we can do—it is also the least we ought to do—is to sit doggedly by the embers of Jewish teaching, by the opened Bible (in Hebrew!) above all, and prepare ourselves for the miraculous moment when the words enflame our spirit. Then we—adults and children alike—will know what we only can guess at now: what it means to be children of the Fathers and covenanted to God.

12. The Changing American Rabbinate

A GENERATION AGO the overwhelming majority of the rabbis in America were either immigrants or the children of immigrants. Even the rabbis of English-speaking congregations, many of whom were chosen in part because they appeared to be completely Westernized, were thoroughly at home in Yiddish, and with the exception of one segment of the Reform rabbinate, the rabbis of all persuasions were overwhelmingly fervent and devoted Zionists.

The great rabbinic careers of the last generation were not really made in congregations. To be sure, men like Solomon Goldman in Chicago, Abba Hillel Silver in Cleveland, and Israel Goldstein and Stephen Wise in New York were the rabbis of imposing congregations. Their careers did not, however, unfold on the stage of what they were doing within their synagogues. Several of these men did indeed at some point come to high office within their specific denominational groups, but that was incidental and often as a consequence of other battles. When Silver became the president of the Central Conference of American Rabbis (Reform) in 1945, that was understood within the Conference itself as symbolizing the turn of its majority toward Zionism. His elevation did not occur for internal denominational reasons. In the minds of everyone the great rabbis of that period had individual synagogues as their base, but they served as such to exercise what was essentially political leadership in the Jewish community and on its behalf in American politics and in international Jewish affairs. Silver is again perhaps the best example. He remained a factor in Republican politics because he could and did produce the necessary Jewish

Reprinted from *Midstream*, vol. 12, no. 1 (January 1966).

votes in Ohio, especially for his friends in the Taft family. As a Zionist leader he translated this power into political leverage against Franklin Delano Roosevelt when the latter faltered on Zionist issues. Stephen Wise led the Reform elements in New York against Mayor Walker. He was as much the leading Democrat among the rabbis of the country as Silver was the leading Republican, and the defeat of Wise by Silver for the leadership of the American Zionist movement in 1946 represented more than anything else the disillusionment of the Zionists with a policy of trusting the Democrats.

Perhaps the most illuminating analogy to explain the role of the leaders of the American rabbinate a generation ago is to be found in the career of Martin Luther King. The generation of Negro ministers immediately preceding his own comprised men of the Negro ghetto who were as incapable of speaking for the Negro to the rest of American society as were the *maggidim* of the Lower East Side in the 1890s. King represented their children, with college training, largely at home in white society, but retaining deep roots within the misery of the Negro ghetto and profound identity with the aspirations of their community. It served King well in the world that he remained a minister of a specific church, because thus the world had to treat him with at least some of the respect that it professes for religion in general.

Nonetheless, King's role was that of a Negro political leader, and his career unfolded on the stage of his people's struggle for its rights. Had he ever become, as was quite conceivable, the president of all of American Protestantism for an elected term of several years as the head of the National Council of Churches, such an event would have belonged to the history of race in America more than to the normal preoccupations of internal religious structure. Rabbis Wise, Silver, Goldman, and the others represented a comparable phenomenon, at a comparable stage in the development of the American Jewish community.

The American rabbi of today is quite clearly a different phenomenon. There exist today many individual congregations as large as or larger than the congregations headed by Wise and Silver. Nonetheless, no comparably renowned rabbinic names have emerged. There are a few specialized reputations in Jewish scholarship, but it is a well-known fact that the scholars among the rabbis have no real power in Jewish communal affairs. There is hardly one rabbinic figure today who commands the attention of the entire Jewish community. This is so at the very time when the majority of the Jews of America are formally affiliated with the synagogue, and when both locally and on a national scale American Jewish life has been prospering. The organized enterprise that the rabbis head, the synagogue and all its institutions, is more powerful than ever before, but the rabbis seem to be less so. Why?

Part of the answer lies in the very "success" of the synagogue. All enterprises in America today—economic, political, and religious —have been undergoing the same shift from viable, small private enterprises to institutionalization. Careers which in the past were made through personal force and creativity have now been transmuted into advancement for service to large organizations. The successful owner of a local grocery store of a generation ago is today the manager of a division for a chain of supermarkets, looking forward to the day when he will be a vice-president of the company as a whole. The very success of the religious institutions in America implies that the central bodies are now much stronger and that they have much more influence—to be blunt, they have many more favors to grant and they are much less beholden to powerful, individual rabbis. On the contrary, those individual rabbis who have the normal human ambition to rise must now take much greater account of the wishes and the needs of their central denominational bodies.

A generation ago the central organs of religious Jewish life were largely dependent for moral and material support on the goodwill of potent individuals, both lay and rabbinic. Now these bodies are so large that they are ever less beholden to any individual. They can, and indeed do, bypass even the most powerful rabbi and deal directly with his congregation and community. This means that status within the general community, and sometimes even within an individual congregation, is much more affected today by the relation of the rabbi to his denominational superiors than it was a generation ago. The result is that rabbinic careers today are ever more being made in semibureaucratic fashion. They tend to be safe rather than picturesque.

Many results flow from the hugely increased size and power of the central denominational bodies. One obvious result (and the one that is heard most often in the mutterings of unhappy rabbis) is really the least important. To be sure, the road to a "leading pulpit" is smoothest for those in favor with the denominational higher-ups, and it is more difficult for the nonconformists. Lesser favors, such as star speeches at denominational conventions and chairmanships of national committees, are also reputed to be likely gifts to those rabbis who do not rock the boat. These mutterings are not entirely justified. None of the structures is so monolithic, or so vindictive, that it really purges the oddball. The truth is that the rabbi of today has very few economic problems, because hundreds of congregations are now paying their rabbis more than decent middle-class salaries. The rabbinate as a whole is short-handed. Therefore, every rabbi with any ability is sufficiently in demand so that even his critics in the national bodies are glad to help him obtain a substantial pulpit. Nonetheless there is much unhappiness in the rabbinate, reflecting a frustrating sense of the decline of the importance of the individual rabbi—and this unhappiness does have something to do with the rising power of the denominations. What has happened has not been willed by the leaders at the top; it was an inevitability.

The growing denominational establishments continue to need increasing numbers of professionals to staff themselves. Many of the bureaucrats are lay people, but many of the jobs cannot be done except by rabbis. Even fundraising, that most secular of occupations, engages the efforts of some of the rabbis who are in the employ of the denominations. Our contemporary seminaries and the institutions that are allied with them are wisely following in the footsteps of a very ancient Jewish tradition, that the givers to schools of Torah feel closer to the ennobling purpose of the appeal if they give the money to a scholar. It is also self-evident that much of the educational and cultural work of the central denominations must be directed by rabbis. The various seminaries have required a number of their own graduates to staff their faculties, and that number increases as the schools grow. For that matter, there has been a remarkable growth in the last decade in the number of chairs in Jewish studies that have been created in various colleges and universities. Many if not most of these jobs have been occupied by ordained rabbis. One other economic consideration needs to be mentioned: the posts in the bureaucracies and the professorships, with preaching on the high holidays and lecturing thrown in, now pay as well as a middle-range pulpit. Such jobs, therefore, appear more attractive to a large number of the ablest graduates than betaking oneself to an initial pulpit somewhere in the wilds.

Two things are happening within the congregations themselves that add to the discomforts of the individual rabbis. In the first place, the synagogues are becoming ever larger and more varied in their functions. In the course of one generation the synagogue school has come to supplement the independently maintained communal school as the dominant form of Jewish education. To almost an equal degree the synagogues have become community centers, and have thus acquired a range of activities that most of them did not have a few decades ago. The administrative responsibilities of the rabbi have, therefore, increased enormously. His predecessors of the past generation no doubt worked just as hard, but they had a free choice of their fields of activities. They had major energies left to devote to larger causes because they were not running institutions which demanded that they attend an infinite number of regularly scheduled staff meetings, board meetings, committees, etc. The individual rabbi may want to study or to devote himself to some communal cause. He may even know that this is the only way to exert real influence on the broad American Jewish community. The obdurate fact remains that he is busy as institutional executive, and that his immediate constituents are justifiably demanding that he should not neglect his specific duties. But busy and tired men who are running to keep up with what is immediately before them do not make major revolutions.

The people who are occupying the pews of individual congregations also differ from their parents a generation ago. In the earlier relationships there was a distinct aura of respect for learning that suffused the encounter between the rabbi and his congregants. This involved not only Jewish learning; it also involved secular knowledge. The rabbi belonged to what was then a small minority of American Jews who had gone to college, and the shopkeepers who sat before him gloried in both his rhetoric and his English accent. On the level of secular learning the congregants of today are as well educated as their rabbi. The congregations are studded with professional people who have spent as many years in graduate schools as did the rabbi, and some of them read much more widely than he does. In the mind of the congregation the rabbi therefore no longer enjoys a unique estate. The congregants presume that the highest reaches of learning in the rabbi's profession, as in theirs, are not being cultivated by him but by research students. On literary, social, and political matters they delight in correcting his misquotations from Yeats, or from the lead article in the latest issue of a quality magazine. The rabbi is decreasingly a man apart. Like many of his congregants he is in a service profession. (This point is even demonstrated by the rhetoric now in vogue for the announcement of new rabbinic appointments. In the past the rabbi was usually "called" to be the "spiritual leader"; nowadays he is generally "elected" by the board to "serve" as rabbi.)

This structure of denominational life, both within the national bodies and the individual synagogues, thus tends to depersonalize the rabbi. There is far less relationship today between the individual talents of the rabbis and the fortunes of their synagogues. A growing neighborhood with a reasonably affluent Jewish community of childrearing age produces, as a matter of course, a large and busy synagogue. Such synagogues succeed just as well as institutions with rabbis of little personal stature—men of drive and learning are not indispensable to their fortunes. A generation ago every major Jewish center in America had at least one rabbi whom people came to hear from all over the city, Sabbath after Sabbath. Joshua Liebman in Boston and Milton Steinberg in New York had the last such congregations, in which their particular pulpit was a sounding board which an entire community heeded. Men of equal capacity are preaching today. Within their congregations on a Sabbath one finds the same human material as in the pews of their more conventional colleagues: the small group of regulars, and the relatives of the Bar Mitzvah. But there is not a single pulpit in America today which leads opinion, precisely because the attendances are institutional rather than substantive.

The decline of the pulpit is part of a general trend in American life as a whole. The lecture platform and the mass meeting are no longer of great consequence in this generation. Mass audiences are addressed today primarily through television and to some degree through the national press and publications. Individual rabbis do appear in dozens of communities on the religious programs of their local stations, but they have little access to national programs. The normal procedure for one of the networks is to turn to the New York office of the denominations or to one of the secular Jewish agencies when it needs "Jewish representation." The various national agencies are indeed quite competitive with each other as they battle for the available invitations. Each national agency constantly bears in mind its own need to show to its givers that it, more than others, is doing an effective job in enhancing respect for Jews and Judaism in America. It is thus no casual concern to any of them that an official clearly identified with his specific organization appear before the cameras to speak for Jewry.

Less parochial motives are also at play. Sensitive issues are constantly being debated, especially in "chat" shows. The national agencies quite properly feel they are exercising their responsibility to the entire Jewish community when someone who is well briefed by them (which generally means someone in their employ or in their top elected leadership) does the talking. The mass media do occasionally select an individual rabbi, but these cases are atypical. Such rabbis are likely to come to the attention of busy program editors only if they have said something scandalous, e.g., that neither they nor their congregation believe in God. But in the normal course the mass media, playing safe themselves, turn to the people they know, the staff representatives of the national Jewish organizations, for quasi-official Jewish opinion. The same situation obtains in relation to the wire services, the national newspapers, and the important magazines of mass circulation. They will cover the occasional rabbinic oddball with great relish, but they will tend to get their serious and continuing Jewish coverage from the officials of the national Jewish organizations.

No individual can make a reputation and exercise continuing leadership in a democratic society unless he can effectively and consistently broadcast his views. Effectively barred as he is from the general media, the individual rabbi has only one alternative if he wishes to influence Jews outside his immediate bailiwick. It is the Jewish press. Here the picture is somewhat different, but not much brighter.

In the last generation the Yiddish press still had a national circulation of several hundred thousand, and its readers were in their forties and not, as today, in their seventies. It covered the Jewish news directly and not by reprinting press releases and handouts. The reputations of individual leaders could be and were made within it. After 1910 Judah Magnes led the newer immigrants of the Lower East Side against some of his immediate peers among the German Jews by the power of the Yiddish press. A number of quite obscure young immigrants, such as Boruch Zuckerman of the Labor Zionists, rose in a few years to a leadership with which even Jacob Schiff had to reckon because they could create a mass constituency. In the great battle in the early 1920s between Justice Brandeis and Chaim Weizmann for control of American Zionism, Brandeis lost the fight because both on the platform and in the press Weizmann swayed the immigrant Jewish masses. Even today there remains one segment of the American Jewish community in which some individual leaders, most of them rabbis, are effectively heard. What remains of Yiddish-speaking Orthodoxy can still be reached over the heads of any of the national bodies, including its own, through the Yiddish press, but this press is now irrelevant to the vast majority of American Jews. They may remember enough Yiddish to understand the jokes at Grossinger's, but what is published in the language does not shape either their opinions on issues or their estimates of individual Jewish leaders.

There are now a number of Jewish periodicals in English which circulate in hundreds of thousands, but not one is a newspaper. Almost every one of the national organizations has its own periodical. Some of them publish articles of substantial merit. However, they scarcely pretend to be anything but house organs. It is both their right and their duty to serve the needs of their immediate constituents. The news that is covered is therefore largely that of the sponsoring bodies, the purpose being to give a picture, in the most positive terms, of their activity. Controversy and criticism are not a staple diet of such journals. These are not the forums in which individuals can get a consistent hearing for any outlook that is at fundamental variance with the existing mood and structure of the contemporary Jewish establishment. The house organs, especially the religious ones, print many articles by rabbis. But even the most critical members of that breed are, of course, gentlemen; when they do write in these forums they know that such occasions are not the proper time to embarrass one's hosts.

With a few exceptions the local Jewish weeklies that are published in all Jewish communities of any size are not much more useful as a platform for any individual Jewish leader. Most exist to publish the announcements of the various local Jewish bodies, plus all of the Jewish "society" news. Their coverage of national Jewish affairs consists almost entirely of reprinting press releases. Most of their editors do not even read the few small, serious journals of Jewish comment where critical opinions do get some hearing.

Annually the various denominations and other national bodies hold conventions, and there is debate. Dissenters do rise to speak their piece, but they are essentially muffled. I have before me a pamphlet containing the resolutions to be proposed for adoption at the biennial convention of one of the major religious denominations. This set of resolutions is typical of the sort of thing that serves as the basic convention agenda of the other denominations, synagogues, and lay bodies. For that matter, substantially the same material appears annually at the meetings of the national secular organizations. The particular resolutions before me divide into two parts. There is, first, a series of statements representing Jewish-flavored, conventional liberalism. The convention in question will declare itself against the Arab boycott of Israel and for increased rights for Soviet Jewry; it will support a liberal American immigration policy and express its concern about the separation of church and state. The rest of the resolutions are self-congratulatory. The assembled delegates will vote their pride in all the many activities of the national body.

What is typically missing from all the convention programs is serious business. In the past two decades I have attended a few exceptional occasions when someone arose to call some major activity or project into question. Such speeches were almost invariably greeted as disloyalty. The national conventions are not constructed to deliberate the working policy of the organizations. They are intended as demonstrations of strength. Budgets are indeed formally ratified, but are almost never seriously discussed. A small coterie of top lay leaders and upper echelon bureaucrats makes the real decisions. The various little Jewish curias remain in continuous session, at the center of power. They may even endure a sharp annual barrage of brickbats, secure in the knowledge that the day after the convention they will continue to do pretty much as they please. The dissenter, even if he is a distinguished rabbi, will go home, where he has no regular access to the decision-making process.

The only real check on the masters of national Jewish affairs is financial. Whatever the men at the top may decide to do they must find the money for it, and this must come primarily from their constituents. In the past the dissenting rabbi was able to exercise some influence by refusnig to cooperate with those appeals for funds which he did not approve. This last bit of veto power is now also vanishing. In the first place the pervasive mood of the American Jewish community is not discriminating. The "givers" of today make their contributions without differentiating among Jewish-sponsored causes out of a feeling that all such endeavors are "good for Jews." When a dissenting rabbi suggests that a particular cause does not merit support, he is wielding a two-edged sword. His own congregants expect that he lead them in being "warm," "good" Jews. It is an open secret, for example, that the American rabbinate as a whole is less than enthusiastic over the fact that a Jewish-sponsored secular, nonsectarian university like Brandeis raises more money each year than all the national religious bodies and their seminaries combined. That this is so is in part due to the brilliance of Brandeis's leadership, but it is equally due to the fact that, unlike the Jewish scene of a generation ago, the climate of today is not hospitable to public criticism and to continuing debate about the values which Jews ought to be fostering with their money. Rabbis therefore are increasingly hesitant to attempt to exercise veto power by inhibiting fundraising in their bailiwicks for causes they dislike.

What I have been describing so far are aspects of social change in the American Jewish community as these have been affecting the role of the individual rabbi. Such is the new context of his labors; but it is not the heart of the matter. The essence of the problem that confronts the American rabbi today much more sharply than it was ever faced by his predecessors is the question of faith and purpose. To what end can the rabbi really lead?

The crisis of Jewish faith is a long-standing one. It is at least two centuries old. In its starkest form it boils down to the question: If one rejects orthodoxy, why be a Jew at all? This is the Jewish version of a question that has been confronting all of religion in the age of modernity: What is the role of faith among men whose primary concerns are of this world? The dominant answer among all the faiths has been that the contemporary function of religion is to play some significant role in the remaking of society. In the nineteenth century, and in the first part of the twentieth, Western Christianity addressed itself, in the name of the "social gospel," to the woes of the underprivileged. In America today the most advanced churchmen make it their prime business to be on the barricades in the battle for racial equality.

In Jewish circles the equivalent of this "social gospel" has been the continuing battle of the Jews to reorder their own situation in the world. During the last century the rabbinate has been in the forefront of the fight for Jewish equality. In America this battle is now over.

The Jewish community itself has few tangible problems. It would be content to stop the social clock at this moment, so far as its own interests are concerned. The rabbinate, therefore, has no local Jewish social tasks left. The remaining issues concern the relationship of American Jews to other communities, especially to the Jews of Israel and to the Negroes in America. Both of these cares involve basic issues and Jewish commitments, and rabbis are inevitably in the middle of the several battles. Nonetheless, it scarcely needs demonstrating that the American rabbinate is very much less involved in Zionism than it was. It is equally clear, despite the presence of rabbis in places like Selma, that race relations were not the major cause preoccupying the American rabbinate. There was nothing in the tenor of rabbinic involvement in the civil rights issue which resembled the urgency and singleness of purpose with which many of these same men picketed Great Britain twenty years before when they were still students at the seminaries. In their heart of hearts the majority of American rabbis are ambivalent, for very serious reasons, about all the immediate, tangible issues of the day.

Let us consider Zionism first. Ever since the creation of the State of Israel the Zionist movement has been wrestling with itself in an attempt to find a new definition. On several levels poststate Zionism in America has inevitably collided with the immediate interests and concerns of the bulk of the rabbinate.

This is revealed most sharply in the area of Jewish politics. Whatever else the concept of the sovereignty of Israel may mean, it certainly has been made to mean this: that in the international Jewish community Israel will not share any real political power with Jewish leadership of the Diaspora. The crucial turning in this new direction happened very early and very melodramatically. Immediately after the creation of the State of Israel there was a titanic falling out between two of its chief architects, David Ben-Gurion and Abba Hillel Silver. To be sure, it was also a case of conflict between two strong-willed men, but their battle turned on a fundamental issue. Ben-Gurion maneuvered Silver out of Zionist leadership in order to put an end to any pretensions of the Zionist movement to real political power in Jewish affairs. In this Ben-Gurion was eminently successful.

There is no Zionist politics in America in the sense of the 1920s to the 1940s. No one can today make a major career within American Jewry through Zionist political activity. Whatever barricades on behalf of Israel remain are occasional ones, when a specific difficult moment arises such as the Suez crisis of 1956. At such moments Israel has been finding support in the widest circles of the American Jewish community. It is true, as old-line Zionists have been claiming, that only they provide the kind of intense and passionate concern for Israel which used to prevail in the heyday of the movement, and that other American Jews are far more tepid, especially when the U.S. government happens to be opposed to some action or position of the Israelis. However, this argument is really irrelevant. Zionist politics will not again become an area in which rabbis make their communal careers because today the only place where those who lead Zionist politics occupy the center of the stage is Jerusalem and not New York.

Deprived of a political role, the existing Zionist structures in America have inevitably been moving in the direction of a primary concern with aspects of Jewish life in the Diaspora. This was symbolized very precisely by the slogan of the World Zionist Congress, in December 1964: "Facing the Diaspora." This emphasis has two possible meanings. The one preferred by the Zionist leaders of America is that Zionism should concern itself with a wide variety of Jewish educational and cultural endeavors of the "survivalist kind." Such a program inevitably sets Zionism on a collision course with the rabbinate.

Since the synagogue in America is to a large degree a "Parent–Teacher Association" of its religious school, the rabbis regard with alarm any serious drifting of Jewish educational facilities, especially those for the young, outside their orbit. There are no doubt sound reasons for this attitude. From ancient times the synagogue has been conceived as a place of study. The rabbi is the one professional Jew best qualified by scholarship and training to concern himself with the perpetuation of Jewish learning and traditions.

However, counterarguments from history and tradition are possible. In the past Jewish education has been the concern not of individual synagogues as institutions which charge membership fees, but rather of the entire community of Jews resident in one locality. A good case could be made for the proposition that it would be "good for Jews" in our day, regardless of the economic consequences to synagogue institutions, that the total Jewish community organize a network of free schools for all Jewish children. Whenever such a notion is broached, it immediately becomes clear that there is one fundamental objection: the synagogues must oppose it. Regardless of the professionally treasonable thoughts of a few rabbis (these men are the rabbinic equivalent of the few American doctors who dare to say a good word for socialized medicine), the rabbinate as a whole will not stake its career in this generation on creating a new structure of Jewish educational and cultural institutions which will bypass their synagogues. That such a venture may be announced under Zionist auspices does not make it more likely to succeed.

For Israeli Zionists, and for a handful of American Zionists, cultural work means propaganda for *aliyah,* i.e., that even Jews in America live in spiritual exile and that they ought to return to their natural home. The merits of this position need not detain us here. It is enough to state that on ideological grounds such Zionists have an excellent case, for Zionism does indeed mean that the idea of the Jews as a lasting minority outside their homeland is an anomaly. But the overwhelming majority of the Jews in America today regard this idea as subversive. For them, their rise to middle-class affluence and to cultural acceptance in the last two decades has been the culmination of their dream of "at-homeness." The hundreds of synagogues that have been built were not constructed to be temporary. Here the rabbi performs a new function. He is no longer the tribune of an embattled Jewry, as Martin Luther King was of the Negro, demanding justice on behalf of the "we" from the "they." The rabbi of today is expected to symbolize the new Jewish role as part of a new American "we." Such a rabbi may still have a good word to say for the *aliyah* to Israel of a handful of Jews from America as a kind of continuing Jewish peace corps, but even that he will say with some circumspection. Being human, the rabbi knows that one of his bright young people might ask *him:* "If *aliyah* is so important, why don't *you* go?" Here, too, Zionism becomes a threat. The rabbi can maintain some peace with his Zionist past, or with some of his rabbinic frustrations in the present, by keeping a small candle burning for the notion of *aliyah,* but this, too, cannot be a Zionist career for the American rabbinate.

There is a more immediate sense, however, in which the bulk of the American rabbinate is currently made uncomfortable by Zionist and Israel realities. The overwhelming majority of the Jews in America belong to the Conservative and Reform groups and, with a few notable exceptions, a large majority of those rabbis who might be major communal leaders serve within these two denominations. Yet it is precisely these two groups that have no organizational connection with the institutionalized life of Israel as it exists today, or with the formal Zionist structure. Since it is not only fashionable but also expected today in the American Jewish community that Jewish leaders be "recognized" in Israel, this creates a vexing problem for the non-Orthodox rabbinate.

This problem assumes two major forms. One is related to the nature of the society of Israel, and the other is the result of the structure of the World Zionist Movement. Amid the complications of organized Jewish life that is so bewildering that only the specialists understand it, there has risen a situation which provides comfort for the American Orthodox rabbinate, while leaving the others increasingly angry.

Jewish religion in Israel is, in the legal sense, an "Establishment," supported by the government and entirely in Orthodox hands. It is a fact that the rabbinate and the whole of Israel's formal religious life are dominated by and represented by a political party, the Mizrachi. In the political structure of Israel each of the political parties is a complete society, with everything from housing projects to banks, and in the case of Mizrachi, also rabbis. But the official Orthodox rabbinate in Israel by law controls the entire gamut of personal status—marriage and divorce—for everyone in Israel. The World Zionist Organization, including its American branch, is organized largely by the counterparts of the political parties that exist in Israel. This means that the Orthodox rabbinate, through Mizrachi, is directly represented in the highest organs of both the State of Israel and of world Zionism, while the American Conservative and Reform Jews—and their rabbis—are on the outside looking in. This results in many annoying little rubs, and a few threatening big ones.

Let me mention a small matter first. There is hardly a rabbi of any consequence today who has not visited Israel recently. There are several setups in Israel for the reception of American dignitaries. The Orthodox rabbis are received by the Israel rabbinate, and their hometown papers somehow or other tend to be very well informed of this. Their individual status is thus subtly enhanced by pictures of them visiting the chief rabbi, or lecturing at a yeshiva, or sitting on the bench as honored guests at one of the rabbinic courts. Their Conservative and Reform counterparts are received with great respect by the Jerusalem office of the United Jewish Appeal or the Bond drive. If they have any academic connections there may be a tea for them somewhere on the campus of the Hebrew University. Some have even attained the ultimate honor that Israel can give—a visit with Ben-Gurion or Eshkol, or coffee with President Shazar in his office. But rabbis are rabbis. They will soon discover that they are not socially welcome to any rabbis in Israel, and if such an encounter is indeed arranged, it becomes quite painful.

Larger issues are, of course, more important. There is an unresolved battle being waged between the Conservative movement in America and the rabbinate of Israel on the issue of religious divorces. Such documents, issued by the responsible tribunal of American Conservative Jews, in due and ancient form completely according with traditional Jewish law, have not been recognized by the official rabbinate of Israel as valid there. "Quiet diplomacy" has so far avoided a frequently threatened testing of the issue in the civil courts of Israel, but it continues to smolder. Whatever the official rhetoric on both sides, the real position of the Israel rabbinate is not that it doubts the correctness of the procedures of the Conservative tribunal. It is, rather, that the Orthodox refuse to recognize that any group of Conservative rabbis, no matter how learned and meticulously legalistic, have any authority in Jewish law and practice. *A fortiori,* this applies to the Reform rabbis. The reverberation of this in America is that it adds another stroke to a picture of a valid Judaism, dominant in Israel, and represented in America by a faithful minority of true believers—the "real rabbis" —i.e., the Orthodox.

More than mere personal pique accounts for the unhappiness of the bulk of the American rabbis with the religious scene in Israel. At the very root of the Zionist vision, even among many Zionists whose rhetoric was secularist, there was the hope that the faith of Judaism would be revitalized in Zion and that this renewed vigor would help sustain the rest of the Jewish world. This may yet happen, but it certainly has not even begun to appear in the last eighteen years. The boldest American rabbi, Mordecai M. Kaplan, has confronted this issue by maintaining that the greatest single need of Israel today is a "religious mission" from American Jewry. What he means is that Israel needs a religious alternative to the two choices that are presently posed there, sharply and almost exclusively: Orthodoxy or doctrinaire secularism.

A few younger American rabbis have been working in various capacities to bring this about. Some have gone to serve as the rabbis of the handful of nascent non-Orthodox congregations; others have worked as teachers in schools and kibbutzim. This is far from a mass movement, and it is hardly likely that it will become one. No substantial number of American rabbis (let it be said in utter frankness) are prepared to leave posts of both considerable responsibility and material security in order to assume the personal risk, in obloquy and insecurity, in Israel, for the sake of a serious struggle for a middle-of-the-road Judaism there. Nonetheless, it is a pervasive mood among the American rabbinate that "something ought to be done." This is a far different stance from the one hoped for two decades ago, in which rabbis envisaged themselves as the channel through which Israeli creativity would flow to the Diaspora.

On several levels, therefore, the American rabbinate is ambivalent about important aspects of Zionism and the life of Israel. To be sure, the rabbis are of one mind about the fundraising activities in support of Israel, but that area of Jewish life must in the very nature of things be led by laymen who are men of large affairs. The inevitable result is that the leadership careers of individual rabbis are by and large being sought elsewhere.

Today the most obvious place is in the arena of social action on the American scene—which means the problem of race. But here, too, the rabbis are in some tension. All of the leadership elements of the Jewish community have been drawn into this issue. A sense of moral compulsion is operating, allied with the feeling that no civic or religious leadership of any persuasion can avoid the question of the Negro without being reduced to irrelevance. The rabbinate has certainly been serving the Negro cause no less than any comparable group of liberal clergy in any of the denominations, and the organized Jewish community has been involved in the race struggle more, perhaps, than any other white group. Nonetheless, it is hardly likely that the American rabbis in their various pulpits will find an adequate outlet, both within the Jewish community and in the country as a whole, by espousing the cause of the Negro.

In the first place no white spokesmen of any kind can be more than allies to the Negro in this battle. The day is gone when that community will allow anyone who is not a Negro to be a major spokesman for him. For example, the beating up of Rabbi Arthur Lelyveld in Mississippi in 1965 was a scandal, but so many other people had been beaten and murdered there that this incident really did not make an enormous amount of difference. Twenty years ago a prominent white clergyman, after such an event, would have been speaking for the Negro cause all over the country. It is common knowledge that Rabbi Lelyveld was fighting a courageous battle in his own town of Cleveland for Negro rights. That qualified him as a notable and useful ally. He would not claim, nor would be even want to maintain, that he was a leader of the civil rights movement. It is today inconceivable that any white man can head a major civil rights organization, as Springarn did for an entire generation as the founder of the NAACP.

In the second place, the rabbinate is far from having solved a certain "Jewish" aspect of the race struggle. Here the hidden, and not so hidden, prejudices of their own constituents are not the issue. Indeed, if that were the only question the rabbis of America would be in excellent position. They could reassume the mantle of prophets and engage in battle with the prejudices of their congregants. This would no doubt bring some immediate discomfort in various individual synagogues, but anyone who knows the rabbinate at all may be sure that its best men would be delighted with such a battle. The essence of the problem is that the rabbis themselves share in at least some of the ambivalence about the Negro that abounds among the laity.

Like their congregants, the rabbis are worried about intermarriage. They, too, have the feeling that a totally open Jewish community that is primarily involved in larger social issues is one that might vanish as a separate entity. The most liberal Christian ministers are comforted by the knowledge that the Negro is a Christian. Such men are willing to accept, and some even to urge, interracial marriages because they regard such an attitude as the highest expression of a contemporary Christian faith. It is true indeed that the Christian interracial couple of today does not need to be lost to the church. The synagogue is just beginning to face the problem of the Jewish–Christian interracial couple. It has certainly not yet arrived at the point of welcoming the phenomenon.

The rabbis who hoisted the standard of Zionism a generation ago during the Hitler years did it for a variety of reasons. One motive that was certainly a factor was that what they were doing would serve to bring Jews who were on the periphery of the Jewish community back to allegiance to it. The situation of the rabbis confronting the Negro problem is more ambiguous. On one level they are convinced that it is their moral duty to help the Negro advance. The rabbis even know that their presence in the civil rights movement is making them encounter many Jews, especially of the younger generation, who are entirely committed to this struggle. What makes the rabbis uneasy and what, therefore, makes it impossible for them to find their fulfillment in civil rights is the feeling that they are not thereby bringing peripheral Jews back to any of the parochial Jewish concerns. On the contrary, a rabbinic effort to identify contemporary Judaism primarily with the struggle for justice may well serve to confirm a notion that few rabbis could possibly want to strengthen: that all that is "in-group" within Jewry is irrelevant and dead.

Out on the picket lines carrying the banners against segregation, many rabbis have been asked by young Jews they never see in synagogue: Why should we survive as Jews? This question has been asked, prominently, since around 1950. For a few years the most contemporary voices in the rabbinate looked for a sense of purpose in a revival of theological thinking. Martin Buber, who had been almost unknown in America, suddenly came to occupy the center of the stage as many of the younger Jewish intellectuals flirted with religious existentialism. But it became clear almost immediately, at least to rabbis, that modernist Jewish theology simply could not sustain the burden they were trying to put on it. The most that one could derive from Jewish religious existentialism was a highly personal sense of encounter with God and with other men. Hasidic texts especially could be an intriguing source for such emotions, but they were not necessarily the only ones, for many of the young could and did wander around among Buber, Zen, and even Catholic mysticism.

The religious situation of the American rabbi is the most difficult that it has been in modern times. Almost the whole organized enterprise of Jewish life in America is today running less on passion and conviction than on momentum and on emotions about togetherness. What the rabbis are doing at this moment amounts to a holding operation. They are using every technique they can muster to relate individual Jews to some function or service provided by the Jewish community. This is why the rabbis are so busy. In this age of anxiety and insecurity people need counseling, so the rabbis have all become pastoral psychiatrists. Since Jews will not come to synagogues in great numbers to pray, the rabbis have devised family services in which birthdays, anniversaries, and the like are honored. Book reviews of best-sellers, antique shows, amateur theatricals—the list could be extended at will—are omnipresent. All of these are now much of the business of Jewish life, not because the rabbis really care about any of them, and not, as some of their critics have been maintaining, because the American rabbis have become vulgar.

The rabbis know that the Jewish religion is, to them, a source of unique spiritual experience, that it represents that by which they are commanded—but they have not the language with which to define such a uniquely Jewish commandment and to convince others to live under its yoke. Therefore, they keep themselves busy, and they keep others busy, with the myriad tangible acts of Jewish life. The corporate enterprise thus continues, while everybody can lay aside, most of the time, the disheartening ultimate questions.

Can the rabbinate survive in its present form and with its present functions?

I think not, because we are now at a historic turning. The rabbinate that Jews have known for two millennia ended in America within the last decade. This hardly noticed event is as historic a turning as the beginnings of the rabbinate in ancient Israel, when the priests of the Temple lost the leadership of Judaism to the nascent class of Pharisaic teachers.

The rabbinate arose then as a new leadership which the Jews

were willing to accept because the rabbis were the arbiters of a system of religious values which commanded their assent. While the early Pharisees were rising to dominance during the last years of the Second Temple the priesthood remained and it continued to perform ritual functions, but these activities became ever more vestigial. The business of Jewish life then became the cultivation of the values commanded in the Talmud, as interpreted by the scholars within that tradition. At the dawn of Jewish modernity in the nineteenth century, the rabbinate secularized this role for a century or so as it led the Jewish community in the name of immediate "this-world" values which an oppressed minority shared: its quest for freedom and equality.

The rabbinate today is, essentially, neither judge nor leader. It is the agent of a remaining powerful and pervasive emotion about Jewish togetherness. The purely religious function of the rabbi has been becoming ever more vestigial for many decades. Indeed, it is as far now from the center of Jewish mass consciousness as were the ritual functions of the priesthood of old. The rabbi's more contemporary role as leader of the Jews in a hostile world, or as moral guide to their political action, is constantly diminishing. He has become peripheral to the major social struggles of this age.

The rabbinate thrived for many centuries by offering Jews a vision of themselves as the servants of God. It then carried on for a relatively short time by holding up the dream of the Jews as servants of their own quest for freedom and, therefore, as trailblazers for all the oppressed. The Jewish community within which the rabbis are working today sees itself, for the most part, as the servant of its own survival. There are no great, individual rabbinic careers because there are no shared Jewish purposes on the American scene grand enough to evoke them.

And I see no sign of such purposes on the horizon.

13. The Changing Rabbinate

You will remember that the rebbe of Alexander was the kind of gentleman who davened with great passion and personally carried through the tradition which good hasidim call *havayes*. He moved. Behind him stood a hasid. Every time the rebbe made a gesture, he instantly made the same gesture. After a while the rebbe of Alexander was very tired of the whole business and he looked back upon his hasid and said, "Stop!" The hasid said, "Why stop? I'm following directly after you, my teacher and master." The rebbe answered, "When I have made the gesture, it is finished, and when you repeat it, it is no longer authentic."

I wrote a piece on the rabbinate back in 1966 and on rereading it I find that I did learn from our teacher and master, Mordecai Kaplan. I did learn from him when one day, in order to save myself a good thrashing, I gave as the outline for a sermon to be given at the seminary synagogue a verbatim account of what he had said on the subject the preceding Thursday. On Monday morning after I delivered this sermon in class, he proceeded to demolish me totally. I turned to him and said with great passion and considerable anger, "Dr. Kaplan, I don't believe in all this either, but this is what you said last Thursday." He looked at me with a typical Kaplan smile and said, "But, Arthur, I've *grown* since Thursday!"

There are one or two things that I think I have learned about the rabbinate, not by reflection nor by theorizing but simply perhaps by living it out a few more years, simply perhaps by watching for seven or eight more years what's happening in the congregation in which I am not a tourist. I think part of our problem is that we are sometimes tourists in our congregations. You have to stay in one place for a generation and then ask yourself honestly what

Reprinted from the Proceedings of the Rabbinical Assembly, vol. 37 (1975) representing a speech given on April 22, 1975, at the 75th-anniversary convention.

you have written large within a generation, within your own congregation. If you are in a place three or four or five or eight years and then go on, you can say to yourself, "I've tried to serve them, I've done it well"—or "I've done it badly"—"the rabbi–congregation relationship has been good, bad, or indifferent." But if you're finishing nineteen years, you cannot say that anymore. You've been there long enough so you are responsible for what is around you. Not the theologians, not *hakhme hador,* not the symposiasts at Grossinger's, but you. Once it really comes home to you that it is not really others who cast you in roles or define your function for you, then it is possible to construct an intellectual and historical analysis.

I would like to begin by disagreeing with myself. What I now know about Jewish history teaches me that the notion that the rabbi's role has become busier or radically different is really not true. I want to deny that proposition. This common coinage that we are now pastoral psychiatrists, group therapists, and hospital visitors, and therefore we should appoint visiting committees and therapists to help us, does not impress me.

Have you read, either in Yiddish or in English, Isaac Bashevis Singer's *In My Father's Court?* Read it! You will discover that Singer's father was a *rov* and a *shtikel moyre horaah* in one of the poorer neighborhoods of Warsaw. He was terribly busy all day, every day, not writing *hiddushe Torah.* He studied Torah and he was busy with *almonot* and *yesomim* and people who got into lots of trouble. He was, after all, an *avi yesomim v'dayan almanot.* As a matter of fact, so were the *zaydes* of some of us.

In the days before I became a politician I wrote a book on the eighteenth-century Jews in France. In our own seminary library we have one of the great eighteenth-century documents: the *pinkas* of the Jewish *kehillah* in Metz from the second half of the eighteenth century. That *pinkas* contains a rabbinic contract for a rabbi much greater than anyone I know, a gentleman known to us as *Sha'agat Aryeh* (in the French sources he is called Asser Léon). In that contract, his *balabatim* defined for him a much busier set of roles than those contemporary rabbis have. Furthermore, they asked him by contract to agree that there are a certain number of things that he will not touch with a barge pole, because they are left for the *parnasim*. Very soon there comes a battle over a *minhag* in the great synagogue of Metz. And the *Sha'agat Aryeh* establishes a personal *minyan* in his own home where he davvens for at least the last twelve years of his life, never darkening the door of the main *shul* in Metz because the *parnasim* had the *hutzpah* not to allow him to eliminate a certain *piyyut* on the second day of Shavuot. I submit that this is a greater *narishkayt* than any of those that modern rabbis have ever faced from a board and, *mutatis mutandis, di zelbe khalerye*. I think that we really have *kankan hadash male yashan*.

As one who spends whatever time he can find on research in late medieval and modern Jewish history, I am thoroughly persuaded that Abrabanel in the fifteenth and sixteenth centuries, a banker and a politician and a representative before the government who wrote *perushim* and dealt with reconstructing a community, was no less split into eighty-seven pieces than the modern rabbi. The Rambam before him, the head of a community involved in innumerable things, deplored the fact that he was not a *baal melakhah ahat*. Were he one of us contemporary rabbis, he would list, in the accents of our own time, a comparable set of complaints, in English rather than in Arabic or impeccable Hebrew. I don't believe that the situation has changed. We are not busier than our ancestors, or split into more pieces.

Some things, however, indeed have changed. Beginning with the end of the eighteenth century two very radical things happened. The ghetto ended, at least in theory, and the halakhah ended for many Jews, at least in theory. I don't have to expand on this. Read a book you all know, Mordecai Kaplan's *Judaism as a Civilization*. Or read a book with more footnotes, available in both German and Hebrew (alas, not in English)—Max Wiener's *The Jewish Religion in the Era of Emancipation*. There you will see a brilliant description of what we are living with: post-halakhic Judaism. We are living it, whether it is the life of Samson Raphael Hirsch, or Geiger, or Frankel, or Schechter. We are living in a situation within which the power of the Jewish community to compel religious uniformity no longer exists. I can put it very simply. There are still in some smaller towns here represented some Jewish country clubs which will not admit you if you don't give to the United Jewish Appeal. There is no organization which will expel you for eating *hazir* on Yom Kippur. So it is very clear that the Jewish community has decided *yehareg ve'al yaavor* applies to its sense of *Judennot,* the needs of the Jewish people, and not to its sense of what is halakhically enjoined in the ritual tradition.

We are essentially in an eclectic religious situation, whether it be Joseph Hayyim Brenner's eclecticism, or Solomon Schechter's eclecticism, or our own. As a matter of fact, this was already predicted in the very genesis of hasidism. Hasidism arose in the middle of the eighteenth century. It is a very strange interweaving of kabbalah and halakhah. It is the kabbalah tamed by halakhah. Within hasidism the notion is created that *tzaddikim,* who are role models, can in the very nature of their lives decide *vos me meg un vos me tur nisht.* It is halakhically inconceivable to davven *Shaharit* at one o'clock in the afternoon. Those people who decided to davven *Shaharit* at one o'clock in the afternoon certainly knew the halakhah. Nonetheless, they permitted themselves as role models to live it out differently, within what they regarded as acceptable limits of choice.

Let's get down to *takhlis.* Solomon Schechter has been so bathed in an aura of mythology that we no longer read him. He's become a kind of totem: we no longer know what the man said. What did he mean when he talked about "Catholic Israel" in his *Studies in Judaism?* Do me a favor: read it. You will find that every time he says "Catholic Israel" he means those Jews living within a contemporary situation who care, who have some sense of what the limits are and who make their choices by what they highlight or what they do not highlight. Schecter is most revealing in an essay in which he wrote about the Bible as read in the synagogue. He makes the point very consciously that the portions of the Bible which the synagogue chooses to read reflect its own set of choices, how much it wants to keep alive and what, without making an ideology out of it, the synagogue decently in practice wants to inter.

Ahad Ha-am, whom Schechter argued with and loved and tried to invite to the United States, said the same thing in a rather more secular way. "We choose within the Jewish tradition," he said. "We live it out with a sense of what is authentic and what is not, and our choices become the new authenticity."

Next, let me discuss what I would call the immanent theology of the Conservative rabbinate, talk of what we say, not about our theories on halakhah. Anybody in his right mind knows that a halakhic case cannot be made for eating *milkhiks* out on *tref* dishes. As a matter of fact, the majority of us do. We make choices; not all of us, but a majority of us.

Once and for all let's ask ourselves not what we usually ask ourselves, in bad conscience, what we have chosen to disregard, but let us also ask ourselves about what we have chosen to emphasize. Let us not construct a theoretical, ideological case, because the young in my congregation are not convinceable by ideology, and neither are the young in other congregations. All of the young, including those who live in our own homes, know very well what we care about and what we don't care about. I very often hear of college students from my congregation who make the Pesach *sedarim* at their various schools. I have even heard of them constructing a *sukkah*. I have seen hundreds of them come home for Rosh Hashanah and Yom Kippur. I have seen dozens of them, when visiting home, come to *shul* on *Shabbat*. I have not seen very many go to early morning *minyan!* Do you know what they're telling me? They're telling me that they've been observing me very closely. There is no point to my saying that their parents have been casting me in the roles of hospital visitor, chaplain, psychiatrist, etc. The truth is that the young have been looking at me and, God love us, at all Conservative rabbis, saying *kazeh r'eh v'kadesh.*

We tend to discuss our problems in externalities because it is much easier to avoid the *atah ha-ish* when you write an article such as I wrote for *Midstream* back in 1966. We say the world around us hems us in. As a matter of fact, the way we can tell that this is not so is not by asking what the Jews do not observe, because we do not. Let me ask about the things which the Conservative movement, and for that matter the American Jewish community, have positively learned from us.

Jacob Schiff was a much tougher chairman of the board than I ever faced, and Schechter was his *rav*. The board of the seminary could have fired Schechter just as easily as a board could fire me. In 1906, in spite of the positions maintained by Schiff and all of his board, Schechter announced that he was a Zionist and the world did not fall in. As a matter of fact, I remember a seminary graduation back in the 1940s when we wanted to sing *Hatikvah* at graduation and some people in high authority at the Jewish Theological Seminary said, "That's a national hymn in the middle of a political argument." We did not prevail at that graduation, but it did not take very long for us to prevail. Why did we prevail? Because *that* we really meant: our Zionism, our passion for *klal Yisrael,* our religious tremor for every Jew. To my knowledge there is no rabbi in the Conservative movement who has ever put up with a notion that even approaches anti-Zionism.

We have fought hard for Hebrew. That choice was made a long time ago by Zacheriah Frankel, who (if you read him carefully) did not believe a lot more than Abraham Geiger. He did not leave the Reform Synod because suddenly on the high road to Frankfurt the *rebbono shel olam* appeared to him and said, "Don't do it." He walked out in the 1840s because he looked at the end of Hebrew. That was halakhically possible, but nevertheless totally repugnant. Out he went because he said, "That breaks the unity of the Jewish people." And he fought for Hebrew, as we have fought for it.

We have fought, oddly enough, or not so oddly enough, for *aliyah.* Why do we as a Conservative movement have the beginnings of a leg to stand on in Eretz Yisrael? Because the intellectual migration to Israel from the United States, beginning in the days when Dr. Simon Greenberg was the first American student at the Hebrew University, has consisted substantially of Conservative Jews. It is not accidental that Henrietta Szold came from within our polity, down to Moshe Greenberg, to Seymour Fox, and to all kinds of others, because we have really cared about Israel.

We have affirmed something concerning intermarriage. If we should find a rabbi within the Conservative movement nowadays using a swimming pool for a *mikveh,* we'll allow it in the framework of a minority halakhic decision. (Personally I think that is nonsense, but I have a right to dissent from such opinion within the rules of our movement.) But find that rabbi co-officiating at an intermarriage and the liberals among us will conduct a battle in which no quarter will be given. Out he will go—and the Rabbinical Assembly does not easily throw people out, not even for the infraction of union rules.

We have indeed defined a persona, an identity, and we have defined it precisely as Solomon Schechter expected we would define it. In seventy-five years, in three or four generations, Conservative rabbis have effectively decided that they will live out certain things with passion, some with medium passion, and some not at all. If one of my *balabatim* were in Hong Kong on a *Shabbat* and heard that his rabbi was also there, quite as a matter of course the said *balabos,* wanting to find his *rav,* would go to the *shul* in Hong Kong. But for most of us, unless we were saying Kaddish, neither that *balabos* nor most of us would expect to find each other there on Tuesday morning at the seven o'clock *minyan.* So what have we really said? We have really said that, in terms of going to the synagogue, we are role models even on vacation.

Many of us have been role models for the notion that Jews should not be ignorant. We have taught, and we continue increasingly to teach. We are increasingly involved in education. We used to say, "We don't want to be Hebrew School principals." In my lifetime as a rabbi, increasingly we cannot be kept away from our teenagers or our adults, or from the notion that as role models we have to suggest that Jews ought to know more.

I could go on trying to define the persona, but I think an excellent suggestion has been made that we have a self-study of Conservative Judaism. If we construct such a questionnaire, I hope we are not going to ask ourselves questions such as "Do you believe in the divinity of the halakhah?" I hope we *are* going to ask ourselves some very precise questions about our order of caring, about our emphases and priorities in actual practice.

We are indeed role models in Jewish life, in competition with other role models: the fundraiser, the *tumler,* the sociologist. Indeed, in my grandmother's generation, when *tsuris* came upon the Jews they went to the rebbe, gave him a *kvitl* and asked him to intercede in heaven. Nowadays when *tsuris* come upon the Jews one of the national Jewish organizations hires three sociologists to do a questionnaire, a quantitative analysis.

There are other role models floating around. There are role

models of Jewish leaderships other than rabbis and in competition with them. But the worst thing is that we are in competition with ourselves. We are really trying to say to ourselves that we don't want these burdens. We would like to imagine, as we confront ourselves, that we don't really carry the whole burden of the continuity of the Jewish tradition, that it is carried by objective factors which are being burrowed under by contemporary disbelief, or that somebody else will carry it now, and therefore we let ourselves off the hook. We forgive ourselves as we see that what is around is failing.

Let me give you what I think is the ultimate example of what our choices mean in the terms of the creation of the persona of the Conservative movement. Solomon Schechter was right when he fought against the board to get Mordecai Kaplan appointed as dean of the Teacher's Institute. I've seen the correspondence; it makes very interesting reading. I've seen some of the Schecter–Adler correspondence, and some of the Ginzberg–Schechter correspondence. Schechter insisted that Kaplan understood him perfectly well. Kaplan's reconstructionism, after all, is a pragmatic definition of what we are really about. So why has it failed to conquer the Conservative movement?

Why don't we behave according to the prescriptions of "Jewish civilization," having picked and chosen among "Jewish folkways"? Because in the very midst of our eclecticism we refuse to let go of the notion that the Jewish people and the *rebbono shel olam* have a direct relationship with each other. We have recognized that unless we stand by that and live with it, then the central and transcendent importance of what we are doing is gone. Then what we are doing is as good as what somebody else is doing, and therefore also as bad, and therefore also as expendable.

These choices leave us with one simple proposition: in the contemporary situation, the rabbi has only his biography, nothing else. He no longer has anti-Semitism to "keep the Jews down on the farm," he does not have an organized community, he has competition. With only himself, and what he is, he feels terribly cold and terribly lonely, and he would like to be able to say like Moses, the very first rabbi and the greatest of them all, "Go send somebody else." But here *we* are. *We* are sent. We cannot avoid it. And the same thing has been going on before our eyes in the last generation in Orthodoxy. Liberal Orthodoxy has now been replaced since the 1940s by a new ultra-Orthodoxy, because Rabbi Moishe Feinstein and the Lubavitcher rebbe are different from the people who set the tone of Orthodoxy in the 1930s. Reform has gone in Zionist directions because the kind of people who are leading it are now fearful of assimilation as they were not in the 1920s.

We modern rabbis choose some values to affirm and to fight for and some to ignore. We will kill ourselves for *klal Yisrael,* for the importance of the Jewish enterprise, for Hebrew, for Israel, for a decent traditionalism, as we will not kill ourselves for *shatnes,* as our ancestors did not kill themselves for the *ben sorer umore.*

And so we are, if we are honest with ourselves, in the most difficult and loneliest situation in Jewish history. We are rabbis who have nothing going for us except our own passion, our own conviction, our own lives, and what we are willing to put them on the line for.

14. *Current Issues in Jewish Life in America and Their Meaning for the Jewish Community Center*

JEWISH LIFE HAS broken out in a rash, which is best described as the prevalence everywhere of the subject: "Jewish Identity in an Open Society." It is currently the chic subject and everybody is discussing it. Why?

American Jews have now arrived to a very high degree at the plenitude of American freedom. For the most part, we are well integrated into American society. I, for one, do not believe that anti-Semitism is completely impossible in America, but the majority of American Jews do not for the moment live with any such fears. Indeed, we are freer of them than we have ever imagined we could possibly be. One result of this happy situation is the crucial turn in the stance of the Jewish community in the whole field of intergroup relations. Two decades ago we were calling meetings about how to enlist other people with us, a minority in need, in the battle against anti-Semitism. We were a disadvantaged group trying to find friends. Today we are that friend for

Address given at the Biennial Conference of the New York Metropolitan Region, National Jewish Welfare Board, March 10, 1965.

others. Today we are calling meetings and attending those called by others to deal primarily with the problem of the Negro.

Certainly a large part of our motivation is the prophetic concern of our tradition with all misery and inequality. Another part is the motivation that comes to us from our historic experience, that freedom is indivisible. Nonetheless, I know enough about human nature to suspect that there is a third motivation. Some of our passion for social justice today derives from a sense that this very passion, in its contemporary manifestation, is a sign of how far we have gone positively in American society. In confronting the question of the Negro, we Jews are appearing for the first time in American history in a crucial issue not as one of the problems, but rather as one of the solvers of problems. We are on the barricades, not for ourselves and by necessity, but for others, by choice and as part of the American majority. That we are doing it at all betokens our growing assurance and security as Jews in American freedom. That we are choosing to do it has some relationship, I think, to our desire finally and at long last to leave our own minority status.

May I emphasize in this connection that in terms of our integration into America and our influence in American society as a whole, our positive estimate of our situation at this moment is truer than we know. We Jews are indeed at the zenith of any possible situation that we may occupy in American society. The five or six million that we represent is still a reasonably significant number in an American population of some two hundred million. We are a sufficient number of voters to have made the difference, as we have done before in many elections, in the closely fought battle of 1960. President Johnson, however, would have been elected without any Jewish votes. It is clear today that the Jewish population in America is static while the country as a whole is growing rapidly. Something like four hundred million people is predicted in little more than a generation. A Jewish population of five million in the year 2000 will be unimportant numerically. Today Jews are crucial to the intellectual and academic establishment, to the whole of American cultural life, but we are likely to loom less large, rather than more so, as the years go by. Negroes will certainly replace us in due course as the dominant element in American liberal politics. It follows, therefore, that this is the high-water mark of American freedom in the sense of significance in the affairs of American society for the Jew. It is a moment to be savored; it is a time in which the pattern of Jewish involvement in the larger concern of America is best set, because so opportune a time is unlikely to recur.

In the very midst of freedom this community of ours is beginning to sense a danger. It is in growing fear of its own evaporation. It is more than a little worried that the enterprise of Jewish life, as a recognizable and discrete endeavor on the American scene, will not continue for many more generations. There is reason enough to worry, for there are indeed signs and portents of a slow erosion of Jewish group vitality.

Everyone who is at all concerned about Jewish life knows by now that the rate of intermarriage is today of the order of one in seven. This fact is, however, a symptom rather than a cause. It is indicative of erosion, but we must ask the question: What are the underlying causes?

Many things could be said in answer to this question that I propose. The very openness of American society today is to a very great degree the enemy of our survival as Jews, and it is about this influence of the open society that I should like to make two observations.

In the first place, it used to be true that as recently as a generation ago, when we were battling for the entry of the Jews into the fullness of American freedom, we presumed as a matter of course that America was divided into a "we" and a "they." This is less true today, happily—but it has brought problems with it. We ourselves, the generation who lived through Hitler, feel less of this "we" and "they," and the kind of young people whom we are raising feel very little of it indeed. Twenty-five years ago the American intellectual and academic establishment was entirely dominated by white Anglo-Saxon Protestants. The writers of the day were Hemingway and Faulkner. The heads of departments at every major university were, with few exceptions, of the same human material. Today the leading name in American letters is probably Saul Bellow. The media names in American sociology are people like David Riesman and Daniel Bell. Humanities de-

partments in the major American universities are almost dominated by Jews. Indeed, to understand contemporary writing and
discussion, it is presumed that one knows, even if one is not Jewish,
a little Yiddish and something about Jewish customs and habits.

The Jews who run the American intellectual establishment
remember that they are indeed Jews. People as diverse as Alfred
Kazin and Leslie Fiedler even know, as do most of the other Jews
who are writers, that their Jewish identity has something to do
with their total stance. Nonetheless, the intellectual world which
is represented by the *Partisan Review,* the *New York Review of
Books,* and the like, is an establishment of Jews, but it is not a
Jewish establishment. The people who comprise it are for the most
part not at all committed to the idea that the Jewish tradition or
the Jewish community shall continue. Whatever may be the Jewish
aroma of their personal lives and thinking (I have officiated at a
few of their weddings and at funerals within their circle), in their
majority the intellectual gods of this day are quite content that
Judaism should evaporate in their own generation. An outsize
proportion of the leading Jewish intellectuals, those of large reputation on the American scene as a whole, are themselves inter-
married. Even those who are not are for the most part not educating
their children within the Jewish community. Since these people
are an ever more notable proportion of the teachers who guide
the Jewish young, that is, our children, both through their writings
and in their professorial activities, it is fair to say—I would almost
say that it is fair to charge—that the very Jews who today lead
American intellectual life are, by precept and example, leading
the Jewish young outside the Jewish community.

Committed Jews used to say to their children that intermarriage would leave them without any direct association with the
community because they would be marginal both to Jews and to
Gentiles. This is not true anymore, for the American intellectual
establishment as a whole is now dominated by such marginal people. The young graduate student on his way out of Judaism, even
as he retains some residual memories and emotions, can now give
us a crashing argument. The very best people on the very best
campuses are waiting to welcome him as one of their own.

A second aspect of the problem of Jewish identity in the open society is a corollary of the verve and passion with which we are moving as a community into the whole field of civil rights and American social advance in general. Let it be clearly understood that I, for one, am profoundly committed to the labor for integration. I am at least as aware as any of our advanced Jewish liberals that such commitment comes to us from the very Biblical roots of our religion. I know that Amos once reminded us that the children of Israel are no better in the sight of God than the children of the Ethiopians. I know the rabbinic texts that proclaim the equality of all men. The rabbis, for example, emphasize that all men are descended from Adam, from one father, and that Adam himself was created from dust collected from all over the world so that no one place can claim that it is superior to another. These teachings demand of us that we labor for justice in society, for justice for all men.

There is, however, an unarticulated premise of another kind hidden in the thinking of many of us about the labor of the Jewish community for social progress. It is the notion that by laboring as a community, by bending our major efforts toward all those purposes which go to make up contemporary advanced liberalism, we shall somehow solve the problem of Jewish survival. The reasoning goes something like this: since we know that some of the best idealism of the Jewish young is today going into CORE and the like, we ought to deputize a few rabbis and other members of the Jewish establishment to march with them. We will thus be joining forces with the young who are leading us. The Jewish community as a whole will prove to be a place where liberalism can be cultivated, and the young will, therefore, actively become part of it. What we are trying to say, at least in part, both here and in our growing emphasis on nonsectarian social service, amounts to an outcry to our children: Why busy yourself in CORE when you can do the same thing through the synagogue?

This premise, and all that flows from it, is wrong on the facts and fallacious in logic. It is not true, factually, in my own experience. I have gone through one famous battle on integration, the battle of the public schools in Englewood, New Jersey. Because I believe in integration I was very much part of the fray, and in the course of the battle I worked together and marched shoulder to shoulder with all kinds of liberals, many of whom are quite marginal Jews. My synagogue, I state it with great pride, was the only institution of religion in Englewood that remained completely united on the side of the angels. My Reform colleague worked at least as hard. Neither he nor I has reaped any "ingroup" dividends from our ringing demonstration of the proposition that Judaism is committed to social progress. Not a single individual who was finding his channel for liberal activity outside the Jewish community has, to my knowledge, returned to the synagogue in Englewood because it provided within a Jewish framework those values for which he had been laboring in some other context. What we did do successfully was to take Jews who were already inside Jewish commitment and teach them that that commitment had bearing on the social scene. This was indeed an important achievement, but it did not realize any hopes for attracting back to Judaism those who were not already rooted in it.

I wish that this were not so, but the failure makes logical sense. The very social idealism that expresses itself in the battle for integration reflects precisely the order of moral values which least differentiates Jews. It is within the context of such moral idealism that people of various traditions within America find each other. To put it in religious terms, morality is that which Jews and Christians have in common. It is that which they also have in common with secular liberals of all kinds. It is precisely this which unites a secularist such as James Farmer, a Unitarian such as the martyred James Reeb, and young Jews by birth such as the martyred Goodman and Schwerner, who are buried, respectively, in the name of Ethical Culture and the Community Church. In the dimension of the social idealism, all of our varying traditions are more nearly one than in any other context. These values and the effort for them cannot, therefore, act to shore up the specific life of any individual tradition, because this is not the place where varying traditions are most discretely different. This is the area in which they are most alike.

We cannot, in all logic, produce our social idealism as the reason for keeping Jews in a separate community. We must rule out completely, both in fact and in logic, the notion that the work of the Jewish community for social progress will maintain the Jewish community as a separate entity.

If these thoughts are true, it follows that the total policy of the American Jewish community must be seriously reevaluated, and in a very critical way. We have been pitching our hopes for survival largely on the presumption that we will do nonsectarian things—from basketball to marching in civil rights demonstrations —under Jewish auspices, and that that will save us. I should like to submit that a Jewish community devoted to nonsectarian internal content is a community whose young will find their nonsectarianism elsewhere. Such a community is in the process of comitting suicide, not because it is not sufficiently intelligent either about its Judaism or about America. It is committing suicide because it has not a sufficiently contemporary awareness of the meaning of the open society or of its real impact upon Jews.

The question therefore remains: What is the future of Jewish identity in America? The Jewish Center movement, and all the other organs of the Jewish community, have been surveying and resurveying themselves for many years on issues such as these. The sociological survey is again today one of the favorite indoor sports of the American Jewish community. The centers began it with the Janowsky report, when I was young and thin, and they are still at it now when I am, alas, no longer either. I suspect that the real issue requires no further sociological analysis, which is my polite way of saying that much of our "surveying" is a kind of neurotic acting-out. We know that we have a problem called "Jewish identity," so every time the question pains us we "do something" about it by having a survey. This relieves us from having to take action, because the action might be uncomfortable. I have profound respect for the discipline of sociology since I spent some years of my life laboring in it, but I should like to submit that all the essential facts are already in. The conclusions are obvious if we could only stop "surveying" long enough to look at them.

It is clear that the American Jewish community today is freer and more secure than any Jewish community the Diaspora has ever known. It is also better educated in the secular sense than any community in the history of the world. If there were any more college degrees in the American Jewish community we would not know what to do with them. Everything has, therefore, changed for the better in the last generation, except one variable—there is less Jewish piety, less Jewish learning, and less commitment to the continuity of Judaism. There is more divorce, more drinking, more immorality, and an ever more marked loosening of family ties. It is clear that this could not have been caused by our lack of commitment to liberalism because no white community in America is as committed as we are. What has happened to us must bear some relationship to the evaporation of inner Jewish values. If we would reverse the trend, the cure cannot be found in the administering of more nonsectarianism, because one of the side effects of our entry into the open society is that we have picked up not only its virtues but also the conventional vices of the bourgeoisie. We must, therefore, look for the cure elsewhere, to our own tradition.

This, by the way, is not merely the partisan estimate of a rabbi. This is in part a theme which runs through Saul Bellow's novel *Herzog*. The book is a journey through all the intellectual and moral worlds of American modernity, generally as represented by more or less alienated Jews. Bellow finds all of them wanting. Almost none of the characters that he has met since he left the ghetto of Montreal impress him as having any real moral stature. The people to whom Bellow's hero keeps returning are the members of his family, and the friends that he made, within the context of a living Jewish community that was permeated with traditional values. Bellow makes this point with the language of a novelist, and at the end we are not quite sure which road to sanity his hero will take. We do know that he can take none of the roads away from his origins which are currently fashionable. That is all that I am saying: none of the roads away from the specifics of Jewish learning and Jewish experience, which may seem in the short run to make us popular and contemporary, can really work. They are self-defeating, even suicidal. We must plunge forthwith into the task of shoring up our Jewish life in a concrete and specific way.

The leaders of the Jewish Centers of the largest Jewish community in the history of the world have an enormous responsibility, before God and before history, a much larger responsibility than in their humility they recognize. They owe a corporate responsibility to something more than a program of leisure time activities. They have it within their power to be a major force for the survival of Judaism. In metropolitan New York there are great needs in the field of transmitting Jewish learning and experience which are not being met by the existing agencies, including the synagogue. Such needs are on the doorstep of the Jewish Centers and it is their moral duty to address themselves to them.

I should like to propose four areas in the field of Jewish education, using the term in its broadest meaning, which I hope leaders of the Jewish Centers will make their own. In the first place, many of them are presently engaged in major programs in preschool education. Indeed, it is well known that some of the finest nursery schools and kindergartens in the country are to be found in these centers. It is, nonetheless, true that as instruments of Jewish education these schools are not what they should be, at least not everywhere. Their admission policies are in many places quite properly nonsectarian. This admission policy has become the reason, in some of these schools, for having very little if any Jewish content in their programs. Such a stance is nothing less than a disaster. Contemporary understanding of education is pointing ever more to the importance of the years from three to six. The experiences and expectations that children pick up then mark them for good or ill for the rest of their lives. Preschool education is the place where we can orient children to a healthy acceptance of their Jewish identity. It is in those years that we can make Jewish experience crucial to all their future outlook—and by the same token the absence of Jewish content from their preschool experience is, in reality, equivalent to saying that we do not want it at the root of being of the young. Were it within my power to make one rule by fiat for the entire New York Jewish community, it would be a ukase that we organize a network of preschool Jewish education so subventioned that all children would go to it; that these schools be located in the one overarching institution of the Jewish community, the Jewish Centers; and that their programs be avowedly and creatively Jewish. This alone would go a long way toward solving the problem of the survival of Judaism. Let non-Jewish children come to these schools if they wish; let them be welcome, but on the clear-cut understanding that they are coming to schools whose main purpose is the education of Jews in Judaism, in its broadest sense.

My second suggestion is that I do not think that even the years from six to fourteen in the life of the Jewish child belong solely to the educational instruments of the synagogue. No one has a monopoly on any aspect of Jewish life, for all of us serve a higher master. In the five boroughs of New York there is the largest proportion of Jewish children not receiving any kind of Jewish education of anyplace in the United States. Part of the reason is indifference, and it is the task of the total Jewish community to address itself with missionary zeal to such lack of concern on the part of many parents. The centers are, I am sure, better equipped to reach such people than the synagogue. There is another more tangible reason why many Jewish children are not in Jewish schools. It is a matter of cost. I am sure that a network of free Jewish schools, where tuition is not an issue, will materially raise the number of Jewish young who receive a Jewish education.

It is clear that for the centers to enter this field would involve them forthwith in a two-pronged battle. The vested interests of the synagogue would complain of the shaking up of their structures, which now rest so heavily on the religious school as the magnet which now attracts families to membership. A major effort by the centers directed at the Jewish education of the children of the unaffiliated must also inevitably change radically the present budget of our whole Jewish philanthropic structure. Millions would have to be found annually for Jewish education. The polite thing for me to do at this point is to pretend that such money could be found, in addition to the funds already being spent in other areas, but I have no such delusions. Some other purpose will have to be less well served if Jewish education is to be served better, and there will inevitably be a titanic battle to effect such a change. The battle is worth having. Synagogues, welfare funds, and centers are only instruments, and their institutional discomfort is of no consequence. It is clear to me that we must do something radical to achieve serious Jewish education for all Jewish children. If we continue to go on the way we are there will be nobody to fight these battles, for Episcopalians do not care about the Talmud and Maimonides.

In the third place, the whole question of Jewish teenagers ought to be addressed. At the moment there is an institutional dichotomy, in that it is presumed that formal Jewish education should be provided in the high school age by the synagogues primarily, and that it is the task of the centers to provide leisure time activity for this generation. I do not know how successful these leisure time programs are, but it is no secret that only a very small proportion of teenagers are in the various learning programs of the synagogues. Many of these efforts are small, weak, and badly staffed. The time has come to make Jewish learning in the teenage generation a communal responsibility. Here, too, the Jewish Community Center can play a unifying role. Let all the institutions of the New York Jewish community unite around an effort in education for this generation. I am aware that there are denominational differences, but the classic texts of our tradition unite us all. Our points of view may differ, but Hebraic learning is our common inheritance. Surely enough goodwill can be found in the various schools of thought, and enough ingenuity and wisdom, to make it possible for a united program to be created. If we were to use such an approach to the problem of rooting our teenagers as Jews, our program could be made into an integrated whole, involving both learning and leisure time activities.

My last suggestion involves the area of adult Jewish education. What exists today is best described as the presumption that one ought to "do something" about Jewish content. Conventionally, therefore, our institutions create lecture series. Having participated in many of them myself, I know that their subject matter is usually not the content of the Jewish tradition but a kind of formalized weeping over Jewish woes. The themes of this moment are intermarriage, why Jewish writers are not "positive Jews," and the like. This may be cathartic, though I must confess that I am bored even with my own lectures on these subjects. Since people clearly prefer to come to hear Erich Fromm talk about a really important theme like love and death, or Walter Kaufmann discuss the meaning of faith, it becomes clear, when the alternatives are posed this way, that "Jewish content" is a failure in the adult education programs aimed at Jews. Of course it is a failure; such programs should fail. It is, after all, neurotic to spend all one's time taking one's temperature, and it is perhaps a tribute to the mental health of Jews that they refuse to come to such "Jewish content." What we have not yet tried properly is serious Jewish adult education.

I would like to propose to the Jewish Community Centers, which can vitally affect the adult programs of two and a half million Jews, that they make a radical shift. The Jewish Centers of New York alone have it within their power to be the publisher of a half a dozen Jewish paperbacks a year. Let these books be both classic texts and modern works, but let us see to it that they are read. Let us program around the idea that we will discuss faith in the light of such a book as the eighteenth-century masterpiece by Luzzatto, *The Way of the Upright,* and that we will consider the meaning of history in the light of Krochmal's nineteenth-century classic *The Guide to the Perplexed of the Day.* Perhaps, instead of going to see Tevye on Broadway, we might read some of the stories together in serious confrontation with the world and outlook of Sholem Aleichem. We might then discover that that master was not nearly as sentimental, or as simple, as Broadway is making him out to be, and that he is to be taken very seriously. The availability of important Jewish books in English (and some are already available) would make it possible for us to create Jewish adult education which would center in a continuing endeavor in study groups, to understand these texts and their relevance to our lives.

Any tradition, any community, must speak to the minds and hearts of those who belong to it. If it ceases to do so, their loyalties will weaken and they will look elsewhere for emotional and intellectual sustenance. The need of our day is the need for roots, and Jews will not find theirs *as Jews* elsewhere than in their own tradition. The fabric of a community cannot be sustained by institutional separatism when the content purveyed by the institutions is no different from that which Jews can find elsewhere. I personally do not need the Jewish community to express my liberalism or my passion for integration. I can, and do, express the first through Americans for Democratic Action and the like, and I am a member of CORE and many allied groups for the second purpose. Of course, Jews as an organized community must serve such purposes, for the sake of decency and their own souls, but the future of integration does not depend on the continuing of a Jewish community. Were it to disband, the battle for liberalism would still go on. I look to the Jewish community for that which I cannot get elsewhere: the specifics of Jewish experience and the content of the Jewish intellectual heritage.

I feel a little ridiculous, and more than a little sad, that I should have to plead with Jews to use their collective energies seriously for specifically Jewish purposes. I am saddened, not only because of my own commitment to the continuity of Judaism, but also—indeed, even more—at the prospect of the intellectual confusions and self-delusions now so prevalent in the Jewish community which make such a plea necessary. Let us hope that a decade hence a plea like this will not have to be given again. If it has to be redone, I am afraid that the audience will by then be even more remote from the emotions that I am reflecting, and that it will, therefore, be that much harder to move. The choice is yours.

15. The Protestant "Establishment," Catholic Dogma, and the Presidency

AFTER MORE THAN a year of discussion, culminating in the statement by Norman Vincent Peale and a number of other conservative Protestants, the "religious issue" in the coming election seems finally to have been defined: it concerns the first amendment to the Constitution, which prescribes that "Congress shall make no law respecting an establishment of religion, or prohibiting the free exercise thereof."

Reprinted from *Commentary,* vol. 30, no. 4 (October 1960).

So far (the middle of September) the public discussion has been fairly temperate in tone. To be sure, some Protestant spokesmen, especially Southern Baptists, are beginning to raise the ghost of a Roman Catholic "octopus" which—in the words of Dr. W. A. Criswell of Dallas—"covers the entire world and threatens those basic freedoms for which our forefathers died." Yet even among the Southern Baptists there has been some gain in reasonableness. The incumbent president of this denomination, Dr. Ramsey Pollard of Memphis, for example, went out of his way at the last national convention in May to reject the canard that the Knights of Columbus take oaths of implacable hatred against non-Catholics.

In any case, the passions of the Southern Baptists, and the even greater ire of the "holiness" sects which compete with them in their own region, cannot be taken as representing the mainstream of Protestant opinion. This opinion is promulgated by such churchmen as Dr. James A. Pike, the Episcopal bishop of California; Dr. G. Bromley Oxnam, the former chairman of Methodism's Council of Bishops; and Dr. Eugene Carson Blake, the immediate past president of the National Council of Churches and the incumbent highest officer of his own denomination, the Presbyterian. All three have recently spoken out with considerable positiveness—in the magazines *Life, Look, Reader's Digest* —against the prospect of a Catholic in the White House (Pike more guardedly than the others). But these men have clearly not been reading any anti-Catholic rewrite of the "Protocols of the Elders of Zion." They know that those faithful to Rome are not conspiratorial agents in a plot to dominate the world, that Catholics owe no political allegiance to the papal state, and that Senator Kennedy's candidacy is not a maneuver conceived in the Vatican. What makes them "uneasy"—the word comes from an article by Blake and Oxnam—is their fear that a Roman Catholic in the White House is likely to be a less than wholehearted protector and defender of the first amendment.

Protestant spokesmen have used two kinds of argument, one having to do with present Catholic policy, and the other with Catholic dogma, to support their contention that Catholics are untrustworthy in their attitude toward the principle of separation guaranteed by the first amendment. At present, say the Protestants, the Roman Catholic church is the major force responsible for maintaining the laws against birth control on the books of Massachusetts and Connecticut. Moreover, despite the grave threat to the whole world posed by the population explosion, the Roman Catholic church is the sole, and to date the determining, opponent of our government's participation in birth control programs abroad. The Catholic community has also been fighting hard for more and more state aid to its parochial schools, and it seems to be looking forward to the day when the bulk of the cost of running the schools, except for that small fraction incurred in the direct teaching of religion, will be borne by the taxpayer. Finally, the Roman hierarchy—both the Vatican and its subordinates in America—has remained silent while, as Pike has remarked "Protestants have been having a very rough time in Spain, in Italy, and in a number of Latin American countries."

The more general and fundamental Protestant argument is based on Catholic dogma. In 1864 Pius IX decreed the *Syllabus of Errors* as infallible doctrine. In this document all the characteristic "stigmata" of the liberal democratic state (e.g., freedom of personal conscience, the free exercise of all religions, public schools independent of the church, and the nonintervention of the state in behalf of the Catholic faith) were declared to be pernicious errors. This listing, the Protestant controversialists affirm, remains orthodox Catholic doctrine to the present, and is even taught in American Catholic schools. As evidence, Blake and Oxnam in their joint article in *Look,* and Pike in his new book *A Roman Catholic in the White House,* quote from a recent Catholic text (*Catholic Principles of Power,* by Msgr. J. A. Ryan and Father F. J. Boland): "The state should officially recognize the Catholic religion as the religion of the commonwealth." Protestant worship and the teaching of Protestant doctrine may be tolerated, Ryan and Boland continue, only if they are carried out inconspicuously and without any attempt to convert Catholics. "Error has not the same rights as truth."

Blake and Oxnam know, and Pike (a convert from Catholicism) knows perhaps even better, that the anathemas of the *Syllabus* (or of Ryan and Boland's text) do not express what all Catholics feel. Father J. A. O'Brien, a theologian from Notre

Dame, emphasized in an earlier article in *Look* (to which, in fact, the one by Blake and Oxnam was the reply) that the Catholic communion in America has never deviated from its support of separation between church and state. It is well known (even Pike attests to it) that most American Catholics, led by their American bishops, strongly uphold the ideal of a pluralistic America which offers complete religious freedom for all. Leaders of the contemporary American hierarchy have often declared their devotion to the Constitution, including the first amendment, and have disclaimed any intention of bending the power of the state to their own religious aims, even in the unlikely event that Catholics were to become a majority in America. Pike quotes at some length and approvingly from the writings of a leading American Jesuit theologian, John Courtney Murray, who has labored hard to define an "American view" grounded in basic Roman Catholic principles, which would affirm the equality of all religions before the state and willingly accept all the implications of a pluralistic society. Blake and Oxnam are, however, convinced that such Catholic liberals constitute a small minority, that even here in America their church does not support their views with any consistency, and that the binding and effective Catholic position remains that of the *Syllabus*. Pike generally agrees, but is rather more willing to grant that for an individual American Catholic like Senator Kennedy there may be some room for personal choice between orthodox dogma and the "American interpretation."

The Roman Catholic community has had little choice but to react defensively to the attack. Its leaders have reminded the Protestants that it was they, and not the Roman Catholics, who enacted the Massachusetts and Connecticut birth control laws back in the nineteenth century when Protestant doctrine was in full agreement on this matter with the Catholic. Why, then, demand of Roman Catholic legislators that they strain their consciences today to undo what they did not create in the first place? On the question of parochial schools Catholics have by and large given two answers. First, they are asking only for fringe benefits, like bus transportation, which the Supreme Court has held constitutional; second, they point out that in a democracy like England church-sponsored schools of all kinds are supported by the state with no harm to freedom—it is even possible, they say, to justify such a system for America by interpreting the first amendment to mean the friendly neutrality of the state among all the various sects, not its separation from all religion. Catholics insist that the quarrel over birth control stems not from their lack of concern over the population explosion, but from their conviction that mechanical devices are contrary to natural law, and they continue to urge further exploration of the church-sanctioned rhythm method. Some Catholics, moreover, have publicly deplored excesses against Protestant missionaries in countries like Colombia and Italy, and certain elements in the church have been consistently anti-Franco. At any rate, Catholics argue, the blame for anti-Protestant incidents abroad belongs not to the church but to mobs. Nor is the picture all of one color. No state is more Catholic than Ireland, and yet other faiths enjoy complete freedom of religion there. On the other hand, Protestant Switzerland still excludes the Jesuits by law, and Lutheran Sweden continues certain legal disabilities of Catholics.

On the matter of basic dogma the Catholic defense has been that the classic Roman Catholic doctrine can only be defined, in the words of the liberal Catholic weekly *Commonweal,* "as a textbook position" suitable to a "sacral civilization." At the end of days when the truth as taught by the Catholic church will have been accepted by all mankind, then the civil and religious order will be one and church and state will be interchangeable. But as a guide for present conduct (*Commonweal* continues), "whether it be applied in the United States or Spain," such words are "out of date, and useless, and even harmful." More eloquently still, John Courtney Murray said two years ago at a seminar convoked by the Fund for the Republic that "the highest political good, the unity which is called peace, is far more a goal than a realization. . . . Religious pluralism is against the will of God. But it is the human condition; it is written into the script of history. It will not somehow marvelously cease to trouble the City."

One might suppose from the arguments of the Protestant spokesmen that Protestant devotion to the principles embodied in the first amendment was absolute and unswerving. However, there is ample evidence—both in the history of Protestantism and in the current state of the American Protestant community—to indicate that the Protestants' commitment to the amendment is itself ambiguous.

Historically, far from adhering to the first amendment as a basic "Protestant principle" (of which the supreme example cited by Bishop Pike is Luther's early opposition to both church and state on grounds of individual conscience: "Here I stand; I can do no other"), the major Protestant sects in colonial America were clearly hostile to Protestant nonconformity. In Virginia (which had an Anglican establishment) any parent who did not believe in the doctrine of the state church could be deprived of guardianship of his children. The dominant Congregational (Calvinist) faith in colonial New England, the church of the Mathers and Jonathan Edwards, even more fiercely dogmatic, most assuredly did not believe that men could be left, in their innate wickedness, to choose their own doctrine and moral standards. Anne Hutchinson was exiled to her death by this church over a point of doctrine, and Roger Williams fled before it into the wilderness.* It was not until the second half of the eighteenth century that the influence of this kind of thinking began to wane in America. Skepticism and deism were now the fashionable philosophies of an intellectual elite for which Thomas Jefferson spoke, and individualistic nonconformist sects like the Baptists and Methodists had become the accepted representatives of a frontier society. An alliance between these two forces—the deists and the Protestant nonconformists—guaranteed the enactment of the first amendment. It is not too much to say that church and state were separated by our fundamental law largely to end the persecution of Protestants by other Protestants on these shores.

So complete has been the victory of Protestant nonconformity in America that even the once-opposing sects have almost forgotten the ancient battle: two of the most eloquent defenders of the so-called Protestant principle today are Eugene Carson Blake, the official heir of their Calvinist tradition in America, and James

---

* Congregationalism remained the established church in Massachusetts until 1833, when finally, and against its will, it was severed from official position within the state.

A. Pike, a bishop of the Anglican communion. Nevertheless, the struggle which resulted in the first amendment is not altogether over, and the "Protestant principle" is still in process of practical and theoretical definition, as it has been since the dawn of the Reformation. Though there appears to be Protestant unity in defense of the first amendment in contrast to some division and equivocation among Roman Catholics, the Protestant ranks are in fact split: the nativists see the first amendment as debarring any Roman Catholic, under any conceivable circumstance, from the presidency, while the more responsible elements recoil from so extreme an interpretation. But then the latter group is itself divided. Just as the problems of the Catholics in regard to the first amendment stem from their doctrine of the "true church," Protestants are, on their side, similarly confronted by a set of difficulties which derive from the universal Christian belief that Christianity is the "true faith."

The major example of the Protestant conflict is in the issue of public schools. Opposing Catholics on state aid to parochial schools, most Protestants still share the almost unitary view of the Catholics that the public schools need greater religious influences. Released and dismissed time, religious "common core" curricula, prayers in home rooms, Christmas symbols and celebrations, have all been fought for not only by Catholics but also by the majority of Protestants. In two cases currently before the courts, in Miami and in Morris County, New Jersey, the Protestant ministry has appeared to testify against the plaintiffs, who have argued that all such practices are contrary to the first amendment. Last spring Dr. J. Calvin Rose, the president of the Greater Miami Council of Churches (Protestant), stated his essential premise: "I can see no reason why we should turn to a pagan concept of life when we profess to be a Christian nation." In the courts, Protestants have argued that the first amendment requires freedom *for,* not freedom *from,* religion—and, practically, in this context religion means, as various observers have pointed out, a kind of lowest common denominator Christianity.

Some Protestants are aware that such thinking is inconsistent. It is not possible to interpret the first amendment both as prohibiting state aid to the parochial schools and permitting religious exercises in the public schools. In the very midst of current controversy about a Catholic in the White House, C. B. Deane, the president of the North Carolina Baptist Convention, insisted before part of his constituency in July that "We North Carolina Baptists might search our souls to be sure that we ourselves are free from compromise. It is so easy to point the finger at . . . other churches and other creeds and say 'I am right and you are wrong.' " There have in fact been instances of turndowns by Southern Baptists and other Protestant groups of state aid to their religious institutions in order to maintain a consistent position on the separation of church and state. Unitarians, whose creed is an ultimate outgrowth of Protestant dissent, have stood strongly against any and all religion in the public schools, as have some highly liberal groups inside the Protestant church. Nonetheless, it came naturally to the lips of a Methodist bishop and a Baptist minister to pronounce this a "Christian country" in invocations before the recent Democratic convention. In short, to the mind of many Protestants and most Catholics, agnostics and secularists are somehow un-American, and Jews are a bit suspect of the disease of secularism because secularists are among their allies in the battle against any religion in the public schools.

Paul Tillich and Reinhold Niebuhr have suggested that, at least vis-à-vis Judaism, Christianity should adopt a policy of complete religious parity, on the ground that each is equally valid revelation. The logic of their stand, as their Protestant critics have pointed out, would tend to lead to the end of missionary activity among all other faiths, not only the Jewish. At most it would make the Christian claim to exclusive possession of ultimate divine truth into a suspended assertion, awaiting proof at the end of time. This is today perhaps even less acceptable to the majority of Protestants than John Courtney Murray's kind of reasoning—concerned with outlining a more liberal and viable definition of the Catholic dogma—would seem to be to the orthodox prelates of the Roman curia. The doctrine of the "true faith," the source of the Protestant dilemma, thus has practical consequences in American public life as surely as the more limited Catholic doctrine of the "true church"—and both involve the first amendment. These two dilemmas—Protestant and Catholic—are real and con-

tinuing; they will be with us after the present election has long
been history.

Given the less than absolute commitment of the Protestant
community to the first amendment, one may doubt that the un-
easiness of its leading spokesmen over the prospect of a Roman
Catholic in the White House is ultimately rooted in fear for the
principle of separation. Pike, for example, finds grounds for ob-
jecting even to Senator Kennedy's declaration—first made more
than a year ago and reiterated strongly at a press conference
last month in Texas—of absolute commitment to the first amendment: "Whatever one's religion in his private life may be for the
officeholder, nothing takes precedence over his oath to uphold
the Constitution and all its parts. . . ." Kennedy's statement, Pike
argues, "would seem . . . to represent the point of view of a
thoroughgoing secularist," and is therefore just as objectionable,
according to the Protestant bishop, as the stand of an orthodox
Catholic. The conundrum with which the ablest of Protestant
cross-examiners has challenged the Roman Catholic running for
the presidency amounts to saying: Are you a good or a bad Catholic? If you are a bad Catholic, I gravely doubt whether I can trust
a conscience that is lacking in piety to God. If you profess to be
a good Catholic, then I cannot trust the church which is the maker
of your conscience, for it will bind you to notions and positions
which are an affront to American freedom."

What, then, is *really* bothering men like Pike, Oxnam, and
Blake? The answer, I think, has to do with the claim of the Roman
Catholic church to be the one true church. Almost every one—if
not all—of the major Protestant denominations believes itself to be
the most nearly correct approximation on earth of the church
invisible, but to the Protestant mind only the church invisible is
the true church. Protestants today (it was not always so) are,
therefore, predisposed to be fairly relativistic about denominational
structures and not to regard it as a matter of the gravest importance if a Presbyterian chooses to become a Methodist or a Quaker.
Nowhere in American Protestantism, except perhaps among the
highest of high-church Anglicans, does the notion exist that a
ministry or hierarchy is absolute guide in matters of faith and
morals. Nor is Protestantism particularly hampered by its own

canon law—which can be changed with considerable ease and with little apology to the past. In theory one may credit this flexibility (as does Bishop Pike, following Paul Tillich) to the ultimate "Protestant principle," i.e., that the individual has the right to express what he believes in his conscience to be God's judgment on both church and state. Actually, for most conventional Christians, the "Protestant principle" in practice means that the individual may accept or ignore as much of the teaching of his church as he chooses. At the same time, neither he nor anyone else doubts for a moment that he feels a sense of ultimate piety to God.

John Kennedy, Roman Catholic though he be, stands clearly within this general tradition. Protestant debaters may call it bad theology when he makes a distinction between what he will do in individual conscience as an officer of government, and what he believes in matters of faith and morals as the member of a church he attends on Sundays; yet this distinction is exactly what the "Protestant principle" involves for most Americans.

As many have noted, Richard Nixon, in having abandoned the pacifism of his Quaker origins while still retaining an involvement in the Quaker meeting, is acting precisely in accordance with ths same principle. Why, then, is Nixon not challenged for being a bad Quaker in the same way that Bishop Pike has questioned the piety of that most "Protestant" of Catholics, Senator Kennedy? Because standing behind Kennedy, if only on Sundays, Protestants see a church which declares as a matter of faith that Protestants are heretics, or, more softly, "separated brethren." The Catholic claim that "there is no salvation outside the church" may be less than absolute. Indeed, a priest was excommunicated in Boston some years ago for being too narrow in his understanding of this principle. Nonetheless, the claim makes traumatic listening for many Protestants—and they do not want to hear its echo, if only in their imagination, every time a president may hear the Mass.

This hidden fear explains why Blake and Oxnam have made a distinction between the presidency and all other political offices. They regard Catholic mayors, judges, governors, etc., with equanimity, but balk at a Catholic president—a completely illogical stand in the realm of actual political practice. On the record, after all, Roman Catholics in local or state offices have been much more responsive to the doctrines and needs of their church than Roman Catholics in national politics. Aid to parochial schools has often been granted by city councils and state legislatures, yet there has never been a formally organized "Catholic bloc" in Congress in its behalf. (Nor has Justice Brennan or the late Justice Murphy been any less stalwart in the defense of the first amendment than their colleagues on the Supreme Court.) If Senator Kennedy has left many Protestants unhappy by the obvious discomfort with which he has discussed the issue of birth control, these Protestants are certainly made much more unhappy by existing practice in Massachusetts and Connecticut. Indeed, Catholics in all areas of national government have for decades shown that they can, somehow, find an accommodation between the needs of the day and the dogma of their church. In the question of birth control, for example, the old scholastic distinction between "sin," which is a religious category, and "crime," which is an act punishable by the state, is available, as a few Catholic liberals have suggested.

Why, then, do Blake and Oxnam, as well as Pike, balk only at the presidency? The answer would seem to be that they have an almost mystical regard for the presidency as the incarnation of "the American way of life," which they tend to identify, for historical reasons, with nonconformist, individualistic Protestantism. Such Protestantism, in the deepest sense, is the American "establishment" as Protestants envisage it, and the presidency is as much its head as the queen of England is the head and highest exemplar of the Church of England.

And thus we come face to face with the true paradox with which Blake, Oxnam, and Pike confront a Roman Catholic candidate for the highest office. They are less fearful of what he will do than they are of the possible consequences of having a non-Protestant as the head of a "Protestant establishment." For example, Blake and Oxnam say: "A Protestant President is free to participate in the many interfaith activities that have been built up so carefully over the years. But a Roman Catholic is not. Even if special permission were granted to a Catholic President by a Catholic Bishop, Protestants can hardly be expected to relish the picture of a President under the authority of any other person with respect to his duties as President." Obviously, Blake and Oxnam know that going to interfaith occasions is not a constitutional "duty" of the president; they are well aware that our earliest presidents were not noted for attending any kind of religious exercise. But their argument does make sense on cultural and emotional grounds. Interfaith activity has become one of the "duties" of any president who would fit the image set by our Protestant-permeated culture. Hence Blake and Oxnam can assert that Catholics are acceptable without question in any other office: "a mayor or senator or governor is not the President. He does not represent or symbolize all the people."

Thus the responsible Protestants have this in common with the nativists whom they have been trying hard to discredit: both groups wish to preserve the image of a Protestant America—an image that would be jeopardized by the election of a Catholic to the presidency. In order to appreciate the force of this sentiment—which is very powerful among the nativists and perhaps only atavistic among the responsible Protestants—one must first recall that all three of the major religions in America have an ethnic aspect and that the struggle, in this country at least, between Protestants and Catholics is in part a struggle between the oldest American stock and the postbellum immigrants.

Since 1865 some thirty-five million immigrants, the overwhelming majority of them non-Protestant and non-Anglo-Saxon, have poured into this country. The first generation came out of hunger and looked to America for bread. In the next generation, the American-born children of the newcomers, the move from the ghettos began and with it some preliminary bids for a political role, at least on the local and state level. Today the third generation is full grown. It has no immigrant memories and it has almost forgotten all the languages brought by the grandparents. This generation is throughly assimilated to the dominant moods and modes of contemporary America. They will allow no one to tell them that they are less American than the descendants of an older majority —nor will they, for that matter, hesitate to force change upon their churches and ethnic groups in order to resolve any differences with American society as a whole. The conservatives in the groups from which they spring may yield with reluctance, and the nativists of the majority may beat the drums of prejudice yet again, but this generation will not be denied the very highest place in America. Whether or not John Kennedy wins or loses on November 8, 1960, the wave of the last century of immigration must eventually crest at the White House.

Nativist bigots know this very well, and they are trying to halt what to a historian must seem inevitable, using the first amendment as their most important "legitimate" weapon. The irony is, however, that responsible Protestants like Blake, Oxnam, and Pike will necessarily be forced by these extremists into giving up their own insistence that Catholics are less trustworthy defenders of the first amendment than Protestants: they cannot but be uncomfortable when nativists quote from them with approval. Indeed, Bishop Pike in a sermon in Detroit on September 4 denounced the nativists with prophetic fervor, and similar declarations were made last month by a large group of clergymen and religious scholars, which Bishop Oxnam joined, after the Norman Vincent Peale statement was released. Responsible Protestants cannot in all conscience argue for debarring Catholics forever from the presidency; all they can do is express doubt as to whether the Catholic community in this country has, as of 1960, "really" arrived at full "political maturity"—which must be taken to mean whether it now thinks of itself and its spiritual polity in the dominant Protestant mode. And in any event, their main objective in the present debate is to get an acceptance by Rome of the equality before God of all the Christian churches.*

It is still impossible to say how these various conflicts will express themselves at the polls in November. Nativist bigotry may very well evoke counteraction in Kennedy's favor, both among Catholics and Protestants. And what of the Jews? It has been held for a long time, with considerable justice, that Jews tend to make common cause with Protestants in the tension areas of American interreligious adjustment, and some observers have therefore reasoned that the "Jewish vote" is likely to go against Kennedy. But

---

* When Pope John announced the call for a Council of Churches a year ago, the prompt response of the Protestant World Council of Churches was that the churches it represents would be willing to attend provided Rome accepted the full equality before God of the Protestant communion. If Rome, however, insisted that it was the true church and the others were there to be reunited to it on some basis, Protestants could not in all conscience take part.

quite apart from the evidence that American Jews do not vote in a bloc on any question, there is also good reason to doubt that the "religious issue" in the present campaign will tend in Nixon's favor among Jewish voters.

In theory, Jews share the Protestant opposition to aid to parochial schools and limits on birth control. They would prefer, as much as Protestants, to find Roman Catholics participating in interfaith activities without any inhibition, for Jews, by far the smallest of the major religious communities, find perhaps the greatest emotional comfort of all in such symbols of equality. Nonetheless, on the immediate matters which confront Jews in their daily lives, Protestants are the source of their discomfort perhaps more often than Catholics. Nativism is a sin disavowed by the Protestant church, but it is a sin of Protestants. So, for the most part, is segregation. The quarrels about restricted housing in the best suburbs (e.g., Grosse Pointe, Michigan) and social restrictions in clubs and hotels generally embroil Jews with Protestants and not with Catholics. In the last two decades Jews have been moving, perhaps more than any other group, to the suburbs, to encounter the Protestant earlier settlers as a considerable bar to their complete acceptance. It is also pertinent that the major cities of the Northeast, which contain the large majority of American Jews, have for decades been mostly dominated by Catholic populations and political machines. Control by Catholics has led to many tensions but a real measure of accommodation has also been evident.

Still, issues involving the first amendment are the fundamental consideration. The public school touches almost every Jewish family, and even a rabbi's children occasionally come home in December singing Christmas carols. Here the Christian doctrine—shared by both Catholics and Protestants—of the "true faith" becomes a more or less painful and immediate issue for Jews. On this problem of religion in schools there is little comfort to be had by Jews from the Catholic church, but in actual practice (because the majority of Catholic children attend parochial schools) the Jewish community finds itself often fighting Protestant majorities in school boards and school administrations. On the other side, there is the support that the absolute separation of church and school receives from some of the most distinguished Protestant leaders, though Jews are more likely to encounter such aid and assent in the higher echelons of Protestantism than on the immediate level of the community.

The situation I am describing adds up to an important new development in American interfaith relations. Jews still look to a significant segment of American Protestantism for a liberal lead, but they are more aware today that their problems are with Protestants as well as Catholics. Because American Jewry now, like the rest of the post-1865 immigration, is in its third generation, it too feels an unquestionable at-homeness in America. It is, therefore, increasingly free in its comment and action on the policies of both the other faiths: in the name of its own need for and commitment to *all* the protections of the first amendment.

As we have seen, the first amendment was the battleground, at the end of the eighteenth century, of a major transition in American society in which the old Protestant establishment was forced to yield to the newer ethos of Protestant nonconformity. Today in American society we are witnessing a change perhaps as important —the full entry of the postbellum immigrant groups into the national life. Though the battle once again seems to be raging around the first amendment, it would appear from the foregoing analysis that the true issue is not the separation of church and state, but the symbolic significance for American life and culture of having a non-Protestant—whether he be a Catholic, a Jew, or an avowed atheist—as president of the United States.

16. Church, State, and the Jews

"THE TIME HAS COME," editorialized the Jesuit magazine *America* in the wake of the Supreme Court decision in the Regents' Prayer case, "for [Jews] to decide among themselves precisely what they conceive to be the final objective of the Jewish community in the

Reprinted from *Commentary*, vol. 35, no. 4 (April 1963).

United States—in a word, what bargain they are willing to strike as one of the minorities in a pluralistic society." Many Jews were offended by the question, and indeed the rhetoric of the editorial was in some ways offensive, but the question is nevertheless a fair one and deserves an honest answer.

The answer, however, must at once be both simple and complicated. Complicated because in order to find the true meaning of the Jewish position on church–state issues, it must be understood at the outset that words like "religion," "secularism," "society," have resonances in Christian tradition and post-Christian secularism that they do not have for Jews. Before the challenge from *America* can be taken up, then, it is necessary to recognize that Jews—even Jews alienated from their own religious and historic traditions—differ from Christians not only in the conclusions they draw from society but in the premises they hold about it. We can, though, begin by stating simply that while there are of course deep differences of outlook within the Jewish community, the overwhelming weight of both feeling and opinion among contemporary Jews is for the strictest kind of separation between religion and the state—and even between religion and society. Nor is this opinion merely a tactical response to the current situation in America; it is in fact the expression of an attitude to society that has deep roots in Jewish history, especially in the Western experience of the last eighteen centuries.

But for Christians, too, there is the matter of the bargain *they* have struck to attain the freedom that American society offers them—a mattter which tended to get obscured in the controversy which raged about the meaning and intention of the first amendment. For the controversy largely centered on the question of how much, if any, support the government of the United States may extend to religious groups as such, or to religion in general. Yet the equally important question of what American society requires of religion in exchange for the freedom it offers remains relatively unexamined.

Stated too simply, the notion of freedom of religion can be misleading. For crucial to the particular kind of free society created in this country is the implicit demand it has always made on religion. What the first amendment grew out of and subsequently determined was less the notion of strict religious "freedom" than the idea of a "compact" to be struck between society as a whole and the religious groups comprehended within it. Society undertook not to coerce any of the various religious sects through the power of the state, guaranteeing the "free exercise" of all spiritual faiths—and on the other side the sects were to pay for this freedom by giving up their right to coerce society.

On this point the lesson of American history is as clear as a human record can be. It was decided long ago by the Supreme Court, for instance, that a Mormon may not practice polygamy despite the serious religious conviction that commands him to do so. Nor is a man, merely by proving that he objects to bearing arms on religious grounds, thereby exempted as a matter of undeniable right from the military draft; such exemptions are granted by individual acts of legislative grace.

Not only in this kind of detail, however, nor only in relation to unpopular minority sects, does American society assert its right to effect the modification of religious practice; by extension this right is carried into the domain of doctrine itself. For while each religious group in American may continue to view itself as the absolute vessel of God's true revelation of Himself—dealing absolutely with those who freely elect to accept its discipline—and while each is scrupulously protected with respect to the requirements necessary to the exercise of persuasion on the broadest scale, they must all renounce their claim on the souls of those who reject their doctrine. It is unthinkable, for example, that in America the Roman Catholic church should sue to enjoin a baptized Catholic from remarrying after a civil divorce. In sum, American society has always asked, and continues to ask of religious groups something previously unknown and almost unimaginable: that each of them, remaining for itself and in private the only true and revealed faith, behave "publicly" as if its truth were as tentative as an aesthetic opinion or a scientific theory.

Now, the concept of the limited state on which the American Constitution is based is not a new one in Western history. Medieval political theory declares the state to be subordinate to natural law and to the authority of the church. In the name of this idea a pope once made an emperor kneel in penitence in the snows of Canossa.

Of course, the limits set for a medieval monarch by the authority incarnate in the church militant were different from those that were defined by a sovereign people for its new American state; nevertheless, the act of limiting the power of the state did have precedents in the political tradition. What was really new—and unique—in the American experiment was the concept of the limited church.

This concept was a construction of history, not of theology. To be sure, it was foreshadowed in the theories of Roger Williams, but it was not through these theories that the idea came to triumph. A recent document produced for the United Presbyterian church, called *Relations Between Church and State,* states the case most aptly:

> Although colonial and subsequent Presbyterians played active and dramatic roles in the evolution of the concept of church–state separation, it is a mistake to assume that this concept has grown out of any doctrine of Christian theology. Separation of church and state in the United States was not a product of theological reflection alone. In a real sense it was a decisively secular development and obtained most of its meaning from the national experience of the United States of America.

Left to themselves, the major faiths of the Western world have not thought about each other very much, except as potential objects for conversion. The American stance on freedom of religion is based on the implicit announcement to each of the various religious groups that the others are here to stay. What name one may wish to give to this announcement is irrelevant. But that it has shaped the religions in America, and in a more positive way than by simply providing them with empty space in which to expand and collide, seems undeniable. So, for example, in the bitter debate about the Catholic faith which marked the political campaign of 1960, when Catholics in America were charged with everything that had ever happened in the Middle Ages or was happening in places like contemporary Spain, they answered in essence that America is different and the Catholics have themselves become different by assenting to the American experiment and by living loyally within it. And this is true. It is inconceivable today in

America that Roman Catholic priests should be involved in the leadership of an anti-Semitic movement—precisely what is happening in Argentina, where the hierarchy has failed to silence priests who are spokesmen for the racist Tacuara organization.

At least to someone looking from the outside, it seems that the 1960 election had certain crucial consequences for Catholics and for America above and beyond the election of a Catholic to the presidency. In the height of the campaign several important statements were made on behalf of the American hierarchy; they amounted to a formal promise to abide by the self-limiting tradition of the sects in America—i.e., to behave in actual practice as one among many churches. It was thus that the Catholics purchased the inevitable ticket of full admission into American society.

This sundering of private faith from public policy is, for good historical reasons, extremely congenial to Jews, for they have experienced public policy over the centuries as a force inimical both to the practice of their religion and the safety of their lives.

Historians have generally emphasized that the Jewish community prior to its political emancipation (which is nowhere more than two centuries old) was dominated by its own "established" faith. To be sure, the ghetto community was monolithic and highly disciplined, but its authority could only operate on people who chose anew each day to resist apostasy. In the eyes of those who wielded the real political power, for a Jew to leave Judaism and become a Christian was considered a virtue; the only kind of apostasy that was ever a crime against the state in Europe was defection from the dominant Christian faith. The Jew who defected was thereby relieved of the burden of persecution and often treated with special consideration. Consequently, the Jews were not merely under persistent pressure and temptation throughout the Middle Ages to convert from their faith; they were the sole community in the Christian West in such a situation. What greater proof than this very fact did the Jews need in order to believe that religion could be sustained without support from the power of the state?

The predominant Jewish experience of the state in medieval Europe was one of cowering before its enmity. A Jew could only hope, in the words of the oft-repeated prayer, that "the hearts of

kings and princes be turned with favor toward Thy people Israel."
Furthermore, the state was usually either neutral or faintly well
disposed toward Jews in an inverse ratio to the influence over its
rulers by prelates. There were occasions in European history when
the church protected Jews from rapacious princes, but these occasions were exceptional. The establishment of Christianity in the
Roman Empire by Constantine, immediately accompanied by persecution of the Jews in the name of the true faith, seemed to fix
the norm for the rest of Christian history.

The experience of all those centuries does, however, bring up
two points that are relevant to the question of present-day America. Jews have come to know, almost by instinct, that their freedom
is safest—indeed that their freedom can only be achieved—in societies where the dominance of the church in public life has been
blunted. Research into modern Jewish history provides convincing
evidence that an early impetus toward the ultimate emancipation
of the Jews came from the seventeenth- and eighteenth-century
mercantilist powers who were no longer thinking of the state as
Christian and who therefore tended to be hospitable to any people
who brought realistic advantage to the country. In the second
place, Jewish experience with inimical rulers can be summarized
in what the greatest of contemporary Jewish historians, Salo Baron,
has called virtually a "law": the Jews and Judaism are better off,
and feel safer, in a pluralist society made up of a number of national groups and/or religious sects than they are in a unitary
political or religious structure. Thus another seed of political freedom for Jews can be found in the agreement in the seventeenth
century to end the wars of religion and to accept religious diver-
sity as the norm of Western Christendom. The multinational and
multireligious Austro-Hungarian Empire was a far happier place
for Jews than a monolithic Germany proved to be.

The rise of the modern secular state, then, was the *sine qua
non* for Jewish Emancipation. For Christianity, however, this same
historical development has meant a position of lesser power in
men's affairs. The power of Protestantism has been affected as well
as the power of Catholicism, but, for various reasons, the Catholic
church has responded with more direct animus against the forces
it has held to be responsible for the declining influence of religion.

The *Syllabus of Errors,* promulgated by Pius IX in 1864, in which the "liberal revolution" and all its implications were condemned, was such a response. Pius IX's censures of the separation of church and state, religious liberty, and public education no longer constitute Catholic doctrine, certainly not in America. It is one thing, however, to make a necessary accommodation to the secular state, and it is quite another to hail it—as Jews have done—as your liberator from age-old oppressions.

In this—which points to nothing less than the different meanings of anti-Semitism for Jewish and for Western history—we have arrived at the heart of the matter. The mainstream of Western thought, both Christian and post-Christian, affirms that the history of the West has been on the whole a good human record marred by many imperfections, among them hatred of the Jew. Therefore, except for the initiators of radical revolutionary movements, few people doubt that Western tradition need only be carried along further in the direction in which it has always been going, with some necessary reforms to broaden and purify its culture. And the eradication of anti-Semitism is generally included among the reforms to be achieved in an ever progressive West.

Many Jews share with the Gentiles this view of their civilization—at least intellectually they do—and they also share in the common belief that reform will suffice to put the Jews at last out of danger. But in that place where the heart stores its forebodings, most Jews do not believe it at all. European history has boasted too many pogroms, auto-da-fés, and death camps for Jews to believe with Olympian calm that these phenomena are an unfortunate but accidental feature of European civilization. The Jews must diagnose the Western tradition as not merely prone to the virus of anti-Semitism but chronically, or endemically, ill with it. For their own safety and for the future lives of their children, Jews must look to a radical change in the very foundations of Western civilization.

This special Jewish need has been little understood; in the light of it, we find that the two main streams of Jewish modernism— Zionism, which has generally been considered a radical solution to the Jewish problem, and assimilationism, which has appeared to offer the solution of gradualist accommodation to Western culture—

exactly reverse their positions. Zionism is in fact the conservative position, basing itself on two propositions: one, that all basic identities are, or ought to be, national; and two, that anti-Semitism is a hideously aggravated but essentially rational response to a national imbalance that can quite simply be rectified. Theodor Herzl, the founder of modern Zionism, asserted that it was the "abnormality" of the Jews' being everywhere a national minority that had brought what were otherwise normal tensions between national groups to the pitch of traditional European anti-Semitism; if the Jew therefore reorganized his identity into the recognized form, all abnormal hatreds would automatically disappear. Zionists, moreover, in their profound understanding of the fact that culture is more than political identity, have been willing to admit that in some fundamental sense Western culture will remain pervasively Christian. There can and ought to be, then—for the sake of everybody's peace and dignity—a comparable Jewish national culture. Such a culture could even be (indeed in Israel it largely is) post-Jewish, but it would at least be as related to its own religious history as contemporary post-Christianity is related to the historic values and experiences of the church.

The Zionist conception of the relation of religion to culture was recently given an important expression in the decision of the Israel Supreme Court in the case of Brother Daniel. A Catholic monk of Jewish birth, Brother Daniel had been admitted to Israel and was, under its law, free to ask for naturalization as a citizen of the state. He sued instead for automatic admission under the Law of Return, the state's provision that any Jew, of any provenance, can automatically demand citizenship in Israel. Brother Daniel demanded to be described as a Jew by nationality and a Catholic by faith. One minority view in the Supreme Court of Israel supported this demand, in the name of the absolute separation of religion and national identity. The majority opinion was delivered by Chief Justice Silberg.

I have not come to preach religiosity and I do not represent any particular view as to a proper future development of the Jewish people . . . but one thing is held in common by all parts of the people which dwells in Zion (except for a minuscule minority), and it is this: We are not cutting ourselves off from the historic past, and we are not denying our ancestral heritage. . . . Only a fool would believe or think that we are here creating a new culture, for—it is much too late! A people which is almost as old as mankind itself does not start *ab ovo*. . . .

The Brother Daniel decision has implications beyond the borders of Israel. Brother Daniel's rights to every consideration for his faith will be guarded zealously, but within a society which is overwhelmingly and publicly Jewish. Just so, one could say that Jews must be politically indistinguishable from all other citizens in America, but that the religio-cultural issues must work themselves out separately. Here as in Israel the state is neutral, but here the majority culture is Christian. Jews must accept the fact that they are a cultural minority and that properly temperate expressions of the majority outlook in our public institutions (e.g., Christmas celebrations in the public schools that are not offensively Christological) are as acceptable as are Purim carnivals in the schools of Tel Aviv. What in the contemporary translation of the Zionist outlook the Jews have a right to ask is that they be treated with every consideration a majority can offer the sensibilities and sensitivities of a minority.

However, the real thrust of Jewish modernity, beginning with the political emancipation of the Jews in Europe, has been in another direction—has, in fact, been tied to the dream of a basic transformation. Its most extreme form, that of belief in total assimilation, is not, as so many Jewish ideologists have claimed, the one most accommodating to Gentile culture, but the most radical in its demands on that culture. The source of this dream in Jewish tradition and consciousness is, of course, the vision of the messianic age, of "a new heaven and a new earth," when all the old order of the world would be overturned completely and Jewish suffering would be brought to an end. The expansive spirits at the dawn of Jewish modernity immediately saw in the beginnings of political emancipation a wholly new possibility for achieving the messianic age—in this world and by human agency. Had not the advanced minds of the Enlightenment envisaged a world in which all "medievalism"—i.e., all artificially imposed differences among men—would disappear in the name of the oneness of humanity? Was not Progress the new deity for their age?

It was inevitable that more than any other single community the Jews should have greeted the radical change promised by the Enlightenment: they longed to be not merely fully protected citizens but brothers to their fellow Europeans. Hence the now-famous passion of so many Jews for all the new eighteenth- and nineteenth-century ideologies, from the Rights of Man to Marxism to the Freudian unconscious. The generous promise of modern movements, liberal and Socialist, was a world in which there would be neither Jew nor Christian. The movements were embraced not only by Jews who wished to give up Judaism and worship at the new altars of man; many fervently religious Jews also became partisans of various secularist political movements because they held out the hope of an end to anti-Semitism.

That hope was not to be realized in Europe, cradle of Western civilization. One need not even go so far as to mention Nazism and communism. The liberal anti-clerical Third French Republic, for instance, after the church was totally disestablished, could not produce a situation of real cultural equality. Public school classes to this day are held on Saturday in France and could never be held on Sunday; so it is possible to raise one's children to be Christian, but impossible to raise them as Jews, without coming into collision with the practices of state institutions. By now, then, the first flush of Jewish fervor for modern secular ideologies has been tempered or rendered timid: anti-Semitism in Europe has certainly not been obliterated, and in some cases secularism has lent it an even greater virulence.

All this makes the encounter of the Jew with America uniquely important. The enormous attraction that this country has always held for European Jews—both those who came to it and those who could not do so—did not merely lie in its open frontiers and economic opportunities. In America was located the one society in the Western world which had no medieval past: no ghetto, no pogroms, no anti-Jewish state. Here the Jew might share as an equal in the creation of that modern dream, the "new man." Here was the last, best hope of the Jew to become a normal part of a national culture. It is interesting to note that the Jews were the only ethnic group in America which in the years of the Great Depression still showed a surplus of immigrants over emigrants. After their untold wanderings, America for its Jews has become not another way station but the end of the line.

Most American Jews thus have an investment in this country that commits them to something far beyond being a benevolently treated minority in a Christian culture presided over by a neutral state. A generation ago this commitment was expressed in the idea of "cultural pluralism," according to which every American was to live in two cultures, the public culture common to all and the subculture of his own particular ethnic tradition. Of course, cultural pluralism proved to be a chimera because all the other ethnic groups chose to become largely acculturated. The grandchildren of the non-Jewish immigrants—as Will Herberg famously pointed out in his book *Catholic–Protestant–Jew*—have maintained only one distinctive characteristic: the religion (but not the ethnic consciousness) of their ancestors. Though Herberg himself was careful to say that religion has, and must have, cultural and social implications, his analysis has been assimilated into the public mind as a blueprint for a secular public culture shared by all Americans, who will differ from one another only in being members of three distinct enclaves of private religious faith. The image is best projected nowadays at presidential inaugurations, where clergymen of all three major divisions of faith offer prayer. For Jews the participation of rabbis in the inaugural ceremonies is undoubtedly far more impressive than is the participation of bishops to Christians. The matter-of-course appearance of a rabbi at the most sacral moment of American civic life is visible proof indeed that they are full co-owners of American culture.

The instance of prayers at the inauguration serves to illustrate a further point: namely, it is simply not true that Jews are completely and consistently fixed in their strict interpretation of the first amendment. Such things as chaplains in the armed services, prayers at state occasions, tax exemptions for religious institutions—while the most doctrinaire member of the Supreme Court, Justice Douglas, would now like to strike them down in the name of intellectual and legal consistency—are no more troublesome to Jewish than to Christian opinion. For these practices extend to the Jews in every respect exactly as to all other denominations in America; no pressure of the majority or of its faith is being exercised upon them. Jews speak of the separation of church and state in absolute terms only on those occasions when they are asked to submit to practices which force them to admit to themselves that their status in America is no more than that of a generously tolerated minority. The first amendment is not the real dogma of the American Jew. His deepest and most messianic need is not a completely secular state; it is a truly equal status in American culture.

The true meaning of the battle which raged over the first amendment, then, is not that it was a confrontation between Christian defenders of the religio-cultural status quo and Jews in a somewhat uncomfortable league with the secularists to alter it. In fact, Jewish pressure on the status quo has far less significance than Catholic pressure to create a change in the balance between religion and the public culture. For one brief moment in history, on the day that John F. Kennedy was barely elected to the White House, Jewish and Catholic feeling and interests coincided. And Jews gave a politician for whom, in his own person, they were certainly far less enthusiastic than they had been for Roosevelt, the largest majority of their votes in history. So, naturally, did Catholics. Since that day, however, Catholics have not merely redoubled their efforts to get tax aid for parochial schools, they have largely replaced Protestants in the van of defending religion in the public schools. These are the very public schools that Catholics once abandoned as being too "godless" at a time when Christianity (i.e., Protestantism) was being much more overtly practiced in them than it is today. Indeed, Catholics have largely replaced Protestants as the guardians of that whole complex of practices once created to serve a sub-Protestant public piety. However one may characterize Jewish policy, it is now clearly in conflict with the new Catholic drive for a more Christian America.

And what of the Protestants in all this? Of course, there is no such thing as one Protestantism in America; that which we call Protestantism is a composite of several often conflicting traditions. In the South, for instance, fundamentalism is virtually a state church. For fundamentalists, devotion to the first amendment expresses itself, as during the 1960 election, in the form of a simple anti-Catholic nativism. Fundamentalists are against any kind of aid to parochial schools on grounds of separation of church and state, but they are equally violent about any attempt to remove Christian practices from the schools.

At the other extreme of theological sophistication are many Protestant leaders who support the absolute separation of church and state for very positive religious reasons. Men like Franklin Littell are eager to keep Protestantism entirely free of any hampering relationship to American culture, and especially to American patriotism, so that the church may unambiguously become what it ought to be, the critic and the conscience of society. The document of the United Presbyterian church cited above suggests to Presbyterians the following position: "Theologically, the church must be aware that the sole constant in its mandate is the fact of Jesus Christ. It is to the Christ that the church bears witness, not to a theological articulation of the place of the political order in the structure of reality." Therefore, in such a practical matter as tax exemption for religious agencies, "the church must regard special status or favored position as a hindrance to the fulfilling of its mission."

But the main impulse of American Protestantism lies somewhere in between. The "stated clerk" of the very denomination for which the above study document was prepared, Eugene Carson Blake, spoke rather differently in the summer of 1960 when he was afraid that a Roman Catholic might wind up in the White House. The grounds for his fear, he said, were that "a Protestant President is free to participate in the many interfaith activities that have been built up so carefully over the years. But a Roman Catholic is not." Obviously, even in the heat of that turbulent summer Dr. Blake knew very well that attending interfaith activities is not a constitutional duty of the president. What he really feared was an impairment of the image of our culture in which the various sects are treated as equals, and religion as a whole is in some deep sense the American establishment. And it was in the same spirit that Bishop James Pike deplored the decision in the Regents' Prayer case.

But perhaps the most significant reactions to the Regents'

Prayer decision came from Reinhold Niebuhr and John C. Bennett, who as leaders of liberal opinion among Protestants on interreligious and social issues took many people by surprise with their opposition to the Supreme Court's strict separationist stand. Niebuhr held that "the prayer seemed to be a model of accommodation to the pluralistic nature of our society" and deplored the possibility of a "consistently secular education that the Founding Fathers certainly did not intend."

There are two things implied in a position like Niebuhr's: one, that religion in America is quasi-established, and two, that the terms of that establishment include only such rituals and restrictions as keep the three main historic faiths equal. From such a point of view one can imagine a public policy that would include teaching about religion in the schools as a fact of culture; experimenting with "shared time"; inclusion of Bible reading in the school programs, but elimination of sectarian practices like Christmas celebrations and the Lord's Prayer; observance of some blue laws, with legal exemptions for Jewish Sabbath observers; agitation to remove such laws as those on the books of Massachusetts and Connecticut pertaining to birth control; but a growing concern, in the name of fairness, for the special Catholic burden of supporting an expanding parochial school system.

As for the Jews, the policy outlined above—though unsatisfying to their particular interests in many details—is nevertheless in essence a fair representation of their own wishes for American society. It grants their cherished desire for a tri-faith image of America. And further it assumes the existence of a genuine religious consensus based not on some lowest common denominator Christianity, but on the Biblical values common to both Judaism and Christianity. Thus Jews and Protestants are actually approaching one another more closely on the questions of church–state relations—in proportion to the growing Protestant acceptance of the mutually self-denying bargain that religious denominations have struck with American society in exchange for their freedom.

Catholic commitment to such a self-limiting pledge is of course far more problematic in the very nature of Catholicism. But even in Catholic thought there is some stirring in a new direction. John Courtney Murray—theologically far too much of a Catholic classicist to entertain for a moment the notion that any other religion than his own is ultimately true—has spoken in a way indicating movement toward the other faiths: "There may indeed be some three hundred religious bodies in America. But there are not that many 'styles' of religious belief. In fact, there are generically only three—the Protestant, the Catholic, and the Jewish. They are radically different 'styles' and no one of them is reducible, or perhaps even comparable, to any of the others."

Official Catholic policy, however, appears to be determined by other, special, considerations. The violence of the Catholic response to the decision in *Engel* v. *Vitale* could clearly not have been occasioned by the excision of a short prayer of little if any religious significance. Behind this response lurked the grave problem for Catholics of the future financing of the parochial schools. Cardinal Spellman's statement on the decision, although his most important concern was for maintaining the Christian flavor of American culture, forthrightly linked the two issues. Such decisions as that prohibiting the Regents' Prayer, he said, tend to "the establishment of a new religion of secularism." The same attitude had been expressed a few months earlier in the Boston *Pilot,* the official paper of the diocese of Cardinal Cushing, which was even more vehement about a suggested breach in the blue laws. The Senate of Massachusetts had already passed a bill exempting all Jewish Sabbath observers, whatever their business, from the prohibition to keep open on Sunday. The editorial in the *Pilot* was willing to concede this right to establishments purveying kosher food and the like, primarily to Jews, but it called any further liberalization a "shocking assault," "unjust and offensive," and evidence that a "carefully organized minority has done its work to destroy the Sunday." The editorial then named the senators who had voted for the bill, clearly asking that pressure be brought upon them. (It was, and the bill was rescinded.) In the heat of that moment it was forgotten that in 1960, in the crucial last week of the presidential election campaign, Cardinal Cushing had assured the country that the hierarchy would never dictate to voters on any issue. And examples of this kind multiply. No one even attempts to deny, for instance, that the bill for major federal aid to education has thus far been defeated by pressure brought to bear on the members of Congress from the Catholic hierarchy, who want a bill that includes parochial schools or no bill at all.

Yet it would neither be true to say that "liberal" Catholic views were merely campaign oratory nor that there is a continuing Catholic drive to "dominate" America (whatever that word may mean in this context). What then is the character of Catholic policy? It seems to me that Catholic demands can only be explained in the light of Catholic conceptions of the future of American society and of America's role in the world. Within America, Catholics are (and from their point of view, it must be said, rightly) fearful of "indifferentism," the sin of believing that one religion is as good as another. To be sure, such a belief does not really operate today among theologians—except possibly for Reinhold Niebuhr and Paul Tillich, who approach it—but it does in a very untheoretical way pervade American consciousness. From the middle of the nineteenth century, when Catholics fought hard for the first amendment, to the present, Catholic policy has really moved in a straight line; for it has always been one of keeping Catholics out of an "indifferentist" consensus. What makes the difference today is that the Roman Catholic church is paradoxically both strong enough—in numbers and in generations of rootedness in America—and weak enough—in the overextension of its economic resources—to join in open battle for a different kind of America, an America in which it might win tax support for creating "a truly pluralist educational order."

An even larger concern of Catholic policy is communism. Christianity as a whole has lost heavily in recent decades, and the Catholic church more heavily than Protestantism. Naturally, the danger from communism is most immediate to the heaviest losers. To the Catholic mind, schooled as it is to think in terms of faith and dogma, the confrontation with communism is a war of ideas between religion and antireligion. America, as the leader of the West, is cast for the role of the knightly defender of the faith. But for America to be true to this sacred mission the Christian character of her public life must be buttressed. Parochial schools will teach the Catholics; and the children of others must get at least enough indoctrination in the public schools to give them an appreciation of the trust which as Americans they bear.

All the various positions in America, religious and secular, have in common their rootedness in a basic cast of the Western mind. The precision of Aristotelian logic and the beauty of Platonic ideas have made of that mind a thing enchanted with tidiness and the abstractions it brings. Life, however, is concrete and diffuse; it is very untidy and its stuff does not fit easily into definitions. The faith–counterfaith definition of the West's struggle with communism in fact contains the seed of America's certain defeat in the world at large. For what America can uniquely offer to the peoples of Asia and Africa is not the vision of a Christian or a Judeo-Christian society but precisely of a pluralistic world order in which all men are permitted, nay encouraged, to pursue their own faiths, hopes, and aspirations.

The taking over of the Western ideological bent of mind by so many Jews on their being emancipated into the modern world seems now to have been inevitable: not only, as we have said, because the new ideologies bespoke a new society that would transcend at once all those centuries of hatred and exclusion of the Jews. The Jew's acceptance of dogmatic Western secular "religions" was also his first instinctive gesture of acculturation to a characteristic Western mode of thought and belief. At its deepest, this is what the abandonment of the Talmudic academy for the European university meant. Essentially, however, the Jew is the product of a tradition which is intellectually unideological. Only for Aristotle is A not non-A; classically the Jew can be at one and the same time a bearer of a universal religion and a particular national tradition, a member of the "chosen people" and the possessor of no special rights or qualities. His history is correspondingly unlogical. The ideological ages and societies have always attempted to do away with the Jew in the name of order. He has flourished where the "theology" of rulers has been tempered by pragmatic common sense.

Thus today the American Jew cannot share in the prevailing Catholic concepts of America and the West. He must, however, equally resist the blandishments of "first amendmentism." Any dogma taken to the extreme is ultimately the enemy of freedom, and, as the Jew should by now have relearned from his experience with modern ideologies, it is his enemy. Constitutional logic by itself could not prevent, say, some future generation's opening the public schools on Saturday for the purpose of intensifying education; in the end, only the untidiness of intergroup arrangement, compromise, and, sometimes, counterpressure will make such a thing impossible.

At the moment some Jews, along with some Protestants, are committed to their own parochial schools and therefore in agreement with Catholics on the question of federal aid. An alliance of this kind must no more be taken as a permanent one than the alliance of most of organized Jewry with secularists to support a strict interpretation of the first amendment. For religious alliances, like political ones, are ad hoc. What is permanent is the continuing network of intentions and special needs of each of the faiths. So, the most parochial and Orthodox of Jews may agree with others that there is need for more religion in public life, but he will recoil when this need is fulfilled in such fashion as to add an iota to the coercive power of the Christian majority over him. Most Jewish leaders would probably have preferred not to have the Regents' Prayer question litigated before the Supreme Court when it was. If the time had really been ripe for the removal of some sectarian practices from the schools, specifically Christian ones like Christmas observances would have been of far greater concern to Jews than a nondenominational prayer. Similarly with the continuing dispute about Bible readings and the recitation of the Lord's Prayer in the classrooms. Jews can accept, and may even strongly favor Bible readings: so central to our civilization is the Bible that not to know it is to be almost uneducated.

However, the protection of the first amendment extends not only to religious minorities all of whom have the Bible in common; it must also shelter the non Judeo–Christians, including atheists and agnostics. In any case, the task of teaching the Bible were better left to religious institutions, since the current practice of reading a few verses without comment in the morning does exercise pressure on the children of agnostics without even beginning to teach the Bible adequately to the children of believers. Jews who are opposed to Bible reading are therefore no more strongly so, nor for any different reasons, than many other people. The Lord's Prayer, however, is another matter entirely; it is a specifically

Christian prayer, and its recitation in the schools is clearly a sectarian practice to which all Jews without exception are adamantly opposed.

So much of the church–state controversy revolves around the schools for the obvious reason that, more than any other institution, it is the schools that shape our culture. For the vast majority of Jews the public school is the object of a primary, tacit commitment; it is the first and foremost institution for their integration into America. Jews are thus perhaps the strongest defenders of public education. Arguments about whether the public school is secular or secularist (it is in truth neither) are irrelevant. American intellectual and civic tradition exerts its influence as much through the general atmosphere of the school as through specific teachings. Everyone is today committed to pluralism, but do we want a completely fragmented America? That which pulls our diversities together into a viable common society—call it Americanism or Americanness—is largely, the creation of the one place where most Americans do spend a crucial part of their lives together. If parochial, or class-determined, private schools were to become the norm for America, we would be going a long step toward erecting a society of coexisting ghettos. This is not to say that some parochial education will not, and should not, continue to exist, but it must not, in most Jewish views, become the dominant or even the equal educational form.

Discussions of religion and culture these days tend to dwell largely on the questions which separate the various religious denominations in America, and we tend to overlook how very much they have in common in the realm of social policy. No major religious group in America is racist; all are devoted to a democratic order in politics; and all their pronouncements on social justice are indistinguishable from one another. It is, then, far easier to achieve consensus in action than in thought or even in prayer. This fact goes with the very nature of the American tradition, with its tentativeness and its emphasis on the needs of the day. Perhaps the only phrase that adequately describes the complicated pattern into which American tradition, law, and religion have become interwoven is "not quite." Religion is neither established nor completely disestablished in America. There is separation of church and state, but it is not absolute. Nothing seems clearer than that there is a body of specifically American attitudes that have to some extent reshaped religious denominational life, but this body of attitudes is neither doctrinaire nor is there complete agreement about its precise nature. Jewish life in America can also be characterized as "not quite." Certainly Jews here are no longer in exile by any traditional definition of that term; but neither are they co-founders of American culture. In most things they are "just like everybody else"; in some, they are uniquely different.

The founding fathers have, in the first amendment, given Americans not a dogma but a clue, a clue to how to live with such complications as we all now face in an undogmatic way: standing separately for various truths, standing together for the peace of society, and delicately avoiding that which is hateful to any of us. These are the terms of the "bargain" that the Jews are willing to strike as one of the "minorities in a pluralistic culture."

17. Changing Race Relations and Jewish Communal Service

IT REQUIRES NO great moral courage to assert, and even to mean, that every American who lays claim to personal decency must be involved in the struggle for the equality of the Negro. "Thou shalt not stand by the blood of thy brother" has been the law for Jews from the very beginning of our history. Amos told us almost three thousand years ago that in God's eyes we are no different from the children of the Ethiopians. Anyone rooted in this outlook is

---

Keynote address at New York Area Conference of Jewish Communal Workers, February 1964, printed in *Journal of Jewish Communal Service,* vol. 41, no. 4 (Summer 1965).

forbidden to walk away in unconcern from segregated schools, slum housing, inequality of job opportunity, and the whole host of other problems which accompany the immoral thing that is segregation. Speaking only for myself, I have acted on the assumption that the task of a rabbi is not only to preach abstractly against segregation but to involve himself concretely in the realities of the battle and to lead those whom he can influence toward comparable action.

On the surface, therefore, the question of Negro–Jewish relations, and of the responsibility of the organized Jewish community toward the Negro struggle, would seem to be very simple. The moral position is clear: segregation is immoral and abhorrent to Judaism. It is prejudice against a minority, and Jews have a clear, and even a self-serving, interest in eradicating any such prejudice in whatever form it may manifest itself. What follows from these principles in the minds of many Jews is, therefore, that the present task of the Jewish community is to devote its major attention to the problem of segregation. Internally, it must make absolutely sure that not a single Jewish institution practices any form of segregation, either in its hiring policies or in the availability of its services and programs to people of all creeds and races. The mandate of this generation, in the light of the acuteness of the problem of race in American society, is for Jews to be in the forefront in the solution of the problem.

This position has many virtues. It is clear-cut; it is contemporary because it ranges Jews on the moral side of the most important domestic barricade; and it is certainly correct as a statement of what Jews ought to think in relation to the moral issues. Nonetheless, it is only a partial truth. To call it into question runs the risk that he who would do so will forthwith be accused of dragging his feet on segregation. In liberal circles to be anything less than vocally doctrinaire is to be open to the charge that one is an "Uncle Tom"—and to be called a white "Uncle Tom" is perhaps even more devastating than being a Negro "Uncle Tom." Nonetheless, this danger must be risked, and precisely for the sake of a true and realistic Negro–Jewish understanding.

There is more, much more, to this question than the moralizing simplicity of what now seems to be the conventional view. Its partial truth, presented to the Jewish community as an exclusive commandment, tends to confuse Jews because they remain with the uneasy feeling that there is something more to their Jewish needs than to make of the content of their community an organization of Jews who are involved, out of some Jewish motivation to be sure, in the struggle for civil rights. Indeed, for Jews this question goes down to the very root of the meaning of Jewish identity, both personal and communal. Our policy in this generation toward the Negro struggle bears relation to how Jewish identity was defined in the most immediate previous generations, when prejudice was more directly our personal enemy. Even then the question was asked repeatedly: Are the Jews in existence today essentially as an association of those opposed to prejudice, i.e., to begin with, anti-Semitism? Is this the principle of unity?

This notion too—that Jewish identity in the modern age, in its lowest common denominator, is created by the fact that all Jews share in the woe of being a minority—is in itself appealing as an analytic concept. It solves several problems.

In the first place it avoids entirely the single most insoluble problem confronting the Jew in modern times, the question of defining his own identity in positive terms. In the modern age this has become the question for warring ideologies and, clearly, no one of their doctrines—not even religion, even in the broadest sense—can be offered as a definition of their identity on which all Jews can unite. The battle against exclusion of Jews by the world is thus not merely a fact which affects all kinds and conditions of Jews, even those who would rather not be Jews at all. It serves the function of helping pragmatically to create a Jewish community in which the broadest spectrum of Jews, shading off into the most peripherally involved, can work together against the common enemy.

In the second place such a conception of the Jewish community has further virtue, in an age which disbelieves in abstractions and is biased in favor of concrete facts, that it makes the common enterprise of all Jews today something tangible, fighting anti-Semitism, in the place of the common enterprise of their medieval ancestors, worshipping God. A Jewish community whose ultimate Jewish business is defense can perform its task through the most contemporary tools of research, public relations, and political action. In the very act of doing this, it may speak of anti-Semitism (indeed, in the logic of its stance, it must) as a relic of earlier bigotries, but the mode of fighting this relic creates among those engaged in it a feeling of contemporaneity far beyond that which is available in any other sector of Jewish life. The "positive Jews" are not merely factionalized and often muddled in their thinking; they are almost all involved in one form or another of defending the past. The battle against anti-Semitism is not laden with such encumbrances.

The very immediacy of this battle against anti-Semitism makes it possible to use it, in the third place, as a vehicle for involving the Jewish community in wider social and political issues. This need not necessarily be so. There is a certain particularism, and even a lessening of one's own dignity, that is inevitably involved when a minority pleads with a majority not to hate it. Over and over again in the last century or so, in many countries, Jews have solved this problem by defining the battle against anti-Semitism as one part of a wider issue that involves not only them but all of society, of the war on all social maladjustments. The battle thus becomes in various forms part of a "popular front" in which the Jew is ranged by the side of many other forces. The very function of the organized Jewish community, on the lowest common denominator level, thus lends itself to being transformed into a seeming accidentally organized association of Jews met together to deal with problems of general import. On the immediate scene of America today the relationship of the Jew to the Negro problem can thus appear quite clear-cut: all Jews are involved in bigotry; it is clearly the business of the entire Jewish community; and bigotry is indivisible.

It is necessary at this point in the argument to underscore that I am not discussing now what there is of obvious truth in this construction. All Jews are indeed concerned with hatred directed against them and they must act intelligently to lessen it. Everyone is involved in the travail of the Negro. My present concern is, analytically, to understand the premises and assumptions on the bases of which such a program is being urged on the Jewish community as its major business, and the uses within Jewish communal thinking and feeling to which this notion is being put. The examination of the premises may perhaps show that this, too, is an ideology, a school of thought which is too simpleminded in its analysis of both the Jewish and the human situation, and that it is much too narrow as a program for action. It is a way of attempting to fill the void left by the evaporation of positive Jewish content within Jewry.

The sense of vacuum which has been created within the Jewish community by the twin processes of the eroding of faith and its becoming factionalized into faiths, i.e., into competing sects and ideologies and varying personal positions, has been solved not only through the battle against anti-Semitism, which is essentially negative, but also through a clear and positive value—Jewish philanthropy. During the last two centuries Jews who have been able to agree on nothing else have found it possible to construct a community in which all share equally, and as Jews, on the basis of an overarching responsibility for less fortunate Jews. As political action, in laboring for the removal of political and social pressures endangering unfortunate Jewish communities, this has engaged the attention of the very same Jewish leadership which has battled anti-Semitism wherever it has made an overt appearance. Jews have not only needed political defense. They have also needed help in the countries of their travail, or to emigrate from them to more fortunate places, or to settle down and to reach some secure station in their new abodes. The various competing ideologies have been offering doctrinaire solutions (e.g., Zionism) to the whole complex of problems which has made the last century the great century of Jewish mass migration, but even this ideology has never swept the world Jewish community. Potent forces have been willing to cooperate with Zionism only to the degree to which an unideological commitment to helping other Jews, wherever they are or might choose to go, would permit such non-Zionists to help in the name of charity.

On American shores this thinking has created communities in every center of Jewish life whose largest joint endeavors are in charity. Federations, welfare funds, and the greatest of the overseas efforts, the United Jewish Appeal, are not the outgrowth of an organized Jewish community. On the American Jewish scene they have acted to create community councils and to engender the cooperation of all the various segments of Jewry, but it is historically true that they were not the creations of such a community.

As a principle of Jewish unity charity is subject to the same processes which apply to the battle against anti-Semitism. The processes are, indeed, already well advanced in the case of those of our charity federations whose purpose is to act on the local American scene. There is classic Jewish warrant for the idea that charity is indivisible, i.e., that we must take care of the poor who present themselves to us without regard to race, creed, or color, but what has been happening has not been primarily rooted in a growing passion for this prophetic idea. The rapid rise of the Jewish community to economic affluence had decreased its own immediate needs; those services that remain, such as family counseling, have become less and less specifically Jewish as the Jewish family itself has become more like all other middle-class American familites, both in its problems and in its aspirations. Our Jewish charitable agencies have therefore been becoming ever more nonsectarian in their clientele and even increasingly nonsectarian in their staffs. Charity, the very factor in Jewish life which began as an overarching form of Jewish identification and of Jewish separatism ("we take care of our own") is now itself becoming something else. It is increasingly a way of saying, at least on the American scene, that the Jews have an involvement in, that they are indeed motivated by some flavor of their own ancient tradition and of their earlier experience of poverty to doing social service work on the general scene. In this image the Jewish community becomes increasingly an accidental association of Jews who are met together to do things that are but one sector of the kind of things that all decent people are, or should be, doing. Like anti-Semitism, charity, which was imagined as a last bastion of Jewish particularism, is thus shading off into an activity which inevitably acts to dissolve the specific Jewish community.

At this point in the discussion the question of value must inevitably intrude. There are those who regard such a process of decent evaporation of Jewish particularism as good. For it to be happening under the aegis, in part, of Jewish agencies which allow some remaining play for the ever more private and subtle residual Jewish emotions of individuals is a useful and honorable thing, for it involves the Jewish community in making an important contribution to the wider democratic society which it is hoped is being born. From this point of view any attempt to brake the process in the name of any emphatic Jewish particularism is wrong on two counts: such effort is, in the first place, trying to make Jews of today accept and act on emotions and ideas which are no longer there; in the second place such particularistic effort is a locking of the door to some degree on non-Jews, and even perhaps on their misery. To do this, it is held, is both immoral and anti-democratic. Those people who are firmly entrenched in such an outlook can, in candor, only be made uncomfortable and perhaps angry by reading further, because the rest of what I have to say will be based on the implications of a different set of premises.

To safeguard any particular identity is not in itself an affront to other people. It was demonstrated very early in modern history, at the very height of the French Revolution, that democracy itself can become a form of totalitarianism. Those who did not conform to the "religion of reason," which was supposed to be good for all citizens, were persecuted in the 1790s as lacking in civic spirit. There and elsewhere, later, any simpleminded view of society which imagines it to be composed only of individuals has generally been the preamble to the creation not of freedom but of mobocracy. In France or in Bolshevik Russia those who resisted such leveling became the enemy. A democratic order does indeed require a considerable refashioning of identities so that people may live in peace with one another. Such refashioning cannot, however, itself become a substitute absolute; otherwise we are exchanging one tyranny for another. Freedom itself is not an absolute, because the utter absence of social restraint can lead only to anarchy and to the rule of the strongest.

We understand that the seemingly unideological and pragmatic description of the Jewish community which undergirds the outlook of those whose Jewish concerns are expressed by the battle against bigotry and by charity is in itself an ideology and a value judgment. It is indeed true that these two enterprises are of particular moment to Jews in their own specific experience, and that they do indeed transcend Jewish individual private concerns to evoke "community," in the most basic sense of shared involvement. Such assertions do not, however, merely include; they also exclude. Clearly, such a stance announces that the Jewish religion has no comparable place as a creator of contemporary community, for it is much too personalized today. Comparably, it asserts that Jewish education is of concern, in all its varieties, or of unconcern, to fractions of the community, but not really to all of it.

What is presumed here is a premise that has never been demonstrated and which, by now, the facts clearly belie. It is that there is less variation among Jews in emotion and commitment to fighting together or giving together than there is toward praying together, living together, or studying together.

Parenthetically, the present drift toward generalizing the battle against anti-Semitism into a wider battle for a more liberal world is not a new phenomenon. Ever since the dawn of modernity advanced Jewish intellectuals have joined revolutionary movements in order to remake the world, hoping thereby to help solve the Jewish problem. The involvement of Jews in general philanthropy is also an older phenomenon. In short, this notion—that Jews can solve their own problems best in a wider framework—has existed for many decades. What is new is that it is now being taught not by Jews in general movements of political and social advance who are outside the community, but by many of the very leaders of the in-group.

The spectrum of Jewish opinion about battling anti-Semitism has thus varied from those like Trotsky who have preferred to do away with it through the social revolution to those within the community who have accepted it passively as a continuing curse about which Jews can do nothing. These stances are no less varied than is present in relation to religion, which ranges from Orthodox Judaism of the ghetto to the feeling that the whole of the Jewish tradition is dead. The fact that the Jewish community has imagined that there is less variation of opinion about anti-Semitism than about religion is based on no demonstrated truth. Its only claim to reality is that the processes of assimilation have always worked first on Jewish faith and practice. Usually a generation or so later they have decomposed the seeming solidarity of the residual community which is based on Jewish defensiveness. Anti-Semitism and charity as factors of Jewish unity are a time lag, the mark of the second generation which is postreligious, but these as principles of Jewish unity are as much a result of the momentum of the positive tradition as are the remaining feelings about Jewish religion and Jewish education. Personalized as all these feelings become in the next generation, they cease to act to form community and they are indeed used as its enemy. They exist only as passing phenomena, as the wake of the positive community that once was.

We are now at the nub of the issue—Is the primary purpose of the Jewish community to help itself disappear, or is it to help itself survive? What is the meaning of that survival?

It is easy to opt for Jewish survival in the name of some specific ideology. Such Jewish positions in the modern age have usually been a form of either religion or nationalism. As we have seen, all these schools of thought suffer from being factions, and none of them can be presented to a substantial majority of Jews as their contemporary *raison d'être*. There is, nonetheless, an underlying substratum of affirmation which is indeed a lowest common denominator on which the bulk of the Jewish community can and does stand.

The intellectual tradition which we have inherited from the Jewish past is common to us all. This too can be, and has been, generalized by some into the notion that Jews are predisposed to intellectual pursuits in general, and therefore that any cultural endeavor is in some subtle sense "Jewish," for it reflects a long-standing Jewish trend. It is also argued that what is significant in Jewish creativity now belongs to the common heritage of Western man, and that if it does not yet do so completely, it is our duty to complete the process of translating it and of contributing it to the common possession of all men. Between the two poles of ideological defense of the tradition, in the name of some factional position and of the desire to assimilate even it into some wider cultural syncretism, there is a feeling which pervades the Jewish community at least as much as its concern about charity or about its own defense. It is the conviction that Jews stand in particular relationship to Jewish learning, and that the transmission of that learning is important.

There is further conviction that the apartness of the Jewish community as a social institution should continue to be maintained. In the first instance, of course, this means that in their overwhelming majority Jewish families feel very strongly that their children should marry other Jews. They look to all the various institutions created by Jews to serve the purpose of cultivating a considerable and a deep sense of particular ease and comfort, a sense of personal sharing, that is specific to Jews in each other's company. This is balanced by another commitment with which it lives in tension, the desire of the average Jew to be at home and completely accepted in the larger American society. For the most part he tries to achieve that second sense through his involvement in American life as a whole in the public schools, through politics, and through all the other ways in which he can meet other people as an individual citizen. He looks to the agencies of the Jewish community primarily to provide him with a specifically Jewish counterpull.

For the Jewish individual, the place where he balances between his Jewish and his general Western identity is within himself, and not in the program of a Jewish agency. The task of the agencies is not to be nonsectarian, while he is left within their confines to his own highly personal inner Jewish resources. It is their task to be "Jewish," i.e., to help provide him with those particularist inner resources which he can use in the arena within which he must work out his destiny as a person, to be a Jew in the larger American society. A Jewish community which does not make it its primary business to provide the individual Jew at the very least with a basic Jewish education, both formal and informal, and with a deep sense of rootedness in the Jewish group—a community which regards that as the private affair of the individual Jew and makes its public business into providing him with nonsectarian programs and nonsectarian company—is guilty on two counts. It gives him less than he needs and wants of the sense of his own Jewish particularity. Moreover, it tries to do within the confines of the Jewish community that which he is doing, and ought to be doing, where it really counts, i.e., it provides the Jewish community as the place for the Jewish–Gentile encounter rather than American society as a whole. There may be some justification for the notion that some of this ought to be done as a sort of training, especially of the young within Jewish institutions, but to make this the primary content of agencies such as the Jewish Community Centers and summer camps is, from the prospective of this argument, both wrong and disastrous. I, for one, can explain it only on two presumptions: that those fostering such a policy really prefer the assimilation of Jews and their commitment to leadership in Jewish institutional life is a corollary to one of Parkinson's laws: institutions exist, and jobs in them multiply, even when neither the jobholders nor even the leaders are any longer committed to the value and purposes of the agencies.

This analysis of the pervading emotions of the contemporary Jewish community has shown, so far, that there are really not two but four factors which combine to make an unideological, pervasive set of concerns. It cannot be emphasized strongly enough that the mass of those who are associated in any real sense with continuing the enterprise of a Jewish community are as widely committed to Jewish education and to some amount of conscious self-ghettoization as they are to charity and to the battle against prejudice. The vast majority of Jews, who are neither assimilationists nor in the Williamsburg ghetto by choice, reflect all four concerns.

What, then, is the difference? It is in the fact that Jewish education and the social community of Jews are factors of apartness and the concern about them commands that for such purposes the Jew abstract himself from his neighbors and remind himself of his past. The other two concerns act to involve the Jew in his neighbors and, at least by implication, they help throw off the burden of his past. This second stance is the high road to assimilation; the meaning of the first is to erect the barricade against it.

In the light of what has been said already about contemporary Jewish attitudes, there is, therefore, a crucial difference between the Jewish and the Negro communities. The contemporary Negro, in all his varieties, is interested in the whole complex of activities which in Jewish context have created the ongoing battles against bigotry and the effort for philanthropy. Every Negro, from the most conservative to the most radical, cares that the excess of human misery which is to be found in his community be lessened by every effective means, from philanthropy to political action, and that it ultimately should vanish. There cannot be a single Negro in

America who is uninvolved, at least in his heart, in the battle against prejudice which is stunting so many millions of Negro lives. To be sure there are fringe groups like the Black Muslims whose program in response to these problems is not the effort to integrate the Negro into American society but rather to separate him further from it. Nonetheless, it cannot be doubted that, even more than among the Jews, the pervading view among the Negroes is that they must fight their way into American society.

The crucial difference between these two groups is on the issue of their particularisms. There is some, and perhaps even a growing, amount of feeling in Negro circles that there is a positive and distinctive Negro culture, and that it is a necessary function of the Negro community to foster it. This is as yet not the dominant view. The total stance of the Negro community is in the other direction, toward the assertion that the Negro has no culture other than the general American one and that whatever pertains specifically to him as a Negro will and should disappear in some future generation which will be color-blind. Certainly, there is no religious or cultural argument within the Negro community against intermarriage. We are, therefore, in Negro–Jewish relations, confronted by two communities which share some purposes but diverge on others.

It is not even true that the Jewish and the Negro interest in bigotry and in human misery are completely identical. In the face of the misery of the Negro masses the Jew does not sit beside him as a fellow sufferer. He is, on the contrary, today economically part of the wealthier elements of white America. Regardless of how Jews may feel on spiritual or ideological grounds, the facts are that from the Negro perspective the slogan "I want what you've got" includes the Jew as one of the "haves." Indeed, it very often means the Jew in the first instance, because the neighborhoods and even the economic positions to which Negroes aspire have often last been occupied by Jews.

For that matter, both the prejudice of the Jew which battles against the Negro advance and his liberalism which associates him in the effort to aid it are forms through which the Jew effects for himself further entry into the white majority. In the satanic complexity of human affairs, the southern Jew who is conservative on race is today more useful to the white leadership than ever before.

Certainly one by-product of official Jewish support for the Negro cause has been to create among Jews involved in the struggle a greater sense of identity and camaraderie with important segments of Christian religious and civic circles. From the perspective of one observer the Jew acts more nearly as part of the white majority today because the Negro problem is acting to cement him within it, and Jews are not unaware of how very much more "American" they are therefore becoming.

On the other hand, the Jewish–Negro encounter today, in the arena of hard economic realities, is evoking an amount of struggle and tension which is beyond the general tensions that exist between Negroes and whites. There is undoubtedly a perceptible amount of specifically Negro anti-Semitism. Whatever its economic causes, its existence owes something to a factor that is seldom discussed. Through anti-Semitism, which is so much the underside of the Western cultural tradition as a whole, some Negroes can, at least on this level, associate themselves with the majority in its immemorial hatred of the Jew.

In sum, the Negro is deprived but is by common consent culturally an insider in our society; the Jew is not deprived, but more than something remains of his being outside the mainstream of Western society and culture—and some of that apartness he continues to will and to want to preserve.

What then can be the nature of Negro–Jewish relations today?

In the first place, the Jewish community must, of course, lend its weight to every area of the battle for Negro rights and to every aspect of the concern for Negro misery. There can be no doubt that all Jewish philanthropic agencies, such as hopsitals and case-work agencies, are obligated to serve all people, without distinction.

Second, the Jewish community has a duty to regard Negro leadership as accountable for any anti-Semitism that prevails within that community. Our awareness of the enormous pools of deprivation which feed it is no argument for excusing it. It is not at all self-evident that the Negro in America today is corporately worse off than the peasants and workers of Czarist Russia. It is demonstrable that the Jewish petite bourgeoisie of that time and place, because of their own unfortunate situation, were much more directly hurtful to the poorest elements in western Russia than

Jews are to Negroes in the Harlems of today's America. Anti-Semitism is no more forgivable in America in 1964 than in Russia in 1881.

In the third place, the Jewish community has an obligation to find areas of association for Jews which by their very nature are particularist. Those institutions and organizations, such as community centers and summer camps, which are intended to serve the purpose of providing Jewish social and cultural ties of the broadest kind should continue to do so and should forthrightly emphasize the Jewish nature of their program. We should not permit a cycle of evaporation of their content, which proceeds from nonsectarian program to nonsectarian membership to the total evaporation of Jewish specificness, so that these institutions then become neighborhood centers or camps financed by Jews for everybody. There are indeed such needs in the community, and Jews ought to participate in them handsomely, but they should do so together with other people in truly nonsectarian and integrated institutions. This should not be done in the name of democratic platitudes whose effect is to dismantle specifically Jewish institutions. A corollary of this emphasis is the notion that institutions of the kind in question cannot be "Jewish" simply by 'closed membership; they must pay far greater attention to the Jewish nature of their program.

In the fourth place, I believe that the day of the Jewish-financed organization representing the Jewish community in the civil rights field, despite all the seeming verve of the moment, is soon to come to an end. Many Jews with primary commitments in the field of civil rights have gone and are going outside the structure of the Jewish community into general organizations. Our major Jewish organizations, which have presently taken up this battle as almost their sole contemporary reason for being, are engaged in committing their own institutional suicide. Those who are converted by them to this point of view will inevitably soon leave them. Therefore, we owe an obligation to say to ourselves and the Negro community that, from the Negro perspective, civil rights is indeed *the* problem; for Jews, from their own perspective, it is one of several problems. It certainly does not outrank *for them* the question of their own spiritual and cultural survival in America, or their concern for the rest of world Jewry. Those Jews who do not assent in general to such a sense of balance are in various stages of leaving the Jewish community. They are perhaps better individual allies for the Negro, but no matter how prominent they may be in Jewish affairs at the moment, such Jews are, as Jews, essentially marginal.

In the fifth place, there will inevitably have to be a division of labor among the institutions which are presently financed by the Jewish community. Those which chose to involve the Jew as an individual citizen in activities like nonsectarian philanthropy and the political and civil rights arena will have to transform themselves into avowedly public institutions, to be directed and financed by a broad spectrum taken from the American people. There is no reason why some of our present Jewish agencies should not appoint white and Negro Christians to their boards and appeal to such circles for financial support. In the negative sense this would mean the end of any shadow of an unspoken presumption that these agencies have some specific "Jewish" purpose which can be imagined as a kind of lowest common denominator Jewish survivalism. From a different perspective it seems to me to be morally wrong to conduct an agency that is interracial and nonsectarian in its staff and clientele and insist in effect that its board be Jewish. There is something of the lady bountiful in this approach. Both Jewish and nonsectarian imperatives would dictate the end of such anomalies.

In the sixth place, those agencies which remain in the specifically Jewish field will owe two kinds of responsibility. It will be their obligation to transform their program in the areas of culture and education so that they are consciously and clearly calculated to increase Jewish knowledge and commitment. Part of their task in character training will be, of course, to produce for society as a whole the kind of people who are motivated, from Jewish sources, to band together with others in the general struggle for a better and more just society. Like every other tradition it is incumbent upon those who speak as Jews to be good citizens. I must, however, again repeat the caution that that is but one aspect of Jewish identity and not the whole of it.

The Negro is today fighting for his rights, and Jews, along with all other men of goodwill, must certainly stand beside him. But Jews are today also continuing to work at preserving and trying to define the meaning of their particular survival and identity in the light of their own tradition and historic experience. Since this is a parochial concern of their own, they must here stand alone.

Our age does not like aloneness; it seems to prefer togetherness on every level. But any serious Jewishness must live in tension between that which unites it with others even in the most moral of struggles and that which sets it uniquely apart.

18. On Negro–Jewish Relations

THERE IS A STORY of Chelm, the mythological village populated by idiots, the wise men of which are notorious in Jewish folklore for always getting things quite wrong, with great deliberation. Having heard of the great European city, capital of all culture, Paris, the wise men of Chelm sent a delegation of two of their number to Paris to bring them back a report. On their return the two emissaries were heard separately, ancient Talmudic principles of the taking of evidence providing that one witness cannot listen to the other. Their accounts were widely divergent, one reporting a city of synagogues and houses of study where venerable Jews sat and meditated on the Talmud; the other, a scandalous city of ribaldry and moral abandon. The wise men of Chelm, failing to harmonize these accounts, concluded that Paris was indeed both cities; it depended on who went looking for what.

I am confronted with a somewhat similar problem. The Brook-

Speech delivered at a panel discussion on Negro–Jewish relations at the Annual Plenum of the National Jewish Community Relations Advisory Council, Washington, June 20, 1973.

lyn that I know and the community within which Bayard Rustin has found the angers stilling and the confrontation politics lessening cannot really be the very same place; or perhaps both are.

I don't know much about the black community, and generally most Jews don't. I understand the black community, I think, as well as any outsider can understand an inside. With very few exceptions—Bayard Rustin being one—people who are not within the Jewish community—within its history, within its feeling tone— simply don't understand it from within. And I think the same is true in relation to the black community. And so I don't want to talk about blacks. I want to talk about Jews.

My credentials as a liberal, integrationist, civil libertarian Jew are good enough to get me invited to this platform; but I refused to march in Selma. At the Rabbinical Assembly convention the night of Selma a plane was chartered and nineteen of my colleagues climbed aboard. I said, "No, I'm going home to Englewood, New Jersey, where the community is 25 percent black; that's where my problems are. It's easier to march in Selma, Alabama, than to integrate the schools in Englewood, New Jersey." The Englewood schools were among the first northern school systems to be integrated, and that integration has stuck—with certain problems that are quite indicative of "where it really is at" in relationship to the Jewish community.

Up to 1966, as Bayard Rustin has said, support of civil rights meant largely the fervid affirmation of moral principle and minimal personal confrontation or involvement. The practical issues—poll taxes, busing, school segregation, etc.—were in the South. Since it has come to the question of changing neighborhoods in the North, it is interesting to note that those parts of the Jewish community that have remained most steadfastly opposed to such change are those that have not moved to surburbia, exurbia, or the high rises and have not sent their children to private schools. In Englewood, New Jersey, where I am rabbi of the Conservative synagogue, the liberal rhetoric of the older kind is heard in various neighborhoods in inverse proportion to the immediacy of integration in those neighborhoods.

There are several Jewish communities. There is the community I have just described. There is the ideological community to which most of us belong, which is ideologically committed to every facet of social advance, and certainly to black advance, for a wide variety of reasons. There is, however, an irreducible community, mostly in the big cities and preeminently in New York, which for economic reasons must make Canarsie its Custer's Last Stand. The typical Canarsie-ite is a white ethnic Jew (or Italian) who bought himself a house on one bounce from Bedford-Stuy, is paying for it with his second mortgage, and hasn't the option to buy a $65,000 house (which is the cheapest he could buy in Englewood, N.J., right now).

These people must face the reality of ethnic, black–white, Jewish–black confrontation; there is no escape for them either geographical or rhetorical; they are locked into their situations—in Canarsie for economic reasons, in Forest Hills for cultural reasons, on the Upper West Side of Manhattan for more subtle reasons.

Forest Hills is a Queens Orthodox Jewish ghetto, as the Lubavitchers' enclave is a kind of *shtetl;* the Upper West Side is a kind of *shtetl* of Jewish intelligentsia which has now produced its own right-wing ideology. The Jewish "establishment"—all of us, not only the national agencies, but particularly the community representatives—does not speak, really, out of rootings in the Jewish poor, of those who must confront the changing neighborhood and stay there, who cannot confront it by getting out. We are not really speaking for a Jewish community anymore, as perhaps we could in an earlier time when we could sing "We Shall Overcome," black and white together, in Selma, Alabama, and fly back to our quasi-private public schools in Tenafly, New Jersey, or in Scarsdale. We are in a different life situation now, and we are grappling with it with very indifferent success.

I think we have been going in several wrong directions. We have been trying to solve these questions ideologically. We have been moralizing. We have been hurling slogans at each other—among them, the slogan of prophetic universalism. Let me say something about that as a card-carrying rabbi, my primary identity: the prophets believed in the law and not merely in universal morality; they were sufficiently nationalistic and ethnic, all of them, to believe in the return to the soil of the Holy Land; they had a very refined and very precise sense of political and social reality. Isaiah did not shrink from suggesting the possibility of alliances of the Jews with Egypt or with Assyria. Similar examples could be multiplied. Prophets—and rabbis (especially rabbis)—don't engage in ideological verbiage but deal with specific cases and specific situations and use their best wisdom and insight to settle the problem before the house—and to settle it for that day, on the notion that it may change in a year or two.

Now, over against the ideologues and moralists are the Jewish powerniks: "good for Jews" or "bad for Jews." I think the very first thing that we have to get through our heads is that "good for Jews" or "bad for Jews" is not merely the politics of narrow self-interest. The worst thing for Jews would be American revolution; the best thing for Jews is ongoing reform. Bayard Rustin holds to the Socialist doctrine that the right kind of social revolution which abolishes poverty for all people will somehow solve or obviate all other social problems. I am not all that hopeful. Maybe that's because I am a Jew.

Many years ago Bayard Rustin lectured at the Jewish Theological Seminary, and afterward I said to him: "Mr. Rustin, take out the word 'Negro' but put in 'Jew' and everything you said will read like Zionist literature." A Zionist writer back in the 1880s, just after the pogroms, commented that those who believed that the Jewish problem would be solved through an adequate social revolution were mistaken. The Jews start too far behind, he wrote, and they are, in Russia, a peculiar and very particular problem.

I don't think that social revolution will immediately solve all the problems we are talking about. I am the kind of New Dealer who believes that radical and ongoing reform, ongoing tinkering with the society, is what is best for all the dispossessed, and for all of those who are in danger.

A fragmented society is not good for Jews. We don't want Watts, of course; but also we don't want Lebanon. The single most unfortunate utterance Mr. McGovern made in last year's campaign was that if elected he would appoint one black cabinet member. The America that I grew up in—or hoped that I was growing up in—does not designate a seat on the Supreme Court as Jewish or a seat in the cabinet as black or allocate 8 percent of jet pilots' jobs to blacks and 42 percent to women, etc., etc. Whatever may be the gloss on affirmative action, merit, etc.—and one of the glosses happens to be that every effort must be made to provide the opportunity for those who have been kept out of the mainstream to get into it—we certainly cannot in the long run do away with the principle of individual merit. Whatever we may do right now—and we must do a great deal to bring people forward and up to that principle—we certainly cannot abandon it in the name of ethnicity.

Whatever their moral commitment—and I think we share a moral commitment to peace and justice in American society—people are moved in the long run and most successfully by what they perceive as their ongoing interests. The other day I asked the seventy students in my class in Jewish history at Columbia how many were in the least troubled in their academic careers, or anticipated any trouble, from the affirmative action program. Among those children of the well-connected not a single one raised his hand. I asked the same question at Brooklyn College the same week, and a majority raised their hands. Right or wrong, that's what they feel. We must deal with that feeling. We in the Jewish end of the civil rights movement, whatever our view of the new Jewish ethnics, must get back among them, include them in our consensus, and talk them out of some of the things that they are doing. If we cannot speak *for* them, let us at least speak *to* them—to persuade them that twenty or twenty-five million angry blacks will certainly not go away; that Jewish power is not enough to contain their pressure; that repression is not the future of the country, and explosions are very bad for Jews; and that we must all join in working for an expanded system with expanded opportunities.

I know, I offer small comfort, not even any ringing declarations. I can only say that at this moment in time the Jewish community is obligated at least to talk to itself and within itself on the broadest possible basis. That's the first thing. We must talk to all its wings. We must try somehow or other to carry as much of the Jewish community as we can into the actual practical labors of making a very complex society move forward. We can deal with specific problems and somehow or other make our principles—

which are sometimes contradictory when taken to their logical conclusions—yield some practical guidance. And we can hope that if we keep tinkering with the society, keep bringing more resources to play, keep putting more people together, keep bringing more elements within the society forward, then perhaps we can escape the explosion.

Let me end in a very odd way. Herman Hickman, you may remember, was a Tennessee mountain boy. Herman Hickman came from Knoxville and had been at the University of Tennessee. They brought him to Yale to be the football coach after several disastrous seasons. Somebody asked him how well he expected to do as the coach and his answer was that he expected to do well enough to keep the alumni sullen but not mutinous. My feeling is that if we can succeed together well enough to keep the country from being mutinous, if we can simply contain it and let it knit itself together, if we can do the job of healing and of reason and of wisdom, if we can pronounce fewer jihads and do more specific tasks of building—then I think we will have done the greatest and the single most necessary thing that there is.

ISRAEL AND AMERICA

19. Is the Jew in Exile?

FOR THE LAST TWO centuries, as Jews have been entering the life
of Western society, they have wanted two antithetical things: to
be like everybody else, and to be quite different. Each of these desires has in its turn given birth to a swear word in the Jewish lexi-
con: "assimilation." This word is in such bad odor today that it
has had to be replaced among Jews by a blander and more academic term, "acculturation." Leading theorists in contemporary
American sociology have been laboring to define a difference between these two concepts, but Jews have shifted from one term to
the other for reasons not to be found in the writings of the scholars. Those who are for "acculturation" regard themselves, unlike
the classic assimilationists, as "positive Jews." In actual practice
this means that they would like to be culturally and spiritually just
like everybody else, but they want to bar the door to intermarriage.

On the other hand, it is almost equally daring and even offensive to say to Jews in Western countries, and particularly in America, that they are in a *galut,* i.e., exile. The presumption of Israeli
leaders, headed by the most redoubtable of them all, David Ben-
Gurion, in maintaining this point, has led to notable and bitter interchanges between him and various American Jews. Even American Zionist leaders of the front rank have joined in expressing

Reprinted from A. E. Millgram, ed., *Great Jewish Ideas* (B'nai B'rith,
1964).

outrage at such a presumption. This estimate of the condition of the Jew outside of Israel denies the great dream of a new liberal world in which the Jews participate as equals. Did not our ancestors come to America in order to experience that which could be found "only in America," the blessedness of enjoying a society of "Americans all"? For anyone to say to American Jews that they are in any sense in exile, therefore, means to many of his hearers that he is calling the American experience a self-delusion. That they react with anger to so threatening a thought is understandable.

The life of the Jew in democratic society is, therefore, characterized by a paradox. Wanting to be just like everybody else, he devotes himself to battering down every wall of exclusion erected against him. Once all the walls, or most of them, begin to fall, he refuses to accept the implications of such events in the lessening of family and communal ties. The uniqueness of the Jew is thus not merely a creation of the exclusion that is directed against him. When it is gone he continues to stand somewhat apart from society, by choice. The real question is not whether this is true as a fact, for that needs no demonstration. What needs to be discussed is the meaning of this stance.

"Exile" and "assimilation" are both words that describe a relation. In this case it is the relation between a majority and one specific minority. Whether the Jews can and ought to assimilate, or whether they are in exile, cannot be considered in terms only of Jewish will and Jewish needs. We are inevitably involved in an estimate of what is America and in some projection of the probable future of American culture and society. Clearly the Jews who remain in Yemen are in exile. Most Jews believe that this is true at this very moment of the Jews in Russia. Certainly the American situation is different from both of these—but what *is* the American situation?

We can define four stages in the evolution of a new, twentieth-century vision of America—and each of these visions has been, revealingly, constructed largely by Jews. At the turn of the century in the midst of the last great wave of immigration, the accepted image of the country was that of a "melting pot"—the phrase is Israel Zangwill's; it was the title of a play in 1908 which was the forerunner of the more famous *Abie's Irish Rose*.

The enemies of Americanism were the hyphenated Americans, who were attacked by Theodore Roosevelt, among others, for continuing to cultivate in the new land loyalties which reached back into their pre-American past. In the stage of Americanization, of losing their blatant and hampering foreignness and of learning the language and manners of the country, most Jews participated in this vision. Several factors, however, acted to make it clear, and not entirely to Jews, that this definition of America was too narrow. Other groups, too, were made uncomfortable by a view of America that was really an extension of the self-image of the then-dominant white Anglo-Saxon Protestant community.

In part, disillusionment set in as it became apparent that even being melted down successfully did not guarantee one's acceptance, at least socially, by the oldest elements in America. A newer image of America was therefore suggested in the second decade of the century, and there, too, the thinker who defined the new concept was a distinguished Jew, Horace M. Kallen. He proposed the notion of cultural pluralism, i.e., a society within which there were to be subgroups, each of which would continue in some part of its life the heritage that it had brought with it. This was to include the language and culture of its ancestors and some considerable concern for the country of its origin. All of these groups would meet together in the larger dimension of American cultural and political life which they would share in common.

This theory of cultural pluralism has recently been refurbished by Nathan Glazer and Daniel P. Moynihan in a study of the minorities of New York City, *Beyond the Melting Pot*. These writers argue, quite convincingly, that not only the Negroes, and now the Puerto Ricans, but also the Jews and Irish continue to remain recognizably different communities, even into the third and fourth generations. The implication of this argument, perhaps even its concealed major premise, is that America is becoming a confederation of minorities whose behavior is comparable and can be explained on the same basis.

The vision of cultural pluralism had the merit, historically, of helping to turn the corner away from the presumption that what colonial America had been was, of right, the continuing rule of its existence. It emphasized that many cultures and several religions had gone into the making of America. It began the naturalization of cultural differences as valid on the American scene. It has not, however, succeeded in achieving its very patent "Jewish" purpose, to reorganize America in such fashion that all of its various communities would so live their lives that the Jews could, in the very act of being themselves, be just like everybody else. There are two keys to the failure: politics and culture. In both dimensions the Jews have acted uniquely and not like any of the other minorities.

During World War I there seemed, on the surface at least, to be a considerable similarity in political behavior among the minorities. Before 1917 the immigrants of German origin, for example, pressed for neutrality and, comparably, there was considerable pro-German sentiment in all divisions of American Jewry. Jews from Germany tended to be superpatriots of their old country; newer immigrants from Russia had little initial enthusiasm for the Allied cause because they detested the Czarist regime. Nonetheless, such similarity in conduct did not last. Pro-Germanism remained a political force in America into the 1930s; it has been demonstrated that Midwestern isolationism before America's entry into World War II was related to the German origins of a major segment of the population of that region. However, the contemporary heirs of such isolationist politics are not German-Americans of the third and fourth generation. Some have indeed, as individuals, disappeared into earlier American families and now form part of the human material to be found in the John Birch societies and comparable groups, but the tone of these groups is more nearly akin to the Daughters of the American Revolution. It came quite as a matter of course that the comanding general in America's war against Germany, Dwight D. Eisenhower, and several of his leading colleagues, were themselves of quite recent German origin. Any remaining loyalties to Germany to be found in the United States today would require those who have them to be internationalist in stance. There are no such German-American organized politics on the present scene.

The Irish in America are another case in point. There was considerable emotional involvement, and practical support as well, in the battle for freeing Ireland from the British. This played some role in American politics, especially during the Wilson years. The traditional hatred of the British predisposed Irish-Americans to neutrality in the early months of World War II. Ireland itself remained obstinately neutral throughout the war, but this was entirely irrelevant in America on the morning after Pearl Harbor. Some specific flavor remains to Roman Catholic politics, which means largely Irish Catholic politics, in contemporary America. This community is considerably more anti-Communist than any other group, but even this is lessening. The Vatican itself has been moving toward coexistence with the Russians. Within America the younger generation produced an intellectual and internationalist like John F. Kennedy rather than a local satrap like James J. Curley as the newest version of an Irish Catholic politician. It is fair to say that in "foreign policy" Irish Catholic politics are rapidly losing their uniqueness.

There are, to be sure, marginal elements of "foreign policy" in the ongoing struggle of the Negro. The identification with Africa and occasional expressions of Negro neutralism in the Cold War do betoken something of the anger of the Negro at his being kept apart in America, but these moods are secondary. The essence of the Negro revolt is in his unrelenting struggle for equality in education, jobs, and housing on the domestic scene. This is equally true of the Puerto Ricans. Puerto Rican nationalism does exist in America, but as in the case of the Black Muslims, each of these groups represents a far-out element, not the prevailing tone of opinion within the Negro or Puerto Rican communities.

Jewish politics are precisely in reverse. For themselves, on the domestic scene the Jews have no major bastions left to conquer. No one really cares much about the continued existence of social exclusion in country clubs and some of the town clubs. There is indeed some emotion about economic exclusion of Jews by some of the largest corporations. Despite the noise that is occasionally made about it, however, the economic profile of the contemporary Jewish community is such that these practices, though hateful, are not really very threatening. Bright young Jews, fresh out of college, can find many places in which to work, even if they are not allowed in any significant number into the bureaucracies of the public utilities. Since the Jews were a have-not group as recently as one generation ago, the memory of their travail and of the battle against it still influences Jewish political behavior to a general sympathy with the dispossessed. The Jews do remain predisposed to the Democratic party and to the politics of the New Deal, but Republican strength is slowly rising among them.

A comparable process is taking place before our very eyes on the issue of race. The top leadership and all the major organizations in the Jewish community are unequivocally enlisted on the Negro side. Many Jews are indeed still personally close enough to their own deprived past to sympathize. For appropriate leaders to demonstrate and sit in on behalf of the Negro, side by side with comparable dignitaries of the churches, is even in some minds one of the most positive forms of being "at home" in America. The taking of such action demonstrates that the Jews have really arrived at their own equality. For a variety of reasons it is therefore fair to say that despite certain unhappy economic encounters between Jews and Negroes, the Jews have been and still are more nearly pro-Negro, in action as well as pronouncement, than any other white group. Nonetheless, there is considerable evidence that this commitment is not absolute. On the local level, all Jewish institutions are not rushing to open their doors on an interracial basis—in large part, to be sure, because of their own concern for cultivating the integrity of Jewish identity as distinct not only from Negroes but from all other American Christians. In candor, it need be added that the Jewish masses appear to be moving toward a position on race less liberal than the views of their leaders and more akin to the outlook that is conventional in comparable segments of the Gentile community.

The processes of acculturation are thus eroding the distinctiveness of Jewish politics in domestic affairs. What remains of this element is not an expression of an existing need; it is sympathy. Jews no longer battle for social reform in their own name; they do it together with and generally for others. The fights the Jews continue to have with other Americans, the issues for which they hurry to Washington with delegations and for which they marshal their maximum resources for the persuasion of others, include the suffering of the Jews of Russia, an unceasing effort to liberalize American immigration policy and, above all, the defense of the State of Israel.

It is necessary, and even useful, to reemphasize here that other groups in America have before, and will again, put pressure on the rest of the country in the area of foreign policy to achieve results which are of more concern to themselves than to the majority. But the point here is that minorities in America (whether their motivation is ethnic or religious) have stayed in the political business, indeed in the business of being minorities, in the long run in order to fight their own immediate domestic battles. Thus the Germans as an organized group are well nigh gone because they have no such battles left to fight.

Irish Catholic behavior has so much in common with the Jewish that the difference between the two is particularly revealing for our present purpose. These two groups have recently been colliding semiovertly over liberalism (especially in the McCarthy years) and openly and directly over church and state. The key distinction between the two communities is, however, not in their disagreements but in the importance to each of its investment in these issues. The second is vital to the largely Irish-dominated Catholic community. It remains in the political arena because of one great domestic issue, parochial schools, which still divides it from others. It is fighting for tax support with the emotion of a group doing battle for something that it regards as essential to its survival in its own terms. The Jews have no comparable domestic concern, not even in ending prayers in the public schools, for they could have afforded the loss of that battle. The one battle that, in their own terms, they cannot ever lose is in "foreign affairs." American Jews may in the future cut loose from the rest of the Jewish world, but no one who knows them can doubt for a moment that this will be the surest sign that the American Jewish community is beginning to disappear. So long as there is a serious Jewish presence in America it will be marked by a continuing, unique kind of politics.

There is an equally striking difference between Jews and the other minorities in the area of culture. The grandchildren of the

Italians, the Slavs, and the rest have become completely assimilated culturally. Only the Chinese have made a serious attempt to teach their traditions, through supplementary education, to their descendants in America into the third and fourth generations. The other European immigrants of the last century have failed to provide Jews with parallels for their devotion to some continuity for their own subculture. To be sure, as Glazer and Moynihan have pointed out, there is still some specific socioeconomic and even intellectual flavor to several of the minorities, but all of them have translated themselves into variants of the American idiom. The nearest parallel is the Irish, in whose case, too, the memory of oppression, religious difference, and ethnic uniqueness have gone together. Nonetheless, even they have not labored to perpetuate Gaelic in the way that many Jews continue to fight for at least some Hebrew.

A new formula, therefore, needed to be found to naturalize what differentiated the Jew, and to find valid analogs for these differences on the American scene. In its turn, the Jewish third generation needed its vision of an America so explained as to make it comfortable. This was supplied, again, almost inevitably, by a Jewish writer, Will Herberg, in his famous book of a decade ago, *Protestant–Catholic–Jew*. Herberg propounded the thesis that regardless of their origins Americans had lost, or were in the process of losing, all cultural and political differences which were based on immigrant heritages. The only divisions among Americans that would be recognized as legitimate in the future were religious ones. The ultimate meaning of the changes that had been taking place in the last century is that America had ceased being a white Anglo-Saxon Protestant country, essentially by having broadened the definition of religion to include the three major faiths. Indeed, to be a good American means to be identifiable within one of the three communions.

From the Jewish point of view this definition has much positive merit. It surrounds the Jews with the aura of American respect for religion, in place of what remains of American distaste for "foreigners." As a religion this small minority is suddenly translated by this formula to the estate of one-third of America. Much of what Jews do corporately can be explained, to themselves and, more important, to others, as a natural expression of religion. Jewish supplementary education is easiest to define in these terms. It has in the last generation become almost entirely a function of the synagogue, and so nothing seems more obvious than that it is just like Christian education. Local federations of Jewish charities are presented as the peer group for Catholic and Protestant charities, and the United Jewish Appeal becomes the counterpart of Catholic and Protestant overseas endeavors. As we shall see, all these explanations are forced, but they can at least be made to work on the surface. What cannot be explained on this principle is the unideological but deep and patent concern of Jews for other Jews all over the world. A century ago Abraham Geiger, one of the founders of Reform Judaism in Germany, attempted an explanation of Jewish identity in that country that was comparable to Herberg's definition. It led him, by its inherent logic, to declare that he was much more interested in how many Jews were admitted as equals to the professions in Prussia than in the battle against pogroms in Russia. Geiger was among those who declared that Berlin was now his Jerusalem; so Herberg has recognized the inherent meaning of this stance by having turned ever more anti-Zionist in the years since the appearance of his book.

Jewish motivations and self-definitions are, however, less important than the estate of America as a whole. There is, indeed, considerable evidence for the presumption that America's definition of itself has been moving away from the identification of the country's official establishment with Protestantism. For example, in the last several inaugurations of presidents of the United States, rabbis have been participating in the greatest of state occasions along with Protestant divines and Catholic bishops. The famous victories of the last several years in the battle for the separation of church and school have also tended to confirm the idea that all religions are now on an equal footing. It can be said with considerable truth that before the national government Judaism is today the equal of the Christian denominations. This is less true in various local jurisdictions, especially in the South with its small Jewish population and its Bible-belt tradition where Protestant Christianity remains pretty much the state religion.

The real nub of the issue, however, is not in the relationship between Jews and Judaism and the state; it is in the estate of American society and culture, as distinct from the state. There can be no denying the proposition that American society, for all its secularization, is not neutral. It is Christian. For all the matters that are crucial to the actual experience of the individual Jew, as Jew, within America, the tempo of life as such has inevitably to favor Christianity and to act against Judaism.

We are by now so accustomed to this mode of living that it usually does not even occur to us to identify it for what it inevitably is, an experience of alienation. The day of rest is Sunday. No matter how successful we may be in getting some legal redress for Sabbath-observing Jews, as a matter of social experience the Jewish Sabbath costs every individual Jew who is mindful of it an act of will. The majority of Jewry has abandoned the Sabbath under pressure of its inconvenience in a society which is attuned against it. What is this if not a phenomenon of exile? Nor is this an economic compulsion, rooted in the need of the Jews to make a living. From the very beginning of public school, field trips, parties, dances, and football games all take place on Saturday as the most convenient time. The Jewish child either participates or abstains; in either case he experiences his radical otherness. For that matter much of the weight, or lack of weight, that is being given to Jewish holidays is related to the pressure of a majority culture. A prime example is, of course, Hanukkah, which has now become that which it was never intended to be, the Jewish equivalent of Christmas.

The distinction is therefore clear. It is possible for the Jew to maintain within our democracy that he is no alien to the state. He could make the same claims about society only if a new order were created in which it would be equally comfortable, or uncomfortable, to be a Jew or Christian. It cannot be emphasized strongly enough that this siutation is essentially beyond change. The kind of reorganization which might alter our society enough to bring the Jew into new relation with the majority would have to be more radical than the Communist revolution. The creation of such a new order would produce one of two results: if it were successful, it would homogenize all identities, after the death of both Judaism and Christianity; if it failed to produce a complete new order, as

Russian communism has failed (and as all of the preceding revolutions since 1789 have failed), the alienation of the Jews would forthwith reappear,

Jews say that they are like all other Americans; they even fervently hope that the others will believe them. The Gentile majority in America, including its own Negro minority, knows that this is not so. It knows that the Jews are different because they are alien to the Christian history and style of the majority in all its components. But do the Jews as an organized community really act (apart from talking) on a different assumption? What they are doing, insofar as it contributes to that fervently hoped-for value, "Jewish survival," is very clearly based on an unexpressed assumption of unique apartness. It is just as clear that this apartness, as it exists, does not fit into a conventionally religious definition of the Jew.

One of the keys to understanding the situation is the battle against intermarriage. It is conducted among Jews more bitterly, and with relatively greater success, than among any other group in America. It makes no difference whether Jews believe or do not believe in any version of the Jewish tradition; they battle with equal fervor against the threat of the intermarriage of their children. Certainly one would be shocked to discover nonbelievers of Catholic or Protestant extraction fighting comparably with their own children. What comes to expression in the Jewish attitude is an implicit assumption of Jewish identity as quite unique. Indeed, paradoxical though it may seem, more of the brooding mystery of what it means to be a Jew is to be found, in all its nakedness, in the anguish of the unbeliever, facing the threat of the end of his family's Jewish identity, armored only with an outcry of pain, than is present in the glib rationalizations of the members of synagogues who give conventional arguments about religion and the home and religious differences as the breeding ground of divorce.

This *sui generis* peculiarity shows in every other area of Jewish life. Jewish charitable endeavor is largely the "synagogue" of unbelievers. The United Jewish Appeal is clearly a different kind of affair than the Catholic Bishops' Fund or the various Protestant denominational appeals for aid to missionary activities overseas. Here, too, the mystery incarnate in Jewish existence is most apparent in negative phenomena. For example, the rabbis, as guardians of the tradition, have on many occasions reacted with outrage to business meetings, overt or semidisguised, held by some of our national organizations on the Sabbath. The occurrence of such a problem among the supposed Christian counterparts of these bodies is inconceivable. It cannot be explained away by maintaining that the Jews are here behaving not like a religious denomination but rather like an ethnic minority. The circles guilty of such conduct are usually led by the most "American," least culturally different from the majority, of all Jewish groups. These are the people who shout the loudest, in a well-bred way of course, that they are just like everybody else. It is their disobedience of the tradition, rather than their devotion to it, which is the indwelling sign of their existential attachment to Jewish uniqueness.

Even the synagogue itself is not in today's America a primarily religious phenomenon. Affiliation is very high, but going to synagogue or believing in God is lower than among any communion on the American scene. This can be explained only on the presumption that this generation is safeguarding the mystery of Jewish identity, while being "absent with leave" for what it regards as its inconvenient details such as religious faith, worship, and piety.

The Jewish education of the young has become overwhelmingly an affair for the synagogue, but the reasons motivating parents to send their children in many cases are not religious. In an undefined but strong sense the intent is to root the young in a feeling of wanting to continue the enterprise of being Jewish, though what that enterprise means is really undefinable, at least by the Jewish mass mind.

Here, too, in considering the attempt to define Jews as a religion, what radically refuses to fit is the actual state of the relationship to the international Jewish community and to Israel. Precisely because national political identities are so exclusive in the twentieth century, much Jewish ink has been spilled in defense of the notion that Jews owe no dual loyalties and that their emotion about Israel is really exactly like that of any other group in America about the place of origin of its ancestors. This makes useful defensive argumentation against those Jews who would really like the ties that bind the international Jewish community together to be severed.

We are so superconscious of what anti-Semites have done and can do with the term "international Jewry" that we are constrained to use arguments to deny something that is patently true, i.e., that there is a Jewish identity that transcends national and even cultural boundaries. Parenthetically, is there not an element of *galut* in this very fear of proclaiming it aloud?

This loyalty to an international Jewish identity can and does involve Jews, and not only enrolled Zionists, in stretching the definition of what is politically permissible to a special minority. Jews who are not opting out of the community expect of themselves and of each other that this concern will, at least in crisis, be well nigh paramount in their lives. In the battles of 1947 for the creation of the State of Israel, for example, a quite estranged Jew, Bernard Baruch (and he was not alone), was expected to lend his large influence—and he did. The contemporary American Jewish community no longer excommunicates anyone for religious aberrations, but it has come close to doing precisely that with the more vehement elements of the anti-Zionist Council for Judaism. This attitude does lead to conflict, not only in the public arena but within the individual Jew's soul. It is the presence of the problem, rather than the various solutions that each Jew may have for himself, that is a positive mark of Jewish uniqueness.

The Jew remains in America what he has always been in the history of the West, a co-founder who is yet a resident alien. In religion he may have lost faith to a greater degree than the Christian majority, but an enormous distance remains even between those who never go to synagogue and those who never go to church. The more committed majority among Jews represents a uniqueness in both culture and politics, an apartness from all other Americans, that they both will and choose. The bourgeois Jew, nonetheless, insists that the Jews are just like everybody else. Since this is patently false it is not surprising that this idea is presently being denied by some of the younger Jewish minds in America. The chic words among the best Jewish writers today is "alienation," which is a way of recognizing the truth that the Jew is irretrievably different. Writers like Norman Mailer and Leslie Fiedler, and a host of others, have the merit of seeing that this fact continues to exist even where Jewish learning or active commitment has evaporated. They may no longer know why, and they may deny those reasons that they do know; yet these writers proclaim that the Jew in his very existence is alien to the world.

Nonetheless, this newest self-definition of the Jew is vitiated because it too is being used for self-delusion. Most of those who speak of the alienation of the Jew add that this alienation is indeed the essential condition of modern man as a whole. In other words, the young literati rebelling against their bourgeois parents are really standing the bourgeois Jewish myth on its head. The Jew is not becoming like everyone else, they say; it is that everyone worth mentioning is really becoming just like the Jew.

There is some superficial truth to this assertion at a moment in American life when so much of its literature is being written by Jews. It seems all the more believable because the new hero of the advanced literati is the Negro. Jewish writers are leading the parade toward identifying with the Negro's alienation—and with his supposed sexiness. Norman Mailer, for one, can thus both castigate white America in the name of justice for the Negro, and defy his own chaste and inhibited Jewish ancestors in the name of salvation in the bedroom, which is supposedly to be learned from the true children of nature, the men and women of African ancestry. A significant part of today's intellectual scene in America is thus an alliance among three elements. It consists of Jews who are alien to their own past, at least in terms of conscious knowledge, and who yet know that their Jewishness has something to do with their feeling of being critical outsiders, even pariahs, in society. A second element is a collection of several kinds of Gentile intellectuals who regard themselves as outsiders, many because they are sexual deviates. The third group consists, of course, of a number of Negro writers and artists. This new antiestablishmentarianism appears cohesive, alienated, and therefore "Jewish." The Jewish intellectuals who act as its spokesmen think that they are more at home among the very best non-Jews, the wave of the spiritual future, than any Jewish businessman has ever felt at a Community Chest dinner.

Here, too, what is crucial is not the self-image of these Jews but what is really developing on the larger American scene. It is becoming ever clearer that some white intellectuals may be casting the Negro for the role of the alienated man, but that is not his own desire for himself. "I want what you've got" is not the slogan of a group which finds virtue in standing permanently outside of society. On the contrary, the very bourgeois suburban respectability which Philip Roth finds shallow is the present end value of most Negroes; nor are their intellectual leaders, including even some of the most radical among them, really so contemptuous of this middle-class world. The Negro revolt is not a plea for a new heaven and a new earth, for the building of a new America on different spiritual and cultural foundations. The Negro is quite simply fighting for the opportunity to enter the bourgeoisie, accepting it as it is. We are thus confronted by a paradox: the white intellectuals, especially the Jewish ones, who have banged the door on middle-class culture to join the Negro in his alienation are enlisted in a campaign to help him attain the very situation they have just abandoned.

The tension inherent in this paradox is already beginning to strain the alliance between the largely Jewish devotees of alienation and the Negro. He is becoming ever more impatient with and contemptuous of those who would cast him for a role that he has not chosen for himself. The most important negative figure in current Negro writing is no longer the white oppressor or the Negro "Uncle Tom"; it is the white (often Jewish) intellectual who is an amateur Negro.

Basically, however, the Negro is a side show for the "alienated." They may even forgive his present drive to become part of the majority and think of it as a necessary but temporary affair. It can be argued that once the Negro attains his immediate goals he will then be free to recognize the true condition of modern man. It is to this situation that forward-looking Jewish intellectuals are supposedly speaking, in concert with the best Gentile voices. But are these Jews and these Gentiles really sharing in a comparable alienation?

True, Jewish and Gentile writers are both alienated from middle-class culture—*but in radically different, indeed antithetical, directions.* Unlike the Jews such alienation among the Gentiles has not always been revolutionary, in the name of some new realm of the spirit yet to be born. It has often been conservative, looking back to an earlier age, before Western man was vulgarized by democracy. Too often to be an accident, and equally among conservatives and radicals, alienation has been coupled with anti-Semitism, sometimes of the most virulent kind. In Gentile minds, to be alienated has not meant merely to withdraw from middle-class culture; this hated word has generally been identified with the Jews.

There is all too much evidence for these assertions. In an earlier generation Henry James, and later T. S. Eliot, chose to live in England, hating American rawness—and the Jews. Theodore Dreiser stayed home, to speak for the poor—and against the Jews. Ernest Hemingway, in his Parisian exile, was not much kinder to the one Jew about whom he wrote; and Henry Miller, who is presently the high priest of the beat generation, has written some nasty pages of anti-Semitism. The tale of Ezra Pound is too well known to need repeating. Nor is this phenomenon confined to American letters. The great and alienated French writer Louis Céline was, even under Hitler, a Jew-hater of the most vicious kind. In the Nazi years the alienated André Gide coolly wrote his journal in which there was little sympathy for those millions who were being killed. It was the not alienated François Mauriac, the greatest voice of the liberal Catholic spirit in France, who suffered with the victims.

The "alienated" Jews have, in essence, agreed with the Gentile attack on middle-class culture; they have even quite openly accepted the identification of this unlovely world with the Jewish bourgeoisie. What they have produced as a defense of themselves, in their own persons, is the plea that they stand apart from and in criticism of the main body of Jewry.

To understand correctly the relationship between alienated Jews and these alienated Jew-haters, we must review one element of modern Jewish history. All this has happened before. A recurrent and tragic motif to be heard in the various attempts of the Jew to enter Western society is his acceptance of his enemy's estimate of himself. At the very beginning of the Emancipation, some two centuries ago, there were Jews to agree, though it was not true, that the Jews in general were moneylenders and economically unproductive. These individuals pleaded for their own right to equality because they personally were different. There have been Jews in the last century or so who have agreed that Jewish culture and manners are inferior; they have merely proclaimed themselves as made over in the image favored by the majority. Are not the alienated Jewish intellectuals really the newest "white Jews"?

The world, however, has a habit of reminding Jews that there are no "white Jews." This was what Hemingway meant in his version of Robert Cohen in *The Sun Also Rises.* Cohen can try his utmost but he remains as alien to the bullfight as to the Mass.

The question here is not whether Marjorie Morningstar and her family are really nice people, or whether it is immoral in Jewish intellectuals to be viciously critical of their own community. Marjorie is boring, and divinely appointed Jewish writers since time immemorial have been denouncing the Jews, usually at very inconvenient and very dangerous times. The essential issue is the vantage point. Does one really enter some wider cultural world by detesting Cohen and, *a fortiori,* Marjorie, as much as Hemingway did? Or is the alienated Jew still irretrievably different?

For modern man as a whole, alienation is not his ultimate condition; it is a phase through which the Western spirit has passed before. There always occurs a change of temper, some form of restoration, in which the former antagonists find that they can meet again and draw nourishment together from some ultimate resource of a culture rooted in Christianity and in Greek experience. Almost without exception even the revolts have been battles within the larger framework of the living tradition of Western culture. Their protagonists may place themselves for a while in the posture of critical outsiders, but they are in their very being of the flesh and bone of the society against which they are revolting. No matter what their programs may say, hidden within them there is always the premise that the world will continue and that the meaning of their work will be, ultimately, to change and modify it but not to destroy it from its very roots. The most alienated Gentile intellectuals can go home again; indeed, they usually do.

To this home an individual Jew can indeed repair, but his own alienation is not sufficient passport. He must burn all the bridges to his Jewish past through radical conversion to the culture and, in effect, to the religion of the majority. Disraeli, Heine, Boris

Pasternak, and Bernard Berenson all chose this path (and paid various prices for the choice), for they knew that they could not abandon their home without entering someone else's. Limbo is only a temporary abode. For all those Jews who stop short of conversion there must always remain a specifically Jewish sense of alienation, which is quite different from any momentary travail of Western man. It is the feeling of being not quite inside a culture even when one dominates much of its literature. It is, in short, not alienation, but exile, *galut*.

So long as anything remains of the Jew's own specific identity— it is even enough that he should merely refuse to give up that label and convert—the Jew remains unique, apart, exiled. Even today in America he has not been melted down. His politics are peculiar to himself. He does not fit into the category of either ethnic minority or religion. He remains a stranger to Christian culture. But the Jew has been battling for two centuries to overcome these barriers, not only in the world around him but within himself. He has imagined a society which will open its doors to him and into which he can make himself fit. The nearest approach to such an achievement is in America, and it is here that the ultimate tragic paradox of *galut* is clearest.

Wherever freedom has existed for several generations without a break, the Jews have never in the last two centuries settled down to be themselves. Even in Central and Western Europe in the nineteenth century, in such towns as Budapest, Vienna, and Berlin, the rate of falling-away was disastrous. In the third and fourth generation it began to approach one-half. Today in America we are reaching the stage of the great-grandchildren of the Russian Jewish immigrants of less than a century ago, and all the indices of disintegration are beginning to rise. Freedom is resulting, in part, in the naturalization of corporate Jewish identity in America; it is also resulting in large-scale attrition. A community which must define itself in uncharacteristic modes; which must will its survival within a society to which it is not congenial; whose continuity is most severely endangered by the very plenitude of freedom which is its most devout wish—such a community is in exile.

But do the otherness of Jewish behavior in America and the

feeling of emotional alienation really amount to exile? That depends, of course, on the definition one gives to that term. In the
classic Jewish tradition exile meant, in the first instance, the notion
that the Jew was outside both society and history; he was waiting
for return to his own land. Meanwhile he suffered the pain of
living in a hostile environment. But even in the medieval period
that did not mean only pogroms. It meant also being debarred
from achieving one's own full identity. The radical change in our
time is that environment is doing away with Jewish individuality
not by attack but by openness. Hence the individual Jew, biologically, is no longer in exile in democracy; it is his Judaism, even
his Jewishness, that is in exile.

In the last two centuries two radical solutions to the problem
of exile have been devised. The very Orthodox have perpetuated
a ghetto by choice; the Zionists have insisted on a complete end to
exile. The majority of Jews have chosen neither alternative. They
have continued to live on, usually pretending that the exile no
longer exists and attempting to find various palliatives for its
unadmitted pains.

An overarching answer does not exist. Perhaps our age was
meant to be an age of waiting. Perhaps it was intended that we
hang on as best we can, incarnating in our oft-tormented ways
the mystery of Jewish existence. Perhaps the beginning of the
cure is in an honest recognition of our estate as *galut*. Perhaps
the great paradox of the Jewish situation is that the only Jews who
are safe as Jews, outside of the homeland to which all will repair
in some messianic future, are those who know that they are in
exile. Perhaps the falling-away, the personal trauma, and the
sheer emptiness of so many Jews are related to an underlying
pervasive delusion that the exile which is specific to the Jew ends
with the last pogrom. Such is the mystery of our being that a new
kind of *galut* begins on the morrow.

What is to be done? The Jewish community has spent the last
century or so in emphasizing its resemblances to all other groups.
It has not really convinced many non-Jews, and it has been all too
successful in convincing Jews and leading them out of Jewish life.
The strategy of the next century should be based on the cultivation

of that which is *sui generis*. That is the necessary precondition of survival. It is also the index of the faith of the Jew in the America which has given him unconditional freedom. The ultimate test of his trust in that freedom will be his willingness to be unique.

20. Israel and American Jewry

As soon as the Arab armies began to mass on the borders of Israel during the third week in May, 1967, the mood of the American Jewish community underwent an abrupt, radical, and possibly permanent change. In general, the immediate reaction of American Jewry to the crisis was far more intense and widespread than anyone could have foreseen. Many Jews would never have believed that grave danger to Israel could dominate their thoughts and emotions to the exclusion of all else; many were surprised by the depth of their anger at those of their friends who carried on as usual, untouched by fear for Israeli survival and the instinctive involvement they themselves felt. This outpouring of feeling and commitment appears to contradict all the predictions about the evaporating Jewishness of the American Jews. What happened here between the middle of May and the middle of June therefore demands explanation.

Unfortunately, it did not occur to any of the research agencies in the social sciences to initiate a disciplined study of the American Jewish response as the events were unfolding. So we have to rely, at least for the moment, on impressionistic reportage. Obviously no single person can have firsthand knowledge of everything that went on during the weeks in question. I myself was involved most directly as the rabbi of a suburban congregation on the edge of New York—in Englewood, New Jersey. At the height of the fund-

Reprinted from *Commentary,* vol. 44, no. 2 (August 1967).

raising activity throughout the country I also addressed a number of rallies and meetings in several different towns. In addition, I witnessed the besieging of the offices of the Jewish Agency and the Israeli Consulate in New York by hundreds of young people who volunteered, when the Israeli army was mobilized, to go to work in Israel. And finally, I have compared my own personal impressions with those of friends who were active in other communities and concerned with other aspects of the American Jewish response. On the basis of all this, let me try to describe the situation, at least in its major outlines, before attempting to speculate on what the extraordinary behavior of the American Jewish community during the crisis may mean for the future.

It is ingrained in the American Jewish soul that the correct response to a danger is to give money. This was certainly the most immediate reaction to the Middle East crisis, but with one important difference: much more money was given by many more people than ever before in history. There are innumerable stories from every Jewish community throughout the United States not only of giving on a fantastic scale by people of large means, but also of the literal sacrifice of their life's savings by people of modest means. It all moved so quickly that the bookkeeping has lagged behind the giving, and exact figures are still not available. We do, however, know that during the little more than two-week period which marked the height of the crisis—between the day when Nasser closed the Gulf of Aqaba on May 23 and the end of the war on June 10—well over *one hundred million dollars,* the bulk of it in cash, was realized for the Israel Emergency Fund of the United Jewish Appeal. This was a fundraising effort unprecedented not only in Jewish experience, but also in the history of private philanthropy in the United States.

It is in itself a significant fact that the drive did not begin from the top. The national board of the United Jewish Appeal met in special session on Monday, May 29, in New York to launch its nationwide emergency campaign, but by that time—six days after the inauguration of the blockade—local campaigns were already under way in dozens of communities which had not waited for anyone to ask them to move. Moreover, it was not only the old-line, late-middle-aged leadership of these communities who were acting in this way. Many people in their thirties and forties who had never participated in organizational Jewish life suddenly emerged to take the lead both in giving and in working. The financial contributions of these newer elements were astonishingly large —perhaps because of a desire to make up for past neglect and a wish, or even a need, to be counted in during a moment of manifest danger.

In my own synagogue a congregation approaching high holiday size walked in on Friday night, May 26, in a subdued and very somber frame of mind. An hour or so later, after we had done something never before done in our synagogue's history—an appeal for money at a service with the calling for open announcements of contributions—the mood had changed to one of elation. Anxiety over the danger to Israel had not diminished, but by giving substantial sums of money we had to the best of our immediate ability enlisted in the struggle and become participants instead of passive spectators. Similar things happened wherever Jews live. If it was true in Israel that more reserves showed up in some places than had been ordered to mobilize, American Jewish fundraising was, in its own way, a comparable phenomenon.

Concurrently, a no less remarkable political change was taking place within American Jewry. The most striking fact was the unanimity of opinion. The pollsters found that 99 percent of all the Jews in America undeviatingly supported the Israeli position. Even when Israel went to war, not a single voice was raised in public among Jews to deplore a resort to arms. Yet in the 1940s there had been a vocal minority within the American Jewish community which kept arguing in public that a Zionist solution to the problem of the European Jewish refugees was against the interests and desires of American Jewry, and during the first days of the 1956, Israel reluctantly settled for an agreement which did not ion—including organizations which were usually pro-Israel—had been more than uncomfortable when Israel launched its attack. In the months of diplomatic haggling after the guns were stilled in 1956, Israel reluctantly settled for an arrangement which did not require Nasser's formal and public agreement and which did not make effective at all any rights of passage for its ships in the Suez Canal. The pressure on the Israeli government to accept such a solution then came largely from the United States, and the White House and the State Department managed to persuade some very influential American Jews to counsel Israel to temper its demands.

Ten years later the picture was entirely different. Even the militant anti-Zionists of the American Council for Judaism, who had always appeared at critical moments to attack Israel, refrained from issuing any public statements until the end of the war, and the mutterings since then have been isolated. More surprising still, a number of prominent Council figures are now actually supporting Israel as devotedly as the most passionate Zionists.

The question of Vietnam might have been expected to be divisive, but it turned out not to be. Many of the Jewish establishments, especially those of the Conservative and Reformed rabbinic and lay bodies, are more or less officially dove-like in their positions on Vietnam. In this they are at one with such non-Jewish leaders of American religious opinion as Martin Luther King and John Bennett. All these people, including several important Christian doves, rallied instantly to the side of Israel and they did not withdraw their support even when Israel went to war. There were, of course, jibes at the Vietnam doves now transformed into Middle Eastern hawks. The reasons advanced to counter these complaints may or may not have been convincing, but the truth of the matter is that no one had the time or the inclination to produce a theoretical case which would harmonize the two positions. American Jews, and some of their friends, acted instinctively in the face of a threat to the survival of Israel, and their concern for the life of the besieged Jewish state was not to be compromised by any embarrassment that might come to them out of any other views on other matters, even one so serious as the war in Vietnam.

Within a very few days, however, a rationale began to be developed. The pro-Israel Vietnam doves argued that American support of the government of South Vietnam represented an involvement in a regime which had no popular roots. The last thing that could be said of the State of Israel, by contrast, was that it lacked popular roots. A similar contrast was drawn between American diplomatic commitments in the two cases: they had always been less than perfectly clear in Vietnam, whereas no one could possibly deny that to support the integrity of Israel has been a solemn American obligation for nineteen years. Why then was it inconsistent to demand that America honor its commitment to a rooted democracy fighting for its life and to withdraw from a dubious venture to prop up an unpopular military clique?

Though this case is reasonable, it does not solve all the problems of the pro-Israel Vietnam doves. The opponents of the war in Vietnam have all repeatedly rejected Johnson's domino theory, and even though the White House has said little overtly to suggest that the president is supporting Israel for comparable reasons—in order, that is, to keep Russia from spreading further into the Middle East—this connection is clearly in his mind. My own reading of my friends in the peace movement is that they hope that the Russian attacks on Israel, violent though they are in public, will indeed lead to such a linkage of the two problems—not, of course, because they want to open another Cold War front in the Middle East, but rather because they think that a tandem settlement of both questions by the superpowers may become possible.

Perhaps the most complicated and difficult problem is to assess correctly what really did happen in the response of American Jewish young people to the crisis. In the last days of May, Israeli consulates and the Hillel directors in the colleges were overwhelmed by hundreds of young people who wanted to go to Israel to take over the civilian jobs of their peers who had been mobilized for the army. By the day war broke out, when the American ban on travel to the area was imposed, some ten thousand such applications had been recorded throughout the country, more than half of them in New York at the offices of the Jewish Agency. On June 5 itself the outpouring of young people completely swamped every one of the bureaus. A high official of the Jewish Agency told me that as he arrived at the front door of the building very early that morning, a cab drew up and a man jumped out, followed by two younger men. He stopped this Agency official and said to him: "I have no money to give but here are my sons. Please send them over immediately." That day this was no isolated incident.

But who were the young people who came? Dr. Arnulf Pins, executive director of the Council on Social Work Education, offered his services to help process the volunteers at the New York office of the Jewish Agency. He had some questions included on the forms they filled out concerning their Jewish educational and organizational background and their involvement in such causes as Zionism, race, and peace. Dr. Pins has not yet had the time to tabulate his results adequately, but he took the trouble to give me a reading of what he found in a random sampling. Those who came in May and who therefore constituted the large majority of the young people who actually did get to Israel before June 5 were from yeshivot and from the relatively small circle of American Jewish youth whose main interests are Jewish. At least a third of all the ten thousand who ultimately came to volunteer had had a substantial Jewish education and a continuing Jewish concern. In their answers to the political questions, another third showed that they had spent their young adult years worrying about race and Vietnam and that they now lacked any organizational Jewish ties. Yet even this group had had some Jewish education in childhood or even into the teens. What seemed to be happening to them was that a dormant loyalty had suddenly been stirred and had become at that moment an overriding passion.

What of the young Jews of the New Left? I am told by friends who are in close touch with these circles that they were, if not enthusiastically pro-Israel in their mood (though some were), much less hostile than might have been anticipated. My own impression is that the Jews of the New Left were on the whole sufficiently Jewish to care, but that this concern was neutralized by their sympathy for Nasser as a "progressive" Third World leader. In any event, unlike many Jews of the old left, the young in the New Left are generally unwilling to look upon the fact of their Jewishness as a dimension of being deep enough to justify a reordering of intellectual and moral priorities at a moment of high drama and crisis such as was experienced last June.

A radical shifting of priorities was, however, effected in another circle of Jewish opinion—the circle which has been most directly influenced in recent years by the spirit of ecumenism. Despite some quite vocal opposition to the broadening of the Jewish–Christian dialogue, the majority view within both religious and secular Jewish organizations has cherished the increasing contact between Jewish and Christian groups and the greater openness to which this contact has led. When the crisis broke, Jews found that leading individual figures within the various Christian denominations—Niebuhr, King, Schmemann, Higgins, and Archbishop Hallinan, to mention only a few—were quick and firm in their public commitment to justice for Israel, but that the formal establishments of both the Protestant and Catholic churches remained largely silent. In the last days of May, as the crisis was building toward war, almost no statements could be elicited from any of these communions even supporting Israel's right to exist.

As soon as the war was over several emergency meetings were arranged between Jewish figures with a large stake in the dialogue and their Christian peers. As individuals (though not as spokesmen for their churches) some of the Christians present had supported Israel's right to life, but the prevailing Christian sentiment in those tension-filled rooms was directed toward the question of Arab refugees and the status of Jerusalem. Israel was denounced as the aggressor in the conflict and there was general discomfort in being pressed hard by Jews to think differently.

The Jewish participants in these discussions had not prepared any statements in advance, and yet they were as one in their answers. Every one of the Jewish ecumenists—including Rabbi Marc Tanenbaum of the American Jewish Committee, perhaps the leading figure in this field—arose in turn and said to the Christians that the existence of Israel was not a negotiable matter for any Jew, and that Jews would regard Jewish–Christian relations in America as greatly damaged if the organized Christian community failed to support Israel's right to live. It was made very clear that Christian emphasis on the Arab refugees, no matter how correct the argument might be both morally and politically, would be taken by Jews as an evasion or worse, because the effect of such talk, if it was not linked to Israel's right of existence, would be to encourage the Arabs to remain obdurate. The day had now come when Jews could afford to dispense with goodwill from the churches if that was the price they might have to pay for their passion for Israel's existence. (Rabbi Tanenbaum and a number of others, however, did concede that the Jewish ecumenists had been at fault in having failed to make clear to their Christian colleagues in the past that Israel is no less important to the Jews of America than such "Diaspora" issues as the Christian roots of anti-Semitism and the theological status of Judaism as a religion.)

These battles were not confined to private meetings. Rabbi Balfour Brickner, speaking at the convention of the Central Conference of American Rabbis, and the present writer, in a column for the *National Catholic Reporter,* said similarly sharp things in public. Brickner and I were answered in a very tough article by Monsignor George Higgins, the executive secretary of the American Catholic hierarchy. Higgins, who had personally been courageously and consistently pro-Israel, was angered by Jewish pressure on the church as a whole to take such a stand, and he accused Brickner and myself of trying, in the name of our ecumenical ties, to blackmail the church into supporting Israel.

At the very least these passions and counterpassions are shaking some of the ecumenical bridges that Jews have been building in the last few years. The issues of Arab refugees and the Old City of Jerusalem will go on being debated, and will continue to have a palpably different weight in the thinking of Christian establishments than they will for Jews. Not even the hardest of hardliners in Israel—and certainly no Jews in America—doubts that Israel has a responsibility to make a large contribution to the solution of the Arab refugee problem. No one denies the international interest of all the major faiths in all the holy places. Nonetheless, American Jewish opinion is overwhelmingly convinced that these matters can be dealt with only as part of a larger peace settlement. Many Christians, the pope among them, are being very precise in their concern about the Old City and the Arab refugees and very vague in their concern for Israel's safety and peace. American opinion as a whole is going to be divided in the months ahead over how the crisis should be settled. The likelihood is that the Jews of America will be arrayed in overt battle, not only with known adversaries but even with some of their friends. The American Jewish community today seems not to be afraid of such a confrontation.

The main outlines of the effect that the Middle East crisis has had on American Jewry are, then, relatively clear. It has united those with deep Jewish commitments as they have never been united before, and it has evoked such commitments in many Jews who previously seemed untouched by them. Very large numbers of American Jews now feel their Jewish identity more intensely than they have for at least a generation, and they are much less worried than ever before about what the rest of the world might be thinking of their feelings or of the actions through which they have been expressing these feelings. This crisis has forcibly reminded many, perhaps most, American Jews that the posture and destiny of Jews in the world continue to be quite unique and that Israel is not a state like all other states. Thus for the moment at least the organized Jewish community in America has a different look about it. It is enlarged and refreshed in numbers and its courage and resolution are high. It will yet have to grapple with the problem of maintaining connection with all the new or relatively new people who worked as Jews at the height of the crisis. Whether it will be able to do so is not at all certain.

Any estimate of what this transforming moment might mean for the future of American Jewry must necessarily rely on an assessment of the factors that underlie the responses we have been examining. Here one can only guess, but I would say that the most widespread influence—on Jews in Israel and America alike—was a revulsion against the passivity of the Jewish victims of the Nazis. "Good" Jews have been largely arguing since 1945 that this passivity was a distinctively Jewish form of heroism, but it is now apparent that many who have interpreted it in this way never really succeeded in convincing themselves. Now, confronted by a threat to Israel's existence, Jews almost universally felt that precisely because of the horrifying prospect that Israel might go down, let it go down fighting. A related element was the memory of Jewish conduct in the United States and, for that matter, in England during the years of World War II. These two communities had made little dent on Roosevelt and Churchill, because Jews were not then bold enough to engage in a vehement confrontation with the two war leaders over the parochial destiny of the Jewish people. The response to the Middle Eastern crisis was a way of saying that, come what might, Jews would not repeat such conduct.

But Israel evoked more in American Jews than a sense of moral reparation for the memory of the passive victims of mass murder. The sense of belonging to the worldwide Jewish people, of which Israel is the center, is a religious sentiment, but it seems to persist even among Jews who regard themselves as secularists or atheists. There are no conventional Western theological terms with which to explain this, and most contemporary Jews experience these emotions without knowing how to define them. Perhaps the point can best be made by recounting an incident. Two days after the end of the war there was a major gathering in New York of Jewish leaders from all over the country, many of whom, as I happen to be able to attest, are remote from the synagogue. Yet when the meeting was concluded with a very simple recitation of the blessing in which we thank God for "having allowed us to live and be present to witness this day," almost everyone in the room wept.

At the deepest level, the American Jewish response was the result of a paradox. Jacob Klatzkin once observed that Theodor Herzl could not have arisen directly out of the East European ghetto. What made Herzl possible, in his bold openness about the situation of the Jews and his straight-backed stance before the powers of the world, was two generations of assimilation in Central Europe. The Jewish community has now undergone two generations of comparable acculturation in America. Because Jews are now so very much at home in America, more at home than Herzl ever was in Budapest or Vienna, it was possible for them in this crisis to be boldly Jewish in very angular ways. Perhaps it did not quite happen ten or twenty years ago because Jews were then more nearly an immigrant group.

It is possible to believe that the Middle East crisis of 1967 occurred at precisely that moment in the history of American Jews when an ascending curve of nearly complete outer and inner emancipation intersected with a descending curve of Jewish commitment. If this is so then such a moment is not likely to recur, for these two forces will diverge ever more widely as the years go by. It is, however, also possible, on the evidence now at hand, to take another view. Israel may, as some Zionist theoreticians predicted a Jewish state in Palestine would, now be acting as a very strong focus of worldwide Jewish emotional loyalty and thereby as a preservative of a sense of Jewish identity. There is some reason for thinking that American Jewish education, despite all its inadequacies, has played a significant role in implanting an often deeply hidden Jewish loyalty in many younger people (and most now receive some Jewish training). Perhaps the force of Jewish commitment and the attractions of the almost completely open society are on the point of reaching an equilibrium which might endure indefinitely or even permanently. If that is the case, then the American Jewish community is realizing, at last, the two-centuries-old hope of the Jewish Emancipation: that Jews and their Jewish loyalties could survive and even find new space in which to express themselves in a free society.

Which of these two interpretations is right I do not know, but in either case it is clear that the Middle East crisis represented a lightning flash which has illumined the landscape of the American Jewish future.

21. Zionism in America

ZIONISM IS SUPPOSED TO make Jews realize how uncomfortable they are in the Diaspora and how such living has too little dignity. In the United States, Zionism has acted to the contrary—to make Jews more comfortable in the Diaspora and a greater force within the society at large. Rhetoric obscures this truth, for do not American Zionists and even non-Zionists march through the streets of Jerusalem proclaiming their assent to the "centrality of Israel," which is the very core of Zionism's Jerusalem platform? The truth is that those from Kansas, California, and even New York who assert this mean not that they condemn their *galut* but that the involvement in Israel gives content and verve to lives they intend to continue to live in the American Diaspora.

Reprinted from the *Jerusalem Post, Special United States Bicentennial Magazine,* July 4, 1976.

It is therefore relatively easy to conceive of a celebration by Israelis of the bicentenary year of the United States of America. This is not more difficult than the Canadian celebration of that event. America's neighbor to the north has a complex relationship to the powerful giant to the south, on which it is overdependent but from which it nonetheless maintains substantial distance. Comparably, as I sometimes imagine, the true emotional border of Israel is not on the Mediterranean but immediately off the coast of the United States.

To define an attitude toward the American bicentennial is, however, much more difficult when "Jewish issues" are involved. Can one praise the United States as the home of a unique freedom and influence for Jews, whose power there is a critical factor in the very building of Israel, without raising the troubling question: Is this American Diaspora therefore unthinkable as an abode for Jews?

From its very beginnings American Zionism has answered this question by insisting that "America is different." Here the Zionist task was to marshal political and financial support. A small elite continued to emigrate to Zion, but the great Zionist crisis in America was not a quarrel between Zionists and others over the question: Is America a fit habitation for Jews? That ideological quarrel was fought in Russia, in Poland, and even in Germany, but never in the United States. Here the Zionists fought within the Jewish community for half a century before they succeeded in making support of the Jewish homeland the almost universally shared central purpose of American Jewish life. More crucial and more difficult still was the concurrent struggle to establish in America the right of Zionists to battle for their political aims.

Politically, the most damaging charge ever hurled against any group in America was that of being a hyphenated American, or, as it was later put, of being guilty of "dual loyalty." This charge silenced the German-Americans in World War I and it acted to keep all other ethnic groups, including the Irish, from having a particular foreign policy of their own for any significant length of time.

The only group in America which withstood the charge, both within its own community and in the politics of the larger society, was the Zionists. American Zionists were crucial to making an end of the "melting pot" image of America in the name of a minority commitment of their own. Horace Kallen and Mordecai Kaplan, who defined the program of cultural pluralism for all Americans, were young Zionists in the early years of the twentieth century. They defined their pluralist vision in those years as a projection of their desire to create an America in which Jews could be themselves. This required a new definition of American society, one which would be hospitable to a community which would maintain permanent links with other Jews, and especially with those laboring to reestablish the Jewish presence in the Holy Land. By now, two generations later, all of the earlier competing ideologies within American Jewry such as Yiddishism, the Jewish Socialist Bund, and anarchism, have faded. Only Zionism has translated itself into a second and third generation. The one commitment that is universally shared in American Jewry is to make sure that the foreign policy of the United States does not turn against Israel. At this bicentenary moment all other major special-interest groups are defined in America by their domestic programs: labor, blacks, ethnics in the big cities, and even big business, except, in part, for big oil. The only special-interest group which is defined by its foreign policy is the Jews.

The great success of Zionism is to have made this acceptable on the American scene. This has represented a profound change in America's conception of itself, and it has consequences in other realms. The insistence of blacks in America for "affirmative action," that is, for acts of special reparation in this generation for three centuries of injustice done to them by slavery, fell on ears which had been hearing for decades the Zionist claim that the Jewish people was entitled to an act in this century of unique reparation for twenty centuries of exile by having its homeland returned to it. All other kinds of dissent from the American consensus, such as the movement against the Vietnam War, became possible in a society which no longer equated, as it had at the beginning of the twentieth century, patriotism with conformity. To reverse the argument, in the America of 1976 a Jewish community deeply devoted to Israel is no longer outrageously unique. This represents a fundamental change in American life from the self-definition of this society at the beginning of the twentieth century.

Within American Jewry, Zionism has also successfully conquered the community's inner life so that the labors that it commands have become American Jewry's "religion."

It is simply not true that excommunication no longer exists in modern Judaism. On the contrary, it has reappeared in new forms. One can, indeed, no longer be excommunicated in modern America for not believing in God, for living totally outside the tradition, or even for marrying out. Indeed, none of these formerly excommunicable offenses debar one today from occupying high offices in positions of Jewish leadership—but that does not mean that all is permitted. On the contrary, the case of the American Council for Judaism, the well-known anti-Zionist body, is instructive. It has been effectively debarred from any participation in Jewish life on any issue, even, for example, a matter as uncontroversial and as universally acceptable as the American Jewish struggle for the rights of Soviet Jews.

The yearning for Israeli leaders with charisma on the part of American Jews, and the emotions which they pour into United Jewish Appeal missions, are to be understood as part of a religious phenomenon, the modern equivalent of hasidim traveling in exaltation to see their rebbe and to spend some time in the uplifting precincts of his court. True, only a minority is privileged or has the stamina to live in the very presence of the rebbe, but the hasidim who participate by retelling his glories and contributing to his support are at least validly within the community. Their memories of the uplifting moments make it possible for them to go back home and live out their winter nights by their own firesides.

The overarching religion of American Jews is therefore not Orthodox, Conservative, or Reform; it is not Hebrew or the national culture. It is pride and glory in American Jewry's sharing in Israel—and it is therefore disappointed in rebbes who do not perform miracles on order, who are sometimes fallible on Yom Kippur when a war breaks out, even as mortal men, and whose courts are not as perfect as dreams would have them.

Most important of all, I think, is a cliché which is even more deeply true than it seems to be. Zionism and Israel have, indeed, provided American Jews with great dignity in the eyes of the American majority. Even in today's less glorious times than those which followed June 1967, Israel remains in America the symbol of achievement against odds and of the kind of pioneering creativity that Americans respect.

Within American society as a whole the involvement of Jews in Israel, the very prodigiousness of their giving and the very impact of their political pressure, has acted to gain respect for Jewish devotion and Jewish power. There may one day, as classic Zionist theory predicts, come an anti-Zionist reckoning for overplaying the Jewish hand in an alien society, but there are few signs of it in contemporary America. The unique passion of Jews for Israel was not counterattacked during the oil embargo of 1973, and it is the cliché of American politics that Israel and its American Jewish connections cannot be treated by anybody as just another problem. The very fact that Jews have felt free enough in America to campaign as many did in the late 1960s both against the Vietnam War and for Israel; against a big military budget and for total support of Israel; for radical social change within American society and against Third World forces—all this is indicative, of course, of as yet unresolved discontinuities in American Jewish conscience. What is more important and revealing is how Jews have come to feel in contemporary America—free to be associated with some of the most striking challenges to the status quo.

Even here Zionism was, and remains, unique. At the beginning of the century in the battles for the rights of labor, in the 1930s as part of the New Deal coalition, or in the fights for racial justice and against the Vietnam War, Jews have been especially prominent in movements in which they were never the majority, that is, they were always part of larger alliances in American life. In the case of Zionism, despite all the rhetoric of earlier times and even of today that, to quote Justice Brandeis, "to be a good Zionist is to be a good American," the American Jewish community has remained steadfast in its support of the Jewish homeland while its allies have shifted across the spectrum. Here, American Jewry has uniquely attacked the foreign policy status quo, with its built-in pro-Arab biases, openly and avowedly in the Jewish name.

The state of Jewish Emancipation in America is thus in the

bicentennial year one in which this Diaspora, perhaps in self-delusion, regards itself as secure and at home in America. There are a number of clouds on the horizon, but none of the visible ones are that of the kind that classic Zionism of the "denial of the *galut*" predicted. The proportion of the rest of the Jews to America is falling because of a small birthrate. The Jewish vote thus matters less even as Jewish political activity continues to matter greatly. The major cities, the very home of Jewish influence until recently, have been almost totally abandoned to blacks, for American Jews are now more and more suburban people. The sources of their power in America are more and more those of a highly educated elite. The rate of intermarriage among the young is of the order of 40 percent, and it has not been stemmed by any means that the American Jewish community has been able to devise, including its large labors for Israel. There is thus real danger that something approaching half the Jews will be lost from the community within the next fifty years.

There are, to be sure, signs of religious and cultural rebirth in some circles of the younger generation. The newest post-World War II immigration has brought with it several enclaves of hasidic and Orthodox fervor, but the very strikingness of Lubavitch and Satmar tends to exaggerate the numbers involved or even their influence. More important for our present purpose is to understand that the two extremes of the American Jewish community, those who are evaporating and those who are living by choice in ultra-Orthodox enclaves, both regard themselves as at home in America. The thousands of de-Judaized young who are "making it" in the larger society may be somewhat nervous on occasion about the future of America and their future within America, but there is no existing American anti-Semitism in this bicentennial year for any of them to be candidates to reinvent Herzl in American accents. Comparably, the hasidic and yeshivah enclaves in American life are asserting that it is possible to live indefinitely in this American *galut* in Orthodox communities, and that there is no necessity to transport the court of the rebbe of Satmar in Brooklyn or the yeshivah in Lakewood, or more than a relatively minor element of the activities of the Lubavitch, to the Holy Land.

That leaves one with the middle group, the majority of American Jewry, which is best defined as being nonassimilationist, non-ultra-Orthodox, with its face turned toward Israel. This part of the Diaspora worries about Israel today as much or more than does the rest of world Jewry, and perhaps even more than Israel does itself. For itself, this mainstream of American Jewry lives with one conscious mortal terror—the fear of its own evaporation. To this problem it has no present answer. An Ahad Ha-amist Zionist would say to this American Diaspora: "Increase your links to Israel, or better still, go on *aliyah* and solve your cultural and spiritual problem." The paradox of the Jewish Emancipation in America, and especially of its Zionist component, is that being busy with and about Israel gives sufficient content and verve to the Jewish experience of the mainstream so that these labors act as a continuing anodyne, even as they are not a cure to this grief. For example, Jews can freely demonstrate in front of the Soviet consulates, or pressure congressmen on behalf of Israel.

The Orthodox are busy with themselves; the alienated Jews are trying to "get their heads together" or are working at their personal careers. Those in the unalienated mainstream have the heady feeling of outsize importance both in America and in Israel precisely because they have a unique and now-accepted cause and self-definition—to safeguard Israel and all Jewry. The very "centrality" of Israel is, in the terrible irony of history, the enemy of its true centrality.

On the surface the situation of the two great Jewish communities of our time, those in Israel and in America, are strikingly different. In Israel the Jewish state has finally been realized, and in America, for all of its uniqueness, the Jews are, as always, in *galut,* a minority within a majority culture. And yet, both these communities share at very least in two fundamental conditions.

In the first place, despite classical Zionism, Israel has not yet become a "normal" state, a country like all others. The American Jewish Diaspora, an effective component of the American consensus which has stretched to accommodate it, is not a Diaspora like all other Diasporas. In the second place, the mainstream in both Jewish communities is somewhere in the middle between Orthodox religious affirmations and severing links with the Jewish past entirely, and in both communities preoccupation with present dangers and present successes is increasingly being perceived as not an adequate solution to the problem of inner meaning.

In American Jewish terms, I can only conclude with a further paradox: there will no doubt be some sturdy Jewish enclaves in the United States a century hence to celebrate their survival as Jews on American shores. The mainstream will survive for another century only if it solves its inner cultural-religious problem. So long as the inner life is almost totally externalized in political and fundraising activities, with a passion for Israel at their center, assimilation will grow by the very side of these prodigious labors. Dissatisfaction with *galut* and true inner turning toward Israel require profound reeducation of an American Jewish community that is marvelously busy—and waiting for content.

At the very dawn of political Zionism Ahad Ha-am foresaw the cultural problems that Herzl could not solve. He was clearly wrong in not believing that a political movement could and would make a profound and miraculous positive change, that it would create the glory that is contemporary Israel—and yet the problems to which he pointed remain.

Perhaps, in honor of two hundred years of the United States and more than three centuries of American Jewish life, his pungent and poignant sentence of 1897 bears repeating: "The salvation of the Jews will come not from diplomats, but from prophets."

ZIONISM AND ISRAEL

22. An Agenda for the Twenty-eighth World Zionist Congress

EVER SINCE 1948, almost the day after the State of Israel was declared, the Zionist movement has been searching for redefinition. David Ben-Gurion immediately proposed a famous, one-word formula: Zionism means *aliyah*. The implication of the sentence was that he who is not working toward emigrating to Israel is not a "Zionist" but rather a "friend of Israel."

In the debate that Ben-Gurion's views aroused, the Zionist movement in the Diaspora in all its wings did affirm the notion that *aliyah* is a prime principle of Zionism. For that matter, today, in 1971, even non-Zionists agree to, and are often even part of, Zionist activities to encourage *aliyah*.

Nor, in actual fact, are the most doctrinaire "deniers of the Diaspora" these days behaving much differently about *aliyah* than those Zionists who still have a good word to say for Diaspora Jewish life. The "deniers of the Diaspora" are identical with many of the forces now shouting at the top of their voices for more money from federations and welfare funds, not for airplane tickets for *olim* on any active theory of catastrophe around the corner, but for day schools in Pittsburgh, Cleveland, or Atlanta. As a matter of present fact, the debate about *aliyah* has thus become quite theoretical and old hat. This seems to leave the original question unanswered and even more plaguing: What indeed is a Zionist, that is, other than a good Jew of this day and place, whatever the day and place may be?

Put in these terms, I think the question is unanswerable, but the terms themselves are dated. The question of what is a Zionist

Adapted from *Hadassah Magazine,* January 1972.

231

has meant in the last twenty years not merely how do we define Zionism ideologically. It has always had about it the aroma of another question: What are the specific functions, rights, and privileges of the Zionist organizations and of the world body as a whole? What do only Zionists do, or have the sole right to do?

Pursued this way, the ideological inquiry is really largely a discussion about the needs or self-images of some Zionists who are still rooted in the pre-1948 past and the discussion must come, as it always has in the last two decades, to an angry dead end.

The trouble with this discussion is that it has looked backward to Zionism before 1948 to ask the essentially negative question: What remains of pre-state Zionism? We should be looking forward to questions about what the next generation of world Jewry will be facing and what it will need to live its Jewish life.

What, therefore, are the crucial problems of world Jewry as they appear at the beginning of 1972, on the way to the Twenty-eighth World Zionist Congress? The most obvious one is the task of upbuilding the State of Israel, of bringing to it all who want and need to live within it. Peace and stability for Israel are still elusive. These are the tasks which are at the head of any budget of continuing Jewish concern.

The most pervasive and worrisome Jewish problem today, at this moment, is, however, the erosion of the quality of Jewish life. Assimilation is not now a doctrine or an ideal. It is even possible that intermarriage as such is less of a threat, statistically and biologically, than was imagined a few years ago. Nonetheless, the quality of Jewish life, its relationship to its own ethos and tradition, is very much a problem, not only in the Diaspora but even in Israel.

There was, for example, a study made of the delegates to the last World Zionist Congress some four years ago. It was found that the great majority of the delegates from the Diaspora knew Hebrew. When they were asked about their own children, the figure shrank to less than half. To be sure the situation has changed for the better in the last few years in a number of areas. The number of students from all of the Jewish world who are spending substantial time in Israel has been increasing. Jewish day school education in the United States has by now won community-wide acceptance, though there are signs in the last year or so that the numbers of students are no longer growing. There are new opportunities on the campus, and not only in the United States, but there is as yet no program by the Jewish community as a whole for allocating resources wisely and effectively to make maximum use of the new opportunities.

Most current discussion about the spiritual and cultural estate of Jewish life centers on the new winds among the young, but that is to miss an even more important phenomenon. June 1967 was a transforming moment, and not merely in fundraising.

There was a deep spiritual dimension in the Jewish response to the events surrounding the Six-Day War. In London, Paris, and New York, Jews in their hundreds of thousands who had not thought about their Jewishness seriously for many years, and their children who had not ever thought about it because they grew to maturity after 1948, suddenly discovered something about themselves that they had not known. Though many had been living other lives, being Jewish was the root of their emotion, the critical, central fact of their own self-understanding. This profound inner turning made it possible for the Jews in France courageously to oppose no less a figure than de Gaulle. In the United States, even those who still call themselves non-Zionists are now, since 1967, comfortable with *aliyah* as an option for American Jews, even for some of their own young.

This spiritual turning is compounded today of two forces, an affirmation and a quest. The affirmation is that Jews all over the world today know that their own inner lives require a living relationship to Israel. The quest is a search for roots, an attempt to make of their Jewishness something deeper than a continuing set of responses to political and financial crises.

This quest for roots appears today in a widely scattered variety of expressions, but perhaps most strikingly in the growing vogue of East European memories, and especially hasidic ones, on the stage in New York—and even in Tel Aviv. Despite these signs of revival the synagogue is in the doldrums and many of the older agencies of Jewish cultural life are having trouble maintaining the loyalty of their supporters. In this atmosphere various individuals and agencies are trying to capture and channelize the new mood with attractive and often competitive new projects. There are many agencies, many committees, many grants, and many plans. What there is not—and what there must be—is a discussion by the Jewish world "in parliament assembled" as to what is required for all of Jewry and what we must all now do, together.

There is an even more difficult and delicate problem before the Jewish world today: not only the inner quality of the life of the Diaspora but also the quality of the life of Israel itself. Just to pose this theme arouses, immediately, all kinds of fears. A few parts of the Zionist movement have been slower than the Jewish world as a whole in learning that Israel's politics and diplomacy are her own affair and that the proper stance of world Jewry is to be supportive of the life of Israel and of the conditions necessary to its creative survival. There is a more pervasive concern—that wide discussion of Israel's internal tensions acts to exacerbate them and that when these concerns spread beyond the borders of Israel such discussion lends ammunition to its enemies and casts its concerned friends in the role of interfering nags.

These are the dangers. Nevertheless, it is better to risk them than to continue the sterile doctrine of "non-interference," which means in practice that the connection between Israel and world Jewry is the export of pride and the import of money and influence.

The State of Israel is sovereign and it is entitled to noninterference in its internal affairs by the Jews of the world, but it is also entitled to their love and concern, to their involvement, and thus to the expression of their high emotion that Israeli society should indeed be perfected, with their help, as a light to all Jewry and a light to the world. By the same token, no one in the Jewish world doubts that the passion of Israel's leadership, from the prime minister on down, for the quality of Jewish life in the Diaspora is a proper concern, and that it is not to be turned aside by slogans about two separate realms, that of Israel and that of local Jewish life.

Israel–Diaspora relations, the nature of our involvement in each other's lives, could thus stand discussion. It might then be discovered that the Jewish life of the Diaspora needs more rather than less spiritual and cultural input from Israel, at very least in the realm of Hebrew and modern Hebraic culture. We might also find that some of the problems of Israel require not only more *aliyah* but also more volunteers to go and work, without necessarily remaining permanently, at specific social tasks. Henrietta Szold went to Israel not in order to settle, though that is what she did, even though she kept talking almost to the end of her desire to return to, or at least revisit, her native Baltimore. She went to do the necessary social task, to organize some nursing where it did not exist—and out of this all the rest grew.

In the last year, the Jewish Agency has been reconstituted, with the accession of the major fundraising bodies. The World Zionist Organization has thus structurally surrendered some power, for it no longer totally dominates the machinery through which world Jewry's financial concern for Israel is expressed. Nevertheless, the Zionist movement has in this realm effectively made it possible to organize all the Jews of the world in a forum, the new Assembly of the Jewish Agency, which will be at once Zionist in its spirit and all-Jewish in its outreach. By the same token the Zionist movement is situated at the very center of all the spiritual and survivalist concerns of the world Jewish community, in all its branches. The Twenty-eighth Congress has the great and historic opportunity to call into being some comparable body, at once Zionist and global, to deal with all of these internal issues of Jewish life.

World Jewry requires an international budget of means and of people to face as a whole all the problems posed today by its inner spiritual needs and questings.

New organizational forms will have to be devised and older bodies will have to change. These are not the central issues, for the reconstitution of the Jewish Agency has already proved that such changes can be made with a surprising minimum of fuss. What is necessary now is the courage and vision with which to create a parallel body, both Zionist and universally Jewish, which will deal with the survivalist concerns of the Diaspora and the quality of Jewish life.

23. Dreams and Responsibilities

IT IS SOMETIMES BETTER TO READ A topical book months after its appearance. At that point some of the facts on which the author has built his arguments have changed and trends that he has perceived do not seem so inevitable. When the subject is nothing less than the one that Eliezer Livneh chose, *Israel and the Crisis of Western Civilization,* one begins to feel that perhaps the author should have let the book wait awhile before he published it. He would then, no doubt, have come to the same conclusions, since one's conclusions on a subject like this are almost invariably based on one's faith rather than on a set of present facts, but at least his facts would not have been dated by events.

What Livneh believes is really not at all as new and modern as his references to such ultramodern questions as ecology and the size of the *aliyah* from the United States would lead us to believe. He is reaffirming some standard, and still moving, parts of the Zionist ideology of his generation. Livneh has no doubt that Zionism is a messianic movement come to make an end of the *galut,* once and for all. This, perhaps, owes something to the existence of anti-Semitism, but it was not primarily created by that phenomenon. On the contrary, the Zionism of the ingathering has as its deepest motive the reassertion in our own time of *netsach Yisrael lo yeshaker*—that the Glory of Israel is eternal.

Livneh never tells us, not in a single line, that he believes in God, and yet he quotes verses from the Bible and passages from the Talmud quite copiously to establish the proposition that Jews have an inalienable right on the Land of Israel. He insists that the meaning of the ingathering is to provide an old-new context for the flourishing of the unique moral and spiritual tradition and culture of the Jews. That tradition is identified by Livneh with the

Reprinted from *Congress Bi-Weekly,* vol. 40, no. 8 (May 18, 1973).

regeneration of man, the individual, through living in smaller communities in closer connection with nature. And he is at great pains to insist that such very current questions as ecology will be solved through the example that Israel is already giving in the use of its resources.

It is clear from this summary that Livneh's essential point is that the Third Jewish Commonwealth now being built has, as its basic *raison d'être,* the fulfillment of the prophecy and responsibility that it should be "a light to the nations." Anyone who has read Zionist literature in even the most cursory way can hear in this summary the echoes of Ahad Ha-am and A. D. Gordon even more truly than those of Harav Kook, whom Livneh quotes more often. On purely intellectual grounds one must ask the question of Livneh that Yechezkel Kaufman asked of Ahad Ha-am: "On what grounds, short of the religious belief in the God—who chose Zion—does he assert the binding character and superiority of the Jewish tradition?"

This is not a purely intellectual question and it has important consequences. Our involvement as Jews with Arabs and Christians in the Holy Land is really historic and secular. Now, if we are to assert with Livneh, on the basis of all the citations that he marshals from the Jewish sacred texts, our claim to sovereignty everywhere (Livneh is of course a maximalist) about holding on to territory, then we have put the whole question on the level of religion. If so, Christians have a right to make their claims maximum in the name of what they believe was revealed to them, and Moslems are certainly entitled to speak the same language and refuse to yield up even one centimeter of the land of the believers. If our charter is indeed the Bible, then why should other people yield to us on what was communicated to them in their sacred books? It is possible for true Orthodox believers to answer this question by saying that they have no choices and that the God of Israel will prevail, but I find it particularly difficult to accept this from the pen of so modern a man as Livneh.

It is true that in history, in the realm of the here and now, we Jews have been involved in this land with our deepest being, but so have others on perhaps different levels but nonetheless real for them. They too have something of, not Diaspora, but at least

outside communities of their own who look to this land. It is possible for these various claims, aims, and histories to be balanced in
some set of conditions which work in the secular world, which are
ad hoc, and which should remove their bitterness because they are
not wrapped in sacredness. To declare holy war in the name of our
Jewish position is to invite it in return, and in that path lies
madness.

On another level, I have difficulty with Livneh's notion that
Israel is going to be—no, is already well on the way to becoming—
the solution of the problems of Western society. Has he driven
by the refineries of Haifa recently and seen the open sewers? Has
he really been in Tel Aviv? Does he really believe that Israel has
solved more of the problems of urban sprawl and the abuse of national resources than any other Western society? I do not yield to him
in passion for the perfection of Israel even though my life is lived
mostly in American *galut*. But let us look with clear eyes and realize
that the problem that Israel, and indeed the Jewish people as a
whole, has to solve is to deal with the fact that our lives have been
as deeply affected and even vulgarized by the twentieth century as
other Western communities. We are yet on the way; we are
certainly not in the lead of those who solved the problems of the
twentieth century.

Livneh's messianic feeling leads him to believe that the ingathering is already sure and certain, for lo! the Americans are
coming. I wish it were so. But the truth is that they are not.
If *aliyah* was ten thousand for the year in which he wrote his
manuscript, 1971, it is little more than half that in 1972. No large-
scale immigration to Israel has ever taken place, not even perhaps
the present Russian immigration, without really serious anti-
Semitism as one of the causes. At this moment there are thunder
squalls here and there in the American Jewish atmosphere, but not
the kind of malignant anti-Semitism which will create mass *aliyah*.

These sharp criticisms do not mean that I do not share most
of Livneh's dream. I am a Zionist and therefore dream with him
of an Israel which will produce a new man. I hope and pray that
this new society may become the creative leaven of the world.
I know that it is not yet, and I think it wrong to counterpose
problems of others not to our problems but to our dreams and

then assure ourselves that we are better. Livneh thinks that we
have arrived. Perhaps because he sits in Jerusalem and remembers
A. D. Gordon. I think that we are still on the way. Having been
so sharp with him, I should be equally sharp with myself. Perhaps
I think this because I still live in a suburb of New York and still
view myself on the way. But there is one virtue in seeing things
from the perspective even of New York. One simply has to deal
with the reality of others' and one's own provincialism. Zion is the
great dream, the deepest hope of our life. Let us not make it
unbelievable by claiming too much of the present.

24. Zionism Today

ZIONISM CAME INTO the world to achieve a situation in which Jews
would not be in the control of the Gentiles and would cease
depending on the goodwill of others. As a matter of fact, from
1967 to 1973 we Jews thought we had it made; Israel was the
dominant military power in the Middle East and we thought it
would last forever. I think when Israeli history is finally written
this period is going to be called "the age of Golda and Arik
Sharon." Despite the fact that they are not notably close to each
other, their rhetoric was the same. From 1967 to 1973, Golda's
position was very simple: "Until the Arabs come in a delegation
and ask to make peace, I like it where I am. . . . Time is on my
side, not on their side." Sharon added that "Israel is the ranking
power among the world's smaller countries. It has finally achieved
military-political sovereignty."

In the American Jewish community, because the leaders of the
United Jewish Appeal did their jobs as brilliantly as the generals

---

Unpublished address, Conference of Rabbis for the United Jewish Appeal,
Miami, December 1, 1975.

in Israel, there was comparably the notion that world Jewry was sovereign because from 1967 to 1973 we were fully able to pay the deficit of Israel. It is only after 1973 that subscription money could no longer make up the difference. For the first time since 1948, we were now really aware that the world Jewish community cannot do it all by itself. After the 1967 War the costs were not that high, and from 1967 to 1973 we could manage it by ourselves. Whatever may have been the croaking voices of intellectuals, dissenters, etc., who wrote occasional pieces in the Hebrew press or made speeches in Jerusalem—I'm, of course, mocking myself—there was a presumption in the Jewish world that there were elements of independence here. It never entered seriously the political consciousness of the Israeli establishment in 1967 to 1973 that the role of the American Jewish community, which was even in those days regarded as vitally necessary, was any diminution of Israel's sovereignty. No one then doubted that the critical decisions of Jewish life, as a matter of right, ought to be made in Israel.

In those "seven fat years" we began to imagine that what classic Zionism wanted had been achieved. What happened in the 1973 War is that in its aftermath the Jewish community gave more money, not less. We're giving more money right now. Israel, militarily, did more astounding things in October 1973 than it did in 1967, because in 1967 the Arabs were badly trained and in 1973 they had an army. The recuperation of Israel after the first defeats in October 1973 was a far more astonishing affair, militarily. Comparably, in the aftermath of the Yom Kippur War American Jews raised twice as much money for Israel as the year before. Israel has now, with American help, a more powerful army than ever. Indeed, James Schlesinger tried to persuade me last year that liberal Jews, if they were pro-Israel, really ought to be in favor of a greater American defense budget. He told me that the professional judgment of the Pentagon was that the Israeli army was three times more effective than it was in 1973, in terms of the sophisticated weaponry available to Israel.

Nonetheless, what has really happened is that we are back in a pre-Zionist situation—that is, Israel lives at the tail end of a long American supply line, in an economic situation where if United Jewish Appeal got seven or eight hundred million dollars next year instead of six hundred, we would still have to go back into the American political process, with all its complications, to get what really counts, which is military and economic aid in the billions—primarily military, but military aid available only in the American political process.

We are therefore again in the situation in which we were from 1945 to 1948 and before, and that is that the very life of Israel depends not only on what Jews can do, on their courage and valor and on their devotion, but on what Jews can persuade others to do. That is the terror of it, because the whole of the Zionist venture was created so that Jews would never have to worry again as to whether the secretary of state liked us today—something we had hoped that we were unlearning, to be counting noses again and again in the American political process, to be asking ourselves what, as a shuttlecock in the Middle East, we add up to.

What are the ultimate costs for the world Jewish community in this battle, what does this mean in terms of the stability of our relationships, for example, with the twenty thousand Jews in Mexico or the several hundred thousand in Brazil, or those in Argentina? Is the issue of Zionism, not yet as a dual allegiance but as a rather unique thing in the world and the relationship of Jews in America to Israel as quite *sui generis,* a quite unmixed blessing? I agree completely that in the short run it looks very good; in the long run, it's *tsuris,* but these are the *tsuris* which we thought we had gotten over and therefore the situation is all the harder to take.

I do not believe that 1967–1973 was anything more than delusional. I said it then. Those of you who have long memories will remember that I spent a good bit of the six years from 1967 to 1973 in consistent public hot water as a Zionist saying "Don't kid yourself. The reality of Jewish history is that you have to deal with all kinds of nasty people who simply won't go away—and the delusions that they will simply go away because we don't like them was a dream, a very nice dream, but we're now down to reality."

What then are our problems of self-explanation? How do we explain? What do we do?

How do we explain? I think if anything is clear, at least to me, the rhetoric of classic Zionism is to try to explain the Jew as being just like everyone else, to create him as a species of some genus—in this case a national identity or nation-state. This rhetoric is contrary to the facts today. The plain fact is that Israel is not a state like all other states; it is, as many people have pointed out, the Jew among the states. If you doubt it, take a look at what keeps happening at the United Nations. Is Israel treated in the United Nations like Albania or Singapore, or is it treated as the corporate incarnation of that dread element called the Jew? It is the Jew; it is the pariah state.

Remember a couple of years ago when this was already building? I remember that U.N. Ambassador Joseph Tekoah had asked me to have lunch with him. The most convenient place, in the interests of his time, was to meet him in the delegates' lounge of the United Nations. I had the feeling as I walked into the lounge with him that people were turning away one by one, and I'll never forget what Joe Tekoah said to me. He said, "You know, Arthur, for the last year or so, being the Israeli delegate in the United Nations has finally given me to understand what it felt like to be a Jew in Germany in 1938." He wore an invisible yellow badge and by walking with him I wore the same badge. Oh, yes, the waiters were still polite, but can you imagine walking through a crowded delegates' lounge of two hundred or so people and not a single person, except Israeli staff, said hello to him—and that was two years ago.

Our situation is not like everyone else's. Israel is a state which is treated by the rest of the world as different, and we treat that state as different, and we are treated by it as different because the involvement of Jews, each in the other, and the various parts of the Jewish people, each in the other, is of a unique quality. Remember, every lie has in it just the necessary element of truth which carries it. The big anti-Zionist lie, the attack on Zionism, is carried by a truth which we like to deny for public relations purposes, the truth that the Jews really are singular. There is no other country with an 80 percent irridenta which has a United Jewish Appeal and you and me around to worry about it twenty-four hours a day.

Zionism was created to make an end of the Diaspora. As a

matter of fact it has both acted to preserve it and to sharpen the angularities of its relationship with the rest of the world. Zionism said, "We will now regularize and normalize you." What it has succeeded in doing by its very political and military successes is to produce an odd kind of reevocation of the unique self-definitions and the unique energies of the Jewish people. Therefore, one can talk about national liberation movements until one is blue in the face. Our propaganda may convince college freshmen but it won't convince others. Zionism is not really the national liberation movement of the Jewish people in any sense in which other national liberation movements recognize it. A national liberation movement is the liberation movement of someone from a foreign oppressor; it isn't the liberation movement of one thousand Jews from Milwaukee proudly wearing Koach buttons on a visit to the territory in which they're not living but in whose liberation they participate with enormous élan and great passion. Zionism is the national liberation movement of a people which feels itself socially, culturally, spiritually, and religiously at odds with its environment and nonetheless uses its involvement in Zion in maintaining that peculiar identity.

I've often said that the Israel–Diaspora relationship is a paradox. Israel uses the Diaspora and looks to it as the ultimate source of its survivalist energies. *Aliyah,* not merely money, is the essential demand. The Diaspora looks to Israel and says that its involvement in Israel is what is going to make it survive. When Israel affirms the centrality of Israel, it really means that all Jewish organizations should devote their primary energies to the preservation of the state. When Jews in the United States say "the centrality of Israel" they mean something quite different; they mean that in the very act of worrying about Israel, Diaspora existence acquires verve and meaning. Now these are peculiar, unique, *sui generis* relationships which come out of a peculiar and unique history about which you can't easily sloganeer. Our problem is that we've been sloganeering with the things which come readily to hand, and the slogans no longer work because the world knows that the Jews are not really like everybody else. The world knows something which the thunderers of classic Zionism as well as the thunderers of classic assimilationism both denied. The Jews are not going to "normalize" themselves in the near future, either as a nation or as individuals within the world.

That being so, the problem today is not how you explain that Zionism is not racism. Everybody knows that Zionism is not racism. The problem is how you explain honestly this unique set of relationships in the world which are the ties among world Jewry. Oddly enough, the anti-Semites are ahead of us. Khrushchev, in the early 1960s, was saying that the trouble with Russian Jews was that they were a bunch of "cosmopolitans." We said the Russian Jews were wonderful citizens of Russia, good Communists, only let them have a few Yiddish schools and let them go to synagogue without harassment. Khrushchev knew something that we weren't yet admitting; he knew that the Jews of Russia wanted out, at least the "Jewish Jews" of Russia did. We say today that these Jews of Russia are really citizens of Israel or of the Jewish world, and that they are precisely what Khrushchev said they were in the 1960s. They are involved by their Jewish identity, in ways in which no other subethnic group in the Soviet Union is involved, with people outside the Soviet Union. We are not going to answer the anti-Semites or the anti-Zionists until we are willing to put on the line not the rhetoric with which we delude ourselves very often as well as others, but the rhetoric of truth—and that is that we are different.

After that, for me, comes the next and crucial question: So what? Why must all identities in the world be symmetrical? Why must all identities in the world fit into certain classic nineteenth-century categories of religion or political state or national identity? What is so immoral about international Jewish closeness, about that about ourselves which Mordecai Kaplan once called very beautifully "the peoplehood of the Jews"? What is immoral about it before the bar of anybody's judgment? I would like to suggest to good Americans on the left who would like to forgive the tens of thousands who are in exile, who refused to share this national purpose in Vietnam because they felt bound by other and, in their mind, higher commitments, and to the good Americans on the right who felt that they could break into the Democratic National Headquarters because they felt bound by higher commitments—

and I don't equate them at all—that it ought to be possible for us, who once suggested to America the notion of the multiethnic country, to suggest to America and to the world that category which alone can bear our self-explanations. It is the notion of asymmetrical identities, identities which are not species of the same genus, identities which don't operate in the same way, and which nonetheless each have a right to exist. This particular approach makes it possible to face the real attack on Jews since the very beginnings of the great hatred. Do you remember the first formulation of it by Haman in the book of Esther? "There is a people, scattered among the nations, unlike all others, which operates by its own modalities, by its own rhythms," and Haman said this people is dangerous. Mordecai countered that the Jews were in their own way loyal to the highest purposes of the empire. It seems to me that our self-explanations are going to have to move in Mordecai's direction.

I have one further observation, and that is that I don't think that propaganda is the answer. Having begun with the 1967–1973 situation and mentioned Golda Meir to break a lance with her, let me conclude by quoting this great lady with profound respect. I once argued with her about something or other in Israel's policy and she looked me straight in the eye and said, "You think you are putting it on the level of *hasbarah*—of how do we conduct our propaganda?" She added, "The issue is really what is our policy to be; why don't you tell it to me straight that you dissent from that policy?"

I do not think that we are going to come to terms with the onslaught of this day because it is not merely an onslaught on our difference; it is an onslaught on what is true. It has been said, very beautifully, that what we Jews have going for us is our indissoluble unity. Well, if you know it and I know it, then I expect the Arabs know it too. If what is going for us is the indissoluble unity of the Jewish people, then it is that unity which has to be defended.

In this particular quarrel there will be no real resolution until by political means the Middle Eastern question is settled one way or another, hopefully on the best, the most spacious, terms we can possibly get. We are in a political confrontation over the future of Israel and the future of the Jewish people which is so intimately involved in this conflict. What is going on right now is very sad, very tragic, very dangerous. It is hopeful only if it can be viewed as the moment with which a much more sober Jewish world assesses its strengths and its possibilities and comes to terms not only with its dreams—dreams are the stuff that keeps the Messiah alive—but also with its realities, and operates in terms of the possible. Fighting back, propaganada, asserting the uniqueness of the Jewish people and trying to explain it, trying to defend the idea that anti-Semitism is the dislike of the unlike—all this is very useful, but ultimately we are in a political crisis and a political crisis is soluble only by political means. One thing I know—we have only ourselves ultmiately, but having ourselves we need to be a wise and discriminating people. It's easy to be victorious, it is even possible to be defeated; the hardest thing of all is to live with attrition, with complexity, with ambiguity, and to find one's way. It seems to me that we as rabbis, we as teachers, we as leaders of the Jewish spirit, are now back in our old classic roles of leading a people which is neither heady with victory nor laid low with despair, but which has to find on a day-to-day basis courage and wisdom.

25. Judaism and the Land of Israel

AS A POLITICAL FACT the state of Israel is a unique creation. Though its legal existence has been recognized by all of the major powers and by most other states, all of its immediate neighbors, the six Arab states on its borders, continue to insist that its presence in the Middle East is a political and moral affront of such magnitude that it entitles them to try to effect its destruction. There have been many revolutions in the twentieth century in the name of national self-determination; Israel is the only example of a new

Paper given at the Jewish Consultation with the World Council of Churches, May 27-30, 1969, Geneva, Switzerland.

state created by a largely nonresident people returning to the homeland of its ancestors.

In our century the tendency of political states, both old and new, has been to conceive of themselves as secular arrangements which represent no particular religious tradition. The State of Israel is indeed largely secular. For that matter, one of the avowed purposes of its creators was to make it possible for Jews to lead completely secular lives as Jews, within their own polity. Nonetheless, Israel was created by Jews to be, and to remain, an essentially Jewish state, that is, to represent something more than a conventional, secular, political arrangement to serve the needs of its individual citizens of whatever condition or provenance. This mystique pervades even the secularists in Israel and is deeply felt among the majority of the Jews of the world, regardless of the nature of their religious convictions or commitments. The multiplicity of often clashing forms of life and value appears, from this perspective, to be the confusion of creativity, the necessary turmoil which attends the effecting of a synthesis between the old and the new. The present is seen as an age of becoming, and the sometimes even bitter internal conflicts of the moment are part of some larger harmony. The national mood in Israel is one of attempting to encounter the twentieth century in terms of its own historic tradition.

The most unusual characterstic of the life of Israel today is its connection with the Jewish community of the world. This theme was stated by one of its earliest constitutional acts, the Law of Return, under which any Jew is a citizen of the State of Israel from the moment of his arrival as an immigrant. Such a law is not entirely unprecedented among modern irredentist movements, but the whole complex of connections between the State of Israel and the world Jewish community is, indeed, unique. Support, both moral and financial, by the majority of the Jews outside of its borders is critically necessary to the development of Israel. The State of Israel regards itself, and is universally regarded, as the spokesman for some Jewish interests, such as the rights of the Jews of the Soviet Union, which are not immediately related to its own position and which, sometimes, in terms of narrowest self-interest, Israel would be best off avoiding. The leadership of Jerusalem remains dedicated to the task of helping to preserve Jewish loyalty and consciousness among the Jews on all five continents.

It is too narrow and even unjust to view this concern as the desire of an embattled nation to keep alive a maximum reservoir of goodwill and support or even, ultimately, of potential new immigrants. The preservation of the Jewish spirit is the fundamental purpose for which the state was conceived by its founders, and this commitment is even more important than the immediate needs which the Jewish settlement in the Holy Land has served during this tragic century, as the major place to which Jewish refugees from persecution could come as of right and not as an act of foreign grace. In turn, the Jews of the world look upon Israel as the major contemporary incarnation of many of their own hopes for continuity. The depth of the emotion which Israel evokes among them is, to be sure, affected by recent memories of Auschwitz. Israel is, indeed, in its very strength, a symbol of the end of Jewish passivity and lack of power to resist slaughter; it does represent an open door for Jews who do not easily in this present age trust anyone else but themselves with the keys to their safety. At the very root, however, Israel and the world Jewish concerns which help sustain it are both based on some of the grand and ancient themes of Jewish religion and of Jewish history. One cannot understand the present unless it is viewed as both a contemporary re-evocation of elements of faith and hope peculiar to Judaism and, paradoxically, as a contemporary tension between this older outlook and newer modes of thought and life.

All of the elements of Jewish religious consciousness were present and, indeed, defined in the very first encounter in the Biblical narrative between the One God and Abraham. The account needs to be recalled, both for what it affirms and for what it excludes: "And God said to Abram, go forth from your land and from your place of birth and from the house of your father to the land which I will show you. And I will make of you a great people and I will bless you and make your name great; and be a blessing." In the next verse the last promise is amplified, "and all the families of the earth will be blessed through you." Abraham obeyed the command and entered the land, where the One God appeared to him, reiterating and amplifying the promise, "and to your children I will give this land" (Genesis 12:1–3). In these encounters Abraham was taken away from all of his original relationships. Community, land, and even the family within which he arose, all represent ties which were broken for a fresh beginning, a covenant with the Lord in which a new community was to be created which Abraham was to found. It was to arise in a particular place, the land of Canaan, which had been set aside for the authentic encounter between the seed of Abraham and the God who founded their community. The life of this community in this land was to exist for a purpose: to demonstrate to all other people how human life is to be lived at its most moral. The implication already exists in the original sending that any falling away from such a standard will represent a breach in the covenant and a defilement of holy soil. Exile is already conceivable as punishment and the ultimate return is already in view as laden with messianic meaning, of redemptive quality for Jews and for mankind.

One can skip the centuries and quote a modern writer from almost our own time, to find these most ancient themes reappearing essentially as they were first pronounced. Solomon Schechter wrote in 1906 in New York: "The selection of Israel, the indestructibility of God's covenant with Israel, the immortality of Israel as a nation, and the final restoration of Israel to Palestine, where the nation will live a holy life on holy ground, with all the wide-reaching consequences of the conversion of humanity and the establishment of the Kingdom of God on earth—all these are the common ideals and the common ideas that permeate the whole of Jewish literature extending over nearly four thousand years."

Both as a fact and as a promise the relationship of Jews to the land of Israel thus appeared as an indispensable element in the original covenant. Jerusalem appears later, at the time of David. It is clear from both of the Biblical accounts of its conquest, in Samuel and in Chronicles, that making the city into the capital is the act which set the seal on the creation of the Jewish Kingdom. The city did not belong to any individual tribe, not even to the tribe of Judah: "And David and all Israel went to Jerusalem" (I Chronicles 14:4), thus acquiring it by action of the entire people and making of it the place to which all Israel would turn. It certainly does not need to be demonstrated that all of the Biblical writers looked to Jerusalem as the essence of the meaning of their faith, life, and hope. In the later years of the existence of the Second Temple, Jerusalem was the center of pilgrimage not only for the Jews in the Land of Israel but also for the increasingly scattered Diaspora. The evidence for this is to be found in all the literature of the period, in Josephus (*Wars* I, 4, 13), Philo (*Laws* I, 68) and the New Testament (*Acts of the Apostles* 2:5). The literature of the Talmud is, of course, laden with accounts of masses from all the Jewish world coming to the Temple, especially to celebrate the Passover. There is a tale, no doubt exaggerated, that on one Passover, King Agrippa had the priests count the number of paschal lambs that had been offered up and he found that the total exceeded 1,200,000 (*Pesahim* 64b). It is well known that in those days, in the century before its destruction by the Romans, the Temple was visited by Gentiles as well as by Jews and there is Talmudic evidence that in the sacrificial cult there was regular provision for acts of prayer and atonement for all of the "seventy nations" of the world.

The connection between Jews and the land was not broken by the Exile. By the third century, the Babylonian Jewish community had begun to overshadow the one which remained in the land under the Romans, and yet Babylonian authorities ruled, as firmly as those in the Holy Land, that either party to a marriage could force the other, by appeal to rabbinic courts, to move from the Diaspora to the Land of Israel (*Ketubot* 110b). Dwelling in the land remained, in the view of most of the later rabbinic authorities, a Biblical commandment of continuing validity, and those of the medieval writers who did not insist on this as a religious good absolved themselves and the people of their generation because of the dangers to life that the journey involved (*Responsa* of R. Isaiah Trani II, 25). This point is perhaps best made by quoting a tale from the third century: Two rabbis were once on their way out of the Land of Israel to Nisibis, where the great teacher, R. Judah ben Batyrah, dwelt, to learn Torah from him. They got as far as Sidon and there they remembered the Land of Israel. They began to weep, they rent their garments, and they remembered the Biblical verses which promised the land to the seed of Abraham. The rabbis turned around and went back to their place in the land, pronouncing that dwelling in the Land of Israel is, in itself, an act equal of religious significance to all of the Commandments in the Torah (*Sifrei, Re'eh*).

In aspiration and in memory the connection of Jews with the land was, thus, not broken by the Exile. On the contrary, the destruction of the Temple and of the Holy City, Jerusalem, and the absence of Jews from their land were regarded as a punishment. Life outside of the Holy Land was possible for Jews, but it was less than the full life, in perfect obedience to God, which could happen only with physical restoration. What has increasingly appeared with the progress of historical research in the last century is that these religious commitments were more than merely visionary. Some Jews continued to remain in the land even during the most dangerous and disastrous times and in every century there were returns to it, sometimes by small handfuls of leading spiritual figures and, on occasion, by substantial communities.

In the early centuries of the common era, access to Jerusalem itself was denied to Jews, though there is some evidence that the Roman emperors of the second century and the one thereafter did permit them to visit the city and to worship on the Mount of Olives and, sometimes, even on the Temple Mount itself. The situation became even more difficult by the fourth century, and there is contemporary evidence from Christian sources that Jews had the greatest difficulty in buying the right to come to pray near the Western Wall, at least on the Ninth of Ab, the anniversary of the destruction of the Temple. The Pilgrim from Bordeaux, the earliest Christian visitor whose written account of his visit to Jerusalem has survived, tells that in the year 333 Jews came every year to that site to "bewail themselves with groans, rend their garments, and so depart" (*The Bordeaux Pilgrim,* pp. 21–22). There are comparable accounts by the Church Father, Gregory of Nazianzus (*Orat. VI de pace,* p. 91), and by Jerome in his commentary to Zephaniah written in the year 392 (*Migne, Patrologia,* XXV, Col. 1354). But with the end of Roman rule in Palestine the prohibition against Jews living in Jerusalem was lifted, and after that there is evidence for an often flourishing Jewish community in that city. During the Crusades the great traveler, Petahiah of Regensburg, was in Jerusalem in the years 1180–1185, and he reports that at the time there was only one Jew, a dyer, resident there, but after the era of the Crusades the community began to rebuild.

It is instructive in this connection that ever since 1844, a half-century before the first stirrings of modern Zionism, Jerusalem has been the one city in the Holy Land which has consistently had a Jewish majority in its population. According to the 1844 edition of the *Encyclopaedia Britannica* the population figures of the time were 7,120 Jews, 5,530 Moslems, and 3,390 Christians, and all of them lived within the walled city. By 1896, when much of the Jewish population was already outside the wall but the city as a whole was still a unit, there were more than 28,000 Jews and some 17,000 Christians and Moslems, combined into roughly equal halves (*Luah Eretz Yisrael,* 1896). The first government census by the British, that of October 1922, found almost 34,000 Jews and about 38,000 Moslems and Christians in the whole of the city. Even at that point, with the Jewish population growth taking place entirely outside the wall, there were still 5,639 Jews in the Old City itself. In 1931, Jews were a majority of 51,000 in the city out of a total population of 90,000, while by 1939 the Jewish population of all of Jerusalem was an even more pronounced majority. However, almost two decades of riots and pogroms by Arabs against Jews in the Old City had made it a dangerous place in which to live, and Jewish numbers in the Old City itself had declined to something over 2,000.

In the last two millennia of its history Jerusalem has been the most dangerous and difficult place for Jews to dwell in of any of the cities of the Holy Land, yet this sampling of population figures is evidence that physical connection to the city remained so precious to Jews that they were willing throughout the ages to risk the dangers and to submit to the suffering. All of the chronicles and contemporary accounts of the Middle Ages substantiate the import of the figures for the last century: whenever the barest possibility existed, even under hostile powers, enough Jews were to be found to cleave to Jerusalem so that across the centuries theirs was the largest continuing presence there. Memories of the past, messianic hopes for the future, and modern Zionism in all its contemporaneity are, indeed, the heirs of the major continuing physical connection with that city.

This clinging by Jews to Jerusalem, even more than to the whole of the rest of the Holy Land, is no accident; it has the deepest roots in the continuing religious tradition and folk consciousness of Jews. It is "the city which I have chosen unto me" (I Kings 11:36) and the one "upon which my name is called" (II Kings 21:4). It was, of course, the place where the Temple stood, the seat of God's presence, even though the heaven and the heaven of heavens could not contain Him. In the imagery of prophecy Zion and Jerusalem are often parallel to all of Israel; both these names are often used to represent not only the whole of the people but also all of its land. For example, "Speak unto Zion, you are my people" (Isaiah 51:16) or "Comfort ye, comfort ye, my people; speak to the heart of Jerusalem" (Isaiah 40:1). The synagogue poets of late ancient and medieval times made much of these themes, and of the hundreds of examples that could be given, the most famous is also the most characteristic. Writing in Spain in the eleventh century, Judah Halevi cries out: "Zion, wilt thou not ask after the peace of thy captive children?" Ironically, this poet and philosopher ended his life as a pilgrim in the Hold Land, where he was supposedly killed soon after his arrival.

In the daily prayers of Jews to this day, one of the benedictions of the silent devotion is a prayer for the rebuilding of Jerusalem; that paragraph represents the hope for the restoration of Jews to the Holy Land as a whole. In the grace which Jews say after every meal, morning, noon, and night, the third benediction reads: "And rebuild Jerusalem, the holy city, speedily and in our day; blessed art thou, O Lord, who builds Jerusalem." All synagogues throughout the Jewish world, from the first one in antiquity to those being erected this very day, have been built in such fashion that they face toward Jerusalem. Its very name has always evoked the memory of a time when all was well, when Jews lived on their land and worshipped God in His holy temple, and the hope for the day when some of this glory would return. To be buried on the Mount of Olives, no matter where one dies, has been regarded for two millennia as the surest hope of the Resurrection, and bodies were being returned from Rome some two thousand years ago for that purpose. To kiss the stones of Jerusalem, even in its destruction, was to be as close to God as man could be. To participate in its rebuilding was the hope of the ages.

In the Holy Land, as a whole, the Jewish presence after the fourth century was, in terms of numbers, of relatively lesser importance. Nonetheless, the realities of Jewish history during the nineteen centuries of the Exile are misstated if there is no emphasis on the important existence of Jewish communities in the land itself throughout the centuries. The Talmud of Jerusalem was created by important schools of Jewish learning in the Holy Land, and these declined only in the fourth and fifth century under Christian persecution. The fixing of the vocalization of the Hebrew Bible, the Masoretic Text, was done by Jewish scholars in Tiberias between the eighth and tenth centuries. At that time, and for the next century or so, both the Karaites and the followers of the Talmudic tradition had important communities in the Holy Land, and, for a while, around the year 1000, academies of rabbinic learning were reconstituted in Jerusalem and Ramleh. These were of such consequence that they shared leadership in the Jewish world, as a whole, with the schools in Babylonia, though the Babylonian academies had by then enjoyed an uninterrupted tradition of almost a millennium. Even under the Crusaders, Jewish communities continued to exist in the cities of Acre and Ashkelon as well as in a variety of other places, particularly a number of villages in the Galilee, in several of which Jews have dwelt without interruption since before the destruction in the year 70 c.e.

At the beginning of the thirteenth century there came the first organized attempt by Jews in Europe to return to the Holy Land, when three hundred rabbis of France and England came there. Some of these men were of the highest intellectual rank. Nahmanides left Spain after an unfortunate disputation in Barcelona, which was forced upon him by Pablo Christiani, and spent the last three years of his life from 1267 to 1270 reconstituting a Jewish community in Jerusalem. Toward the end of the fifteenth century, the almost equally important Obadiah of Bartinora, the author of the standard commentary on the Mishnah, left Italy for the

Holy Land and he, too, reinvigorated the Jewish community in Jerusalem.

From the beginning of the sixteenth century there was an important growth of the Jewish population in the Galilee and, especially, in the town of Safed. Exiles from Spain, after the final expulsion of Jews in 1492, arrived in the country in some numbers and within a century there were eighteen academies of Talmudic studies and twenty-one synagogues in Safed alone. Indeed, the most important spiritual stirrings and creativity within Jewry during the sixteenth century took place there. There was even an abortive attempt to reconstitute the authority of the ancient patriarchate, which had lapsed under Roman persecution. The studies of both kabbalah and Talmud were pursued with renewed creative élan, and it was in Safed in 1567 that Josef Karo published the *Shulhan Arukh* which was almost immediately accepted by the bulk of world Jewry as the authoritative summation of Jewish law and practice.

Until the end of the seventeenth century, the overwhelming majority of the Jews in the Holy Land were either Sephardim, of Spanish extraction, or Orientals. Central and East European influence, however, became prominent in the year 1700, and has existed in unbroken continuity into the contemporary era. A group of several hundred people arrived from Poland under the leadership of Rabbi Judah the Pious, and even though the destiny of this community was not a happy one, these immigrants were followed by others. Toward the end of the eighteenth century there were disciples of Elijah of Wilno, the greatest Talmudic scholar of the age, as well as a major group of relatives and other followers of his great antagonist, the founder of hasidism, Israel Baal Shem Tov. Both legalists and ecstatics within East European Jewry could not then imagine the continuity of Judaism without a living link to the soil of the Holy Land.

Throughout these centuries economic conditions in the country were generally difficult, and the Jews suffered perhaps more than did other communities. Those in the Holy Land were constantly sending letters and even personal emissaries to their brethren in the Diaspora asking for support, and one of the prime sources of our knowledge of medieval and early modern Jewish history is in what remains of these exchanges. It was a well-established tradition throughout the Jewsh world that these continuing requests from their brethren in the Holy Land took priority even over local charitable needs.

The Jews in the Holy Land were, to be sure, living largely from foreign alms, and in this they were seemingly parallel to Christian pilgrims and monastic orders in the land during that era. But there were two important points of difference: Jews who came to the Holy Land did not cluster around a variety of holy places, for from Jewish perspective, dwelling in the land anywhere was the fulfillment of religious commandment. In the second place, their very presence in the land had radically different resonance among the Jews of the world than the Christian or Moslem presences had among their brethren elsewhere. This often embattled and struggling Jewish community, repeatedly reinforced by new arrivals and always in connection with the whole of the Diaspora, was a constant reminder to the majority that it was living less than the ideal religious life and that return to the land was the ultimate goal. Maimonides, in the twelfth century, had defined this consummation as not necessarily an eschatological event attended by miracles and cataclysms. The restoration would happen in a natural way, by a change in the political situation which would allow Jews to return to their homeland as part of a universal process ushering in a final age of justice and peace. This view did not become the dominant one, for messianists continued to dream of a cataclysmic "end of days."

Hopes of immediate return were aroused more than once through the ages. For a brief moment in the sixteenth century, when the melodramatic David Reubeni appeared in Rome to offer some supposed military support to Pope Clement VII against the Turks, there was even talk of such a restoration in the highest Christian quarters. The false messiah Shabbetai Zvi had half the Jewish world, and even some Christians, convinced that the miraculous restoration would take place in the year 1666. During Napoleon's campaign in the Middle East in 1799, he summoned the Jews to rally to his banner with the promise that he would help restore them to their land. We know that this offer resulted from some conversation with younger elements of Jewry in the Holy Land. For that matter, the first stirrings toward making an end of living essentially on alms began before the middle of the nineteenth century. Sir Moses Montefiore, the leader of English Jewry, and various forces of the French Jewish community, especially the Rothschild family, worked to teach Jews in Palestine to become artisans and even farmers. Central European philanthropists even created a school for these purposes in 1854 in Jerusalem. It was followed in 1870 by the founding of an agricultural school, Mikveh Israel, and within the next two years two Jewish farm colonies were established. The career of modern Zionism began in 1881, as a direct result of large-scale pogroms in Russia, but already in that year, before any of the new immigration to the land began, the American Consul in Jerusalem, Warder Cresson, wrote to his government that there were then a thousand Jews in the country who were deriving their livelihood from agriculture.

This ancient and ongoing connection to the land and the messianic hopes which this connection both exemplified and helped to keep in being were the spiritual and emotional climate within which modern Zionism arose. In the immediate situation of the last decades of the nineteenth century the bulk of the world Jewish community, which was then to be found in Europe, found itself confronted by three situations. The most searing and immediate was virulent hatred of Jews, and not only in their major place of settlement in Russia. While millions were on the move from that country after 1881, it occurred to several of the intellectual leaders of Russian Jewry that in their newer homes these emigrants might ultimately be as much in danger as they had been in the places from which they were fleeing. Such phenomena as French and German anti-Semitism toward the end of the century raised the question whether the more liberal part of Europe, in which Jews had been formally emancipated, would honor, in bad times, the promise of equality for all.

In the second place, what seemed then to be the most hopeful of contemporary political ideas was the example of those peoples who were working toward their own national independence. Liberal nationalism was being proclaimed, not in the name of dominance over others, but in the name of a creative future for all the historic communities which would both be autonomous and live in concert with each other. This was the great dream of Mazzini, and the earliest major theoretician of Zionism, Moses Hess, responded to it as early as 1860 with acceptance and profound emotion.

The third situation, and the one perhaps most difficult to define, was the inner spiritual estate of Jewry itself. The dissolution of older values and identities, and especially of the religious, which was engulfing the younger intellectuals of all the traditions of the Western world, was felt with particular poignancy among Jews. The new age was revolutionary and upsetting of the older faiths, but for the Christian majority the continent of Europe, its monuments and most of what men had built on that soil, and its very languages represented the continuity of Christendom. The revolution was occurring for Christians in a context which could ultimately assimilate even these tensions into some new synthesis. But from the Jewish viewpoint, though Western secularity required an act of personal conversion to the mode of life which descended from the majority tradition, those Jews who were willing to undergo this conversion, such as Heine and Disraeli, found themselves less than completely accepted. The nineteenth century thus taught some Jews that it had been possible for them to be authentically themselves in the century before, while still in the ghetto, apart from society, whereas in the new, half-emancipated age that followed, it was much more difficult to find their own mode of encountering modernity, either as individuals or as part of their own historic community. The nineteenth century was sufficiently open to Jews intellectually for them to experience all of its problems; it was sufficiently closed to deny them the possibility, even if they had wished, to disappear as individuals in modern society. They remained sufficiently rooted in their own older heritage to regard their community as an ultimate spiritual good, worthy of both survival and inner refreshing. They were sufficiently men of their day to feel that their own involvement in their particular past and in the land sacred to their spiritual tradition was in keeping with the contemporary belief that historic communities and peoples were worthy of preservation, for their own sake and for the service of humanity.

The tragedies and torments of the twentieth century and the

achievements of the Jews of Israel have confirmed the direst of these predictions and some of the greatest of these hopes.

It cannot be emphasized enough that even the greatest of opportunities that the open society made available to Jews raised for them severe questions of spiritual survival. The rights of equality, wherever they have substantial meaning, were given to Jews as individuals, and the continuity of their community perforce had to be defined as a matter of private belief or, at its most organized, as a religious association parallel to that of contemporary Christian churches. From the Jewish perspective such redefinition, enshrined in the modern slogans of the separation of Church and State or of religion and culture, was a far more difficult and devastating charge than it was for the Christian majority in the Western world. For Jews, the holy congregation of all Israel, which means the reality in this world of all that Jews do in community, is the fundamental premise of their identity and tradition.

Classic Jewish interpretation of the Bible has always insisted that Israel "according to the flesh" is what is meant by Isaiah's prophecies concerning "the suffering servant." It is the individual Jew's experience of the Jewish people, of its corporate life, way, and history which mediates for him between the individual and God. When the richness and inner integrity of the life of that community is attenuated by either persecution or assimilation, or when belonging to the tradition becomes so privatized as to represent a bewildering variety of personal choices, that which is specifically Jewish in the consciousness of Jews will act, as it had acted in the last century, to recreate a living Jewish community on the Land of Israel. For the rest of world Jewry this community represents the indispensable contemporary center which ties Jews to one another and which encourages them to believe that their own lives, though cast in different molds and under minority circumstances, are viable. Its very creation some two decades ago represented a turning away from despair in the aftermath of the Nazi years and the rekindling among Jews of belief in the future. To use one of the clichés of the contemporary "theology of hope," the Jewish people in the 1940s had ceased believing in either the *humanum* or the *futurum*. It regained belief in both in 1948, when the State of Israel was established.

There can be no doubt that the Zionist reconstitution of a national Jewish community in Palestine in our time was an act which derived both from the ultimate wellsprings of the historic Jewish faith and from the immediate necessities of a stormy contemporary age. This does not mean that all the trappings of political statehood and all the acts of sovereign power are here being presented as commanded, valid, or necessary. On the contrary, what saves any nationalism, any sense of historic community and kinship, from becoming exclusivist, from the arrogance of "blood and soil," is conscience. It is even more wicked to assert that there is no salvation outside one's own nation than to pronounce that there is no salvation outside one's own church. The conscience which protects us from both such assertions has become manifest in the modern age both in secular forms, such as the United Nations Declaration on Human Rights, and in religious pronouncements by all of the major Western faiths. This most fundamental of our moral convictions has as its source Biblical prophecy. It was Amos who said to the Jewish people of his time that in the eyes of God, chosen though they were by Him, they had no more rights than the children of the Ethiopians, and that his bringing the Jews from Egypt was paralleled by his bringing the Philistines from Caftor and the Arameans from Kir. Here we are confronted by the universal element, the command of the living God of all the world, which enters as a radical demand into the midst of every human particularity and keeps it under judgment. Indeed, the meaning of community for Jews is that they live in the real world of action and choice, in this world, and the meaning of their chosenness is that they are subject to the most severe and searching of moral judgments: "Only you have I known from all the nations of the world: therefore, I will visit upon you all your iniquities" (Amos 3:2). For men of religion, indeed for all men of conscience, both elsewhere and in Israel, its acts, like those of any other people, are under judgment.

It needs to be remembered in this connection that the Zionist movement has itself, at least during part of its history, been of two minds about the demand for a sovereign Jewish state. Statehood, as such, was not even in the Zionist program from the days of the

Balfour Declaration in 1917 until almost all the Zionists, with the doors of Palestine completely closed to Jews, had little choice but to opt for sovereignty in 1948.

In accepting in 1917 the last reformulation of the Balfour Declaration, Weizmann and his colleagues knew that they were agreeing to some form of bi-national existence with the Arabs in Palestine. This was all clearer in the exchanges of 1919 between the Emir Feisal and both Felix Frankfurter and Chaim Weizmann. It was against any increase in Jewish numbers in Mandate Palestine, and not against a Jewish state, that Arabs made riots in 1921. For that matter, the repeated stoppages in Jewish immigration by the British authorities under Arab pressure, especially during the 1930s while Hitler was becoming an ever more murderous menace, was what made it clear to the Jews that any increase in their numbers, any possibility of having the legal right to buy land, or even the ultimate safety of their community could not be left to the goodwill of others, of which there was all too little. From the Jewish perspective, partition, and even statehood, were not hoped-for consummations but, rather, dire necessities. For that matter, even the very military might of Israel is less a source of pride and of national chauvinism than of fear of the constantly threatened destruction. It is certainly beyond doubt that the present choice of Israel is either its own sovereignty or its ceasing to exist, not only as a state, but also as a community.

It would be morally obtuse to presume that there has not been from the very beginning of this struggle, and that there is not now, especially as one contemplates the continuing misery of hundreds of thousands of Arab refugees, much justice on the side of Arab anger. Repeated attacks by Arabs since 1921 on often defenseless people; their tendency to assassinate or to threaten to assassinate their own moderates, as well as their continuing refusal to negotiate any kind of détente with Jews; and the treatment by the Arab governments of their refugee brethren from Palestine tend to undercut their standing in the court of moral opinion. For that matter, convinced though I am that the falls from grace among Jews throughout this half century have been very much less, and almost always reactive, the creators of the new Jewish life in Israel have not always been, and are not today, invariably prophets and angels. We must, however, get behind the often horrifying details of this half century of struggle to the basic moral issue.

From the point of view of the Arabs in Palestine at the end of World War I, the Balfour Declaration was at its very root, even in its most limited application, an act of injustice. They were not impressed by the legal argument that all of the land in the region had not been sovereign for many centuries and that no local population in Palestine had had sovereignty over the country since the end of the second Jewish commonwealth under the Maccabees. The Arabs of Palestine regarded themselves as morally entitled to their own development and unquestioned national life, untroubled by the claims or needs of others. It did not do to assure them, as Weizmann and others tried to do repeatedly, that Jews were coming to the land not to dispossess them or to take from them any of their rights, and certainly not to deny Arabs any of their personal or communal rights. The Arabs of Palestine presumed, correctly, that anything approaching freedom of Jewish immigration into Palestine would soon produce a large and dynamic Jewish population, the existence of which would block the way to the attainment of a Palestinian Arab State. For them to agree to live permanently with the inevitable constraints of another people of equal standing was already quite intolerable.

As is well known, some of the noblest of Jews, such as Magnes and Buber, who kept dreaming of this bi-national dream, could not find any substantial Arab counterparts with whom to work seriously toward its realization. Taking into account the Jewish emotion about the land, the dynamism of a highly trained people and the vastness of the need of millions of Jews for refuge, the Arabs were right, from their point of view, in fearing an open door would soon reduce them to a minority. Against this, they went into desperate battle almost at the very beginning, and they continue to insist that to have denied Arab nationalism in Palestine what would have been a normal development anywhere else is a grave injustice.

To be sure, even had there been no modern Zionism, it hardly needs to be demonstrated that the Holy Land is not like all other lands and that Arab nationalism in that country would have had a far different road to travel than that in Iraq or Egypt. All of the major Biblical faiths have continuing involvements in the Holy Land which they regard as their right and which no sovereign nation, including the Israelis today, can deal with in the most simplistic categories of national sovereignty. The denial by a sovereign Jordan of access by Jews to the Western Wall during the twenty years of its occupation of the Old City and the destruction of all but one of the more than fifty synagogues to be found there, as well as the desecration of the cemetery of the Mount of Olives, was such an act of sovereign revenge on the Jewish adversaries of the Arabs. The possibility of such an occurrence in the midst of political tension of any kind in the future must be guarded against on behalf of all the faiths and in relation to all the political sovereignties of the region, not excluding that of Israel.

Nonetheless, without Zionism there would have been an Arab majority and perhaps ultimately an Arab State of some kind in Palestine. There is, thus, great pain and pathos and considerable stature to the Arab case, and many of the actions by which it has contaminated do not blind Jews to its moral importance. Nevertheless, I submit that an objective assessment of the moralities of the situation must arrive at different conclusions. An Arab majority and a sovereignty in Palestine and, in particular, over that part of post-partition Palestine which is now Israel, is not vitally necessary to the survival and creativity of the whole of the Arab national culture and history, or to the Islamic faith. The great centers of Arab continuity and survival are elsewhere. A viable Jewish people in the land is, however, indispensable to the survival of the Jewish spirit in our age. If we are to presume, as all men of good will must, that the disintegration of either of these great traditions, the Jewish or the Arab, would be a catastrophe of the first order, then it is our moral duty to work toward the conditions that make this impossible. What reversed a rapid trend of worldwide Jewish disintegration was the élan and hope which Zionism and the State of Israel have brought both to Jews and to Judaism. Even to contemplate making an end to the Jewish state for even the most moral of reasons, that its existence denies to

Palestinian Arab nationalism sovereignty over the whole country and that we are horrified by the present misery of Arab refugees, is to put one's moral priorities in the wrong order.

In the world of human action all of our judgments can never occur without some cost, for justice can only be proximate and there is always some right, and often great right, on the side of those whose aims we do not accept. This is the human condition at all times and everywhere, and it is nowhere clearer than in a consideration by ethicists of this grievous conflict. It would, however, be a trap and a delusion not to get our moral priorities in the right order. Indeed, a hasidic teacher once said that Satan does not seduce us by proposing wicked action; he is at his most effective when he asks us to labor for the good, while keeping us from understanding that this labor is in the wrong order of priority and thus destructive of other, greater goods.

For the continuity of Judaism and Jews the State of Israel, not in terms of its culture at this immediate moment but because of the revivifying possibilities that it alone can afford, is today a prime necessity for all men who care that the Jewish ethos should flourish and make its own kind of contribution to all of mankind. Once this is accepted as the moral good of the first order, it then becomes possible to say that the immediate next order of moral concern is that every justice be done to Palestinian Arabs short of such action which would result in the end of the Jewish State. At a moment of political and moral resolution of tensions, when the day of peace begins to come into view, then the return of some former Arab residents to Israel, large-scale compensation and the resettlement of the bulk of the refugees on a permanent and creative basis among their Arab brothers in the large expanses of the Middle East must all be undertaken. Precisely because Jews have been involved inevitably in this tragedy, by their very coming to the land and, more important in my view, because Jews are children of the Biblical tradition, justice for Arabs should and will involve them in large and generous action.

At the very core of our concerns is not the tense and unhappy present, but the past from which it flowed and the more hopeful future for which we are laboring. That past involves us all, but it involves us in different qualities. Our interests are very deep, but they are not exactly parallel. Perhaps the best statement of this that has ever been written—it is the best that I know—was once formulated by a distinguished scholar whose own religious root was in the Anglican tradition. Writing in his *History of Palestine,* James Parkes defined these historic involvements as follows:

> The intimate connection of Judaism with the whole life of a people, with its domestic, commercial, social and public relations as much as with its religion and its relations with its God, has historically involved an emphasis on roots in physical existence and geographical actuality, such as is to be found in neither of the other religions. The Koran is not the history of the Arab people; the New Testament contains the history of no country; it passes freely from the Palestinian landscape of the Gospels to the hellenistic and Roman landscape of the later books; and in both it records the story of a group of individuals within a larger environment. But the whole religious significance of the Jewish Bible—the "Old Testament"—ties it to the history of a single people and the geographical actuality of a single land. The long religious development which it records, its law-givers and prophets, all emerge out of, and are merged into, the day to day life of an actual people with its political fortunes and its social environments. Its laws and customs are based on the land and climate of Palestine; its agricultural festivals follow the Palestinian seasons; its historical festivals are linked to events in Palestinian history—the joyful rededication of the Temple at the feast of Hanukkah, the mourning for its destruction on the ninth of Ab, and above all the commemoration of the original divine gift of the land in the feast of the Passover. The opening words of the Passover ritual conclude with the phrase: "now we are here, but next year may we be in the land of Israel. Now we are slaves, but next year may we be free men." And the final blessing is followed by the single sentence "next year in Jerusalem" (pp. 172–173).

Turning to the present, the most hopeful recent utterance by an Arab on the future of the Holy Land is by George Hourani, in a paper in November 1968 which addressed itself to themes which are essentially the same as our own. Speaking as President of the "Middle East Studies Association in the United States," Mr. Hourani considered "Palestine as a Problem of Ethics." He ruled out the notion that the modern Jewish settlers in the land had no moral right to be there; he was even inclined to consider the proposition that Jewish historic presence in the land granted Jews, even from his perspective, some substantial claim of residence and that on this point "the Arab case is not quite so unequivocal as most Arab spokesmen have claimed." Hourani climaxed his argument as follows:

> Given residence in considerable numbers, and a strong sense of national identity among Jews, it is reasonable that they should enjoy independence in a part of Palestine, on just the same grounds as the Arabs in theirs. To be absorbed as citizens in an Arab state, even as a federal province, hardly assures them of a flourishing future. Here it can be said that the drive for a Jewish state was self-fulfilling: given that drive, the feelings on both sides became so hostile that a bi-national state could not be expected to work in the foreseeable future. The logic of partition is the same today as it was under the British Mandate, the previous period of forced marriage. Both parties want to be in Palestine, but they are not there for love of each other; the driving force of both is to lead their own lives in freedom from each other. Both are happier with a whole half than with sharing the whole.

In concluding, it is meet that we return to the place and to the text with which we began. The place is Jerusalem and the text is, of course, the Bible, where Amos, like all the Prophets, began by announcing his ministry as follows: "And the Lord proclaimed from Zion and raised His voice from Jerusalem." His book concludes with: "Behold, days will come saith the Lord . . . and I will return the returnees of My people Israel and they will build up waste cities and they will plant wineyards and drink their wine, and they will plant gardens and eat of their fruits. And I will plant them upon their land and they will not again be uprooted from their land which I have given them, saith the Lord, their God."

It is in the Bible that Jerusalem as a city is indivisible: "a city which is joined altogether." Not only in the Bible but throughout its history, Jerusalem has been a unity, the one city of the one God, not only in itself but as the very essence, the living heart, of the Holy Land. In the religious consciousness of the Jewish people, a restoration to the Holy Land is inconceivable without the Holy City in which since the days of Melchizedeck, even before Abraham, God had spoken to man. To be sure, in the most ecstatic of messianic visions in the Bible it was imagined that not only Jews but all the nations would look to Zion. In the unrolling panorama of history, something of this has indeed been realized, for Christians and Moslems do indeed turn toward the Holy City and their interests in it are precious and important to Jews, as they are to all mankind. Be it remembered, however, that it is only in the system of Jewish religions law, as it has been handed down throughout the ages, that Jerusalem as a whole—not merely the site of the ancient Temple—occupies a special place. In the Bible itself it was already prescribed that the second tithe was to be used either as food to be eaten only in the city of Jerusalem, or as the wherewithal with which to finance a trip to this most sacred of all sites. For the other great religious traditions Jerusalem is the place of memories in which sacred events once took place; for the Jewish tradition, the whole city is indispensable if the Jew is to be able to live the life of performing all of the commandments enjoined by the Bible. Therefore in ancient times, by the waters of Babylon, weeping as they remembered Zion, Jews said: "If I forget Thee, O Jerusalem, may my right hand wither; may my tongue cleave to my palate, if I do not remember Thee; if I do not put Jerusalem above the greatest of my joys."

Because we descend from our various religious and cultural pasts, all of them rooted in events involving the Holy Land, we are seated here together. We may look back from various prespectives upon the events of the last half century and be saddened by much of what has happened and wish that it were undone. History does not, however, permit us to unscramble eggs.

It is the task of men of peace, mindful of the realities, to bring reason and conciliation to bear. It is certainly not our task to encourage continuing war even with the most moral of rhetoric.

It is not only Israel and the Arabs of Palestine, or Jews and the Arab world, who remain under judgment. So do we, here. Great are the peacemakers for the name of God himself is Shalom.

26. Some Reflections on Zionism Today

CLASSICAL ZIONISM ASSERTED THAT it understood and could tame anti-Semitism; that it could either sustain or make an end of the Diaspora; and that at the very least, it would create in Israel a normal nation among the nations. As a matter of fact, all of these propositions have been disproved by history. Since it is impolitic to say such things out loud, Zionist discussion has been sterile in recent years.

The most pervasive theme of Zionism is anti-Semitism. Late in the nineteenth century Zionism in both its Herzlian and Ahad Ha-amist versions presumed that anti-Semitism was a constant at a certain temperature, sometimes so uncomfortable and even scalding that some died of it in pogroms, but not so vicious and effective that it could destroy all of Jewry. For Ahad Ha-am anti-Semitism was a condition of Jewish life and indeed the guarantee that the Diaspora would continue to exist as a separate entity. The modern Jewish community would exist and would continue to wrestle with its inner spiritual and cultural problems with the aid of a "spiritual center." For Pinsker and Herzl, anti-Semitism was a rational factor, the hatred of the unlike, the most aggravated form of national tension and therefore, paradoxically, it could be turned to positive use to help build the Jewish state. Anti-Semites were

Reprinted from *Forum*, Quarterly of the World Zionist Organization, 1976, no. 25 based on the opening lecture at the Twelfth American Jewish Congress Dialogue, June 29, 1976, in Jerusalem.

supposed to share with Jews in a common interest, the normalization of Jews, so that the problem would no longer exist to trouble either side. In the Herzlian version, and even in the Ahad Haamist, there was some notion that the Jewish center or state, once created in the Land of Israel, would either cure anti-Semitism or at the very least temper it.

All of these predictions about Zionism have been disproved in the twentieth century. Anti-Semitism in our century has been both radically worse and radically better than Zionists imagined. In the first place, demonic anti-Semitism, and not only of the Hitlerian kind, has been an important contemporary mutant of the ancient disease. Even the medieval church was willing to imagine a remnant of Jews persisting to bear witness in their degradation to the truth of the church. The anti-Semitism with which Jews had seriously to cope in the twentieth century almost succeeded in destroying them utterly. It could not be tamed to become the major force moving the international community to cooperate in evacuating Jews from Europe into their own country.

If in Europe the experience of anti-Semitism culminated in the death camps, in the United States a reverse process has occurred. The most "American" of the American Jewish thinkers, Mordecai M. Kaplan, did indeed posit a "Zionist" kind of anti-Semitism, one that would be sufficiently alive in the U.S. to provide a container within which Jews would live without being so virulent as to destroy them. In fact this was true until World War II, but it is clearly not true in the most recent generation. To be sure, some pockets of social discrimination remain. In recent years Third World and other forms of liberal-left counterattacks on Jews, and especially on the connection of American Jews to Israel, have appeared. In actual fact American Jews have been living in recent decades in a society in which hardly any of their personal choices are determined by anti-Semitism.

Whatever Jewishness is alive in America today comes least from rallying together against one's domestic enemies and most from the continued momentum of positive Jewish attachments, of which the most contemporary manifestation is the tie to Israel. The dominant motif in the U.S. of the Israel–Diaspora connection is that it is both a source and an expression of positive Jewish pride. It is, indeed, the great and paradoxical achievement of Zionism in its American version to have made the Jews of America, as one among the various major political groups, to feel as normal as any group can feel among the remaining abnormalities of Diaspora living.

It would perhaps be a useless exercise in semantics or social theory to argue about the correct definition of the present tension between Israel and the Arabs. Is it the newest mutant of anti-Semitism appearing in the Arab world for the first time, or is the contemporary tension but a modern version of older hatreds between Jews and Arabs? Are the present tragedies temporary, soon to pass when peace is made? For my present purposes these issues are not important. In the here and now, it is clear that the Jewish state—which was supposed to settle in reasonably comfortably in the Middle East, either as one normal political state among the rest, or as a renewed religio-cultural community with a center in Palestine—has been created by neither prescription. Right now Israel is not the existing cure of tension between Jews and others. On the contrary, its existence and the tie of world Jewry to it is the single greatest present irritant to those who hate Jews.

To turn to the second theme—the question of the Diaspora— here, too, none of the Zionist theoretical models fit the present reality. Toward the end of the nineteenth century two kinds of Diasporas existed, at least in the consciousness of Zionists. The one in Western Europe was in the process of assimilation and disappearance and, in the Zionist view, it continued to exist Jewishly largely because of anti-Semitism.

The East European Diaspora was Jewish more because of its own inner energies and commitments than because of persecution. The various schools of Zionism presumed that the Diaspora could move in one of two directions, either negatively to vanishing in the West effectively and in maximum comfort, or positively to assert the desire to live full spiritual and cultural lives as Jews. The debate between Ahad Ha-am and Herzl about the future of the Diaspora was not really joined over the issue of whether the Diaspora was a good that needed to be preserved in its own right. It was over an estimate of what was possible, given the conditions that Jewish statecraft was likely to face. To be sure, Herzl cared little about the inner Jewish content of his Jewish state, and Ahad Ha-am's central passion was for Jewish values and not for the modes of Western national life.

Nonetheless, for both of them the options before the Diaspora were two: (1) whether to cease being Jewish; or, given the opportunity, (2) to affirm that Jewishness either through *aliyah* to the state or through making the Jewish heritage the active center of one's contemporary life, wherever one might live. Neither of them imagined a Diaspora which would have the opportunity to emigrate to a Jewish state and would choose not to; which would have the opportunity to affirm a serious Jewish culture and freedom and would largely neglect that opportunity; and which would, paradoxically, make of its labors on behalf of the Jewish state—fundraising, political support, emotional involvement—the dominant content of its Jewish life.

To put it in the starkest terms, in the Herzlian vision, as Ben-Gurion knew very well and kept insisting in the 1950s, the existence of the state meant that free Diasporas should come and join it. In the Ahad Ha-amist vision the existence of a Jewish center in the land had to be followed by a sharp rise in the cultural temperature of the Diaspora. What neither imagined is a Diaspora which would give itself content and at-homeness in freedom by the very verve of its political and economic efforts for the State of Israel, and which would, indeed, become a great success in the eyes of America precisely because of these efforts.

In America, Zionism has contributed not to the discomfort of the Jews in the Diaspora but rather to the acceptance of themselves and their acceptance by others. It has provided the Jews of America with a set of *mitzvot,* the labors for Israel. The only offense for which Jews can be "excommunicated" in the U.S. today is not to participate in those efforts. Intermarriage, ignorance in the Jewish heritage, or lack of faith do not keep anyone from leadership in the American Jewish community today. Being against Israel or apathetic in its support does.

I turn now to the question of the normalcy of the State of Israel today. This theme is, of course, the most delicate of all I have raised—especially, to be perfectly blunt, when discussed in Israel by a Jew from the Diaspora. What Israel might become in its own right is not here the issue. The state may be fortunate enough to settle its problems with its neighbors and live in the next generation in some semblance of political normalcy. It may come to terms with its own inner tension between its pervasive secularity and its ties to the Jewish past. I, for one, suspect that the foreseeable future for the State of Israel, as for the rest of the Jewish people, will bring no clear-cut solutions. But none of the predictions about the future of the State of Israel or the prescriptions for attaining that future make much difference to Israel's essential and continuing uniqueness. It is the other side of its Law of Return, that constitutional act which marks the State of Israel forever as uniquely Jewish.

In the Jerusalem platform of the world Zionist movement the fundamental affirmation is "the centrality of Israel." In that document what is meant by this term is that the building of Israel is the central and dominant purpose of all of world Jewry. The state thus exists with a Diaspora that lives to applaud it, to help it, to take pride in it, to be uplifted by it, and, at least in the minds of the Jews of the Diaspora, to help guarantee their continuity as Jews. In the crassest terms, what the state is required to return to the Jews of the Diaspora in exchange for their concern is to make a fundamental contribution to their morale, to the sense of security and the well-being of the Diaspora, and certainly that of the U.S. The "centrality of Israel" as understood in the free Diaspora does not mean that the Diaspora regards itself as in the process of building itself into the state. It means, on the contrary, that the labors for the state are the prime preservative of the Diaspora.

What we have today, and for at least a generation to come, is a Jewish world which our Zionist fathers imagined not, in which the largest Diaspora, that in the U.S., derives much of its sense of security out of working to lessen the insecurities of Israel.

What remains, then, of classical Zionism? There remains at the very least one fundamental proposition, an order of value. In no version of Zionist thought is it possible to assert the notion of the coequality of Israel and the Diaspora, not even of a Diaspora on which Israel may be overdependent. To assert the paradigm of "Jerusalem and Babylonia" is to maintain that there is no difference between living in one's own language and existing, even in power and freedom in a culture such as the American, which may be unique in not being alien to Jews but which certainly is not totally one's own. What is striking about Jewish discussion in America today is that the least learned Jews, the oft-condemned *machers* of the United Jewish Appeal and the street demonstrators on behalf of Soviet Jewry, accept and act on the presumption that Israel is more important than "local needs."

The contrary notion that the Diaspora is coequal in the scale of Jewish values is argued today by two elements. There are some professors of Jewish study and theology who want to justify the significance of their own careers, and there are activists of the political left who care at least as much about the revolution, whatever that may be for them, as they do about their Jewish specificity. The brute instinct of the Jewish masses is better. Even amid their ease in suburbia they know that Israel is Jewishly superior and they act on this faith. This sense of the priority of values is not derived in the U.S. from a sense of political inferiority. The Jews of the U.S., the very people who accept Israel's Jewish community as superior to themselves, do not at this moment feel less powerful or secure than the Jewish community in Israel.

In the years between 1967 and 1973 there was a historic moment in which part of American Jewish identification with Israel was indeed rooted in admiration for military glory and power of a state, but this is not the mood since 1973, as it was not the mood before 1967. This means that the Diaspora's respect for Israel is not for its power, and certainly not for its efficiency, but for its cultural and spiritual superiority as the incarnation of the most intense Jewishness available in our time. Never mind the definition of that Jewishness, on which the Diaspora is even vaguer and hazier than Israel itself; it is in this area that American Jewry continues to treat Israel in all of its diversities and discontinuities as a homeland and even as a teacher. The charisma with which Israeli leaders are endowed in American Jewish mythology is mostly that which accrues not to statesmen but to religious leaders. Again, a paradox—the very secularity of Israel is seen through the glasses of the Diaspora as holiness.

If Zionism continues to mean today a scale of priorities, a rank order of Jewish experiences in which Israel is held as first, it does not mean today in the Diaspora that the state is a tool for normalizing the Jewish people. On the contrary, Zionism means today for those who affirm it (and quite clearly for its most vicious enemies, those who pass resolutions condemning Zionism as racism) that the Jews of the world are a unique community. Jews are *sui generis* in the contours of their international relationships. To be a Zionist means to want to maintain that uniqueness.

Here, too, one can quote the old Talmudic sentence: "Go and see what the people in the street are doing"; that is, do not ask the official thinkers but look at experience. The world Jewish community is today being attacked for the unparalleled intensity of its connection to Israel, and Israel is attacked for maintaining its peculiar relationship to world Jewry. Those who defend that unique interrelationship are defending it in the name of the right of the Jews to be themselves. Israel is insistent on its Law of Return, but in the U.S. Jews have fought a comparable battle. They have successfully beaten down all the charges that the intensity of their concern for Israel is a form of dual loyalty. That, indeed, has been their greatest internal political victory in the last generation—to make America accept the idea that its Jewish minority, convoked primarily in politics as a pro-Israel pressure group, has the right to that activity. In the U.S. today every other pressure group exists in order to achieve some domestic objective. Only the Jews exist as a recognizable political group united on a foreign policy issue.

Zionism thus means today that Israel is not a state among the states, and that the American Jewish Diaspora is unabashedly a group not analogous to any other. To be anti-Jewish means today to demand that the Jews be more "normal"; to be pro-Jewish, or positively Jewish, means to accept the notion that the Jews have the right to live out their unconventional lives.

This assessment of where Zionism is today leads to the following conclusions: in the first place, the political style of the Jewish world as a whole is not appropriate to its present mood or to its realities. Statism was possible as the foundation of policy only so long as one operated with the image of soon to vanish or politically storm-tossed diasporas, which an ever stronger Israel would save and redeem. It is simply not appropriate at a time in which the storms are worldwide, and the most important of the diasporas is clearly at home in America in the very act of laboring for Israel. There is no way of assessing the relative importance of the various fronts on which world Jewry must fight today for its creative existence, but clearly the battle in America for assent to and support of Israel is one of the several on which we dare not ever lose.

The notion that this front, along with all the others, can be commanded almost exclusively from Jerusalem is left over from older Zionist rhetoric and mindset. Israel lives on behalf of and through world Jewry as surely as it does for itself, and the distinctions between those problems which are purely Israel-centered and those which belong to world Jewry are ever more artificial. I suspect to a very great degree that these distinctions are being maintained today in order to defend earlier statist conceptions of Israel's preeminence in world Jewry. What, indeed, is the question of American military and economic grants to Israel all about? Is it a matter only of Israel's security and defense that is within the purview of Israel's decisions, or is it not also a question, in American politics and public opinion, of the power of Jews in the U.S. to help persuade the rest of the country—and therefore an issue which requires sophisticated judgment in the U.S.? Is the settlement at Kadum, beyond the pre-1967 borders, an Israeli domestic concern only, or does it not also have enormous fallout affecting the very role Jews are playing today on that vital front which determines the political attitude of the U.S. on the Middle East? Israel's defense and security concerns might mean, on the narrowest grounds, that no one but Israeli cabinet ministers and generals should decide on battle orders and defense positions. This argument becomes something of a shibboleth when it is used to describe geopolitical assessments and decisions involving great power concerns, which involve in a serious way the role of American Jews within American public life.

I have no formula to suggest as to how the process of consultation ought to take place. There has been more such consultation in recent years than less, and the logic of events will increase this trend. Perhaps one ought to think seriously about the formula that was rejected out of hand some years ago when it was proposed informally by one of the most distinguished figures in Israel

(Menachem Begin) that a kind of Jewish "House of Lords" be created. This suggestion bristles with great difficulty. Our enemies might seize on it to "validate" the "Protocols of the Elders of Zion." Here, at last, international Jewry would be caught sitting together to plot against the world. There is the further difficulty that such a body would consist of citizens of Israel and political nationals of other states—and yet is that such a difficulty? Each one of our existing international frameworks, and especially the World Zionist Organization, are affected in one way or another with political concerns on behalf of world Jewry, and several of our international Jewish bodies such as the World Zionist Organization and the World Jewish Congress have in various forums semigovernmental status. The civilized world accepts the notion that "the house of Israel is not like all other nations." In the battle which led to the creation of the state, not only Palestinian nationals such as Moshe Sharett but even citizens of the U.S. such as Abba Hillel Silver appeared before the U.N. to represent world Jewry in support of a Jewish state. Such Americans were in open conflict with the policies of their own government.

The years immediately to come are fraught with dangers the likes of which we have not experienced since 1948. World Jewry must be rallied together politically in joint thinking. I do not mean here to deny either the sovereignty or the preeminence of Israel's political leadership, but the leadership of the rest of the Jewish world has to be brought into the ongoing process of thinking and planning to deal with all of the ramifications of our interrelated problems. If we once and for all exorcise the Israel statist political model and return to a conception based on the political uniqueness of world Jewry, modes for serious joint consultation and action will be found.

In the cultural realm, which is normally regarded as much harder to define, the situation seems to me to be more clear-cut. To be sure Israel has grave internal cultural problems, but they are of a far different order than those of the Diaspora. Israel may not yet have found the answer to the question that was asked in the very earliest days of the state: Are we still Jews? To be Israeli, even at its most secular, means that one is Jewish, perhaps even despite one's self, and certainly that one is potentially very Jewish indeed. In the free Diaspora it is Jewishness itself which is evaporating amid politics and action on behalf of Israel. Here, a vast rescue operation must be mounted and for this purpose it does not matter whether one "affirms" the Diaspora or "denies" it. The American Diaspora might experience a catastrophe and have to flee or it might not, but meanwhile it is bleeding profusely—not economically, not politically, not in its success in American culture, but from its Jewish heart.

At this moment, the prime task of Zionism in the Diaspora is to mount a rescue operation so that every Jewish child receives some kind of Jewish education, some direct experience of Israel early in his life and is challenged with the possibility of opting himself for *aliyah*. In this endeavor the preeminence of Israel is clear. I must add that it is a tragic sign of the weakness of Zionism in the U.S. that it has had so little cultural impact. In interwar Poland the Zionist movement, in the very midst of all kinds of religious and other educational expressions, created its own schools and produced a generation, some of whom survived Hitler, that proved to be a critically positive factor in Israel and the Jewish world as a whole. Today there is no Zionist education in the U.S., no schools, no teaching seminaries, no commitment by Zionists to the notion that the education of a Zionist kind of Jewish personality is of prime concern. In the U.S. there are only Orthodox and some Conservative day schools and a variety of congregational schools, almost all of them decently Zionist in spirit, but very few, even among the day schools, are bilingual, speaking Hebrew as well as English. There are younger Jewish activists around in the U.S., but very few younger Zionist intellectuals.

Here, too, the question is not what specific program one can suggest. I argued a year and a half ago at the plenum of World Jewish Congress that world Jewry had to guarantee a free Jewish education to every Jewish child, no matter how expensive, as the prime preservative task of our day. In that address I maintained that we must approach the young people in the Jewish world outside Israel and lead them to accept the demand that each give a year or two to a Jewish service corps to do their share in a world in which their peers in Israel all go into the army. Here, too, formulae do not matter. The commitment does. If we were to get beyond pious verbiage in which at all our international Jewish gatherings we affirm the importance of Jewish education and culture and instead put into this endeavor half of the kind of effort that we put into fundraising we might be redeemed.

Of course Israel is in danger and defending it is the prime objective of world Jewry, but strengthening and preserving Jewishness, wherever it might be, is an almost coequal purpose. It requires now, even in the midst of crisis, very nearly coequal energies. They are available to be evoked if we but will it.

I know that these remarks are in less messianic and visionary accents than those of the founders of Zionism. I cannot see radical solutions to make an end to the problems of the Jews of the world, either with the Gentiles or with ourselves. To be utterly candid my sense of three generations of Zionist achievement, including the state, is that some very fundamental new things are present in the Jewish world. We now do battle in our own name; we have the capacity to receive Jews into a Jewish state if that need should arise; and, above all, Israel is the magnet to draw Jews toward their own center. On the other hand, we are not "like all the other nations." Our uniqueness has not ended. It has only been recreated through different means, both in tragedy and triumph, and as far as the eye can see that uniqueness will remain.

I am a Zionist not because I may carry an Israeli passport, but because I am a citizen of world Jewry, of *am Yisrael*. The task of Zionism in our time is to educate our children for that pervasive citizenship, and to create the modes of joint endeavor, with Israel as the center, which will create and retain that citizenship.

Heinrich Graetz defined Jewish history, in a phrase which has often been mocked, as being the history of literature and suffering. By that he meant that what has united the Jews throughout the ages, amid all kinds of political and social changes, was their joint commitment to a spiritual heritage and their joint involvement in each other's problems. Pragmatically, which is the only way Zionism can be defined for all Jewry today, it seems to me that it is these two motifs which both unite us and which are our present tasks.

Let us therefore consider how we can labor together to outlive those who wish ill to all of us, and to hand on the Jerusalem both of flesh and blood and of eternity to all our Jewish children everywhere.

27. *Letter to an Arab Friend*

YOU AND I HAVE BEEN meeting in recent years in out-of-the-way coffee shops in New York, at obscure tables in the back, like illicit lovers. Our encounters have indeed been something of a courtship. Although we have both known that political decisions are not in our hands, we have, nonetheless, persisted in talking together. Yet, I suspect our motives are not the same. I am sure that you have come to these conversations with one overriding purpose in mind: to work toward "moderating" American Jews. You know that the support of American Jews and the hosts of sympathizers of Israel whom they lead is critical to Israel's strength and, yes, to its stubbornness in defense of its interests. You have therefore been looking for American Jews who would be less fervent in their support of Israel's most tough-minded policies. And you have every right to this endeavor; it flows naturally from your perception of the Arab self-interest.

But why have I come to our coffee trysts? I have not come hoping to persuade you of my views on what a settlement in the Middle East ought to look like. What I have hoped is that you, who are sophisticated enough to understand the Israelis, might ultimately understand me. I know that you know that Israel is here to stay, that the Israelis regard their state as their native land, and that no diplomatic legerdemain can change their fierce determination to live in their country on terms which they regard as

Reprinted from *Moment,* vol. 3, no. 4 (March 1978).

viable. You are, in your context, a "moderate." You understand that it is not important whether you approve or disapprove of the recent historic events, both diplomatic and military, which produced that state. You have faced the fact that Israel exists and that its patriotism is real and ineradicable. This was what President Sadat recognized when he took the step of flying to Jerusalem.

But what you have never understood, my friend, is me. You have told me as much. How is it, you have asked, that someone who is an American, and whose children continue after him in the United States, is so very much involved with Israel? You have even thrown the Palestinians up to me, telling me that those who have found their way into the Western world are not Palestinian nationalists in any serious sense. Why, you therefore ask, am I a Jewish nationalist, a Zionist? Well, here I am (and there are five million or so like me in the United States alone and millions more wherever Jews are free to express themselves) for whom Israel is the emotional center. You have been too polite, or perhaps too politically wise, to ask the even more pointed question: How is it that in all the major countries in which Jews are present in significant numbers, and especially in the United States, this marked uniqueness of the way Jews feel and behave is accepted and is permitted to be politically significant?

It is more important today than ever that you hear my answer to these questions. These days Egypt and Israel, no matter how bumpy the road they shall travel in 1978, are inexorably moving closer together. The alternative is chaos, worse than the armed truce we had before; accommodation will be found. The road to that accommodation is not easy, and it will no doubt become still more difficult before it is completed. Since so much of the diplomacy is being conducted before TV cameras, it is apparent that both sides understand that they are doing battle not for pieces of territory in the Sinai, the Golan Heights, or the West Bank, but for world public opinion, and especially opinion in the United States. There are many signs that the conversations, at least between Egyptians and American Jews, are moving from occasional meetings in secret to public dialogue across a broad front. President Sadat is himself engaged in trying to persuade American Jews; so, too, more quietly, are others.

Therefore, lest you and I, my comrade from the New York coffee shops, disappoint each other and mislead our friends, I think the time has come for me to describe what it is that motivates us—which really means, does it not, of what can you persuade us?

First, there is this: Jews like myself, even those who live in the United States, cannot forget the Nazi years and many centuries of pogroms which preceded them. It is no use to argue, as you sometimes have with me, that the Arab world is not to blame for these memories, that you were not the makers of Auschwitz. You maintain that unlike the Christians, Moslems did not persecute Jews; the present generation, therefore, owes us no recompense, certainly not in Palestine. Jewish debaters invoke the Almohades in Spain in the Middle Ages and paint the exodus of Jews from all the countries in the Middle East after 1948 as confiscatory and heavily tinged with persecution. To tell you the truth—a truth which I do not know that you ever fully accepted in our coffe shop meetings—both sides of this argument are irrelevant. It is a fact that almost all Jews are, in varying degrees, worried about the possibility of persecution even in the freest society. That means that Jews have a profound commitment to the existence of an airfield and a port somewhere in the world to which they can go *as a right* and without asking anyone for permission—and that can only be in Israel. Whether we fared better under the Arabs than under the Europeans simply makes no difference. What matters is not being under any more.

Perhaps you will understand this better if I tell you a personal story. My family came to the United States from Poland in the early 1920s when I was a small child. All of my mother's family was left behind, including her father, all her brothers and sisters, their husbands and wives and their children. In the 1930s we tried desperately to get them visas to somewhere, to anywhere. The United States, then in the midst of a depression, had its doors almost totally closed. (The quota on Polish Jews meant a sixteen-year wait for permission to come.) Palestine under the Mandate was closed even tighter—and so even in the face of the Nazi threat the American government of goodwill under Roosevelt and a British Mandate government which Arabs regarded as too soft on Zionism failed to save my mother's family. All of my relatives on that side were murdered by Hitler. What has remained with me is the iron determination that never again shall Jewish life have to depend on the goodwill of others.

I want to say this in a different way, which may not make any sense to you—but let me try it anyway: I suspect that an argument can be made for the notion that Egypt under what amounted to British rule was governed with reasonable efficiency and that it really did not make a terrible difference that certain European clubs were closed to Egyptians. You, who understand the depth of such an affront (even though your life was not endangered by it), who understand what it means to be a second-class person in one's own country, will surely understand the indelible hurt of two thousand years of Jewish dependence in every country, the reason it is simply intolerable to be required always and everywhere to find a friendly and protective non-Jew. President Sadat went to Yad Vashem, to the memorial to the six million Jews murdered by the Nazis, during his visit to Jerusalem, and he walked by a line of trees planted in honor of Gentiles who risked their lives to save Jews. Every time I walk there I am inspired with reverence for those who are so honored. Yet my feelings are ambivalent. Must the lives of Jews always depend on the presence of such people? There are always too few of them. There were too few to save my family.

From your point of view it is no doubt terribly unfair that this history of mine and these needs express themselves by recreating a Jewish state after two millennia in the Arab Middle East. I understand your hurt, which is why I have been a "dove"—that is, I am one of those Jews who seeks for every possible accommodation because my feelings about my own irreducible needs are more pained than triumphant. I do not, however, want to deceive you: for all my flexibility, I am a Zionist; I cannot and would not and do not yield on the essence of my connection to Israel.

My involvement in Israel is, paradoxically, even more intense than your link to the Palestinians. Each of us is very nearly the opposite of what he appears to be. On the surface you and the Palestinians both speak Arabic and live in the same cultures in the largely Arab Middle East; I live my life in the United States and I am writing these lines in English and not in Hebrew. And yet—

deeply though you feel for the Palestinians, passionately though you have labored for them—what happens to their cause will not, for good or ill, fundamentally change your own sense of yourself. Your feeling of security—sheer, physical safety for yourself and your family—is not bound up at all in what happens to the Palestinian cause. For me, even though my life seems to revolve mostly in other orbits, Israel can never be a cause outside myself. I live near New York and love and trust America—but I cannot sleep the night anywhere unless I know that I can never be trapped, or made completely homeless, or killed, as was my grandfather. As much as any Israeli (perhaps even more, emotionally) I need personally to know that the Ben-Gurion Airport and the port of Haifa are securely in Jewish hands.

Do not imagine that Israelis are all made happy by these feelings of mine. Yes, they know that because Jews have this continuing nightmare about Auschwitz, Israel can depend on almost unquestioning support from the Diaspora. Nevertheless, Israelis are annoyed, and sometimes even furious, with their most ardent Jewish supporters in the United States. Israelis have been insisting for at least a generation that it is the prime duty of every Jew to make *aliyah,* that is, to come to Israel to live. This, however, is an internal argument within the world Jewish community. Its meaning to you, my comrade of the coffee shops, is almost a paradox of paradoxes: you can lessen American Jewish support for Israel only by letting Israel feel totally secure, and therefore you are more likely to encounter public doves in Jerusalem than in New York. Those who guarantee an "insurance policy" (in this case the Israelis) assess the risks more or less realistically; the insured, the American Jews, tend to be more worried.

But Israel is more than a kind of national insurance policy for world Jewry. My fundamental involvement is not conditioned or even created by anti-Semitism. Israel is a creation of a kind of Zionism which I think even a man of culture and goodwill such as yourself does not really understand.

Perhaps I do you an injustice, but I think that you have become comfortable with Zionism by thinking about it as a kind of nineteenth-century European nationalism with the unique (and to you upsetting) feature that it had as its first object a land in which the bulk of the Jews had not lived for twenty centuries, even though they had remembered it in their religion and culture.

Let us not spend any time in repeating all the well-known arguments as to whether this return was right or wrong, for we will continue to differ. The trouble with the conventional description of Zionism, about which "we" have been arguing and fighting for eighty years, is that the essential revolutionary truth about Zionism is still obscure, in part because Israel itself does not yet fully live it. I do not know that this truth will set us free from all the accumulated angers; it may even increase them—but let us as least try to understand why you and I, like magnets, both attract and repel each other with unusual force. It is not because we are "brother Semites" but because our fundamental situation in the last century, our deprivations, and our needs, are parallel.

At its very core Zionism was an outcry by Jews who had lived in the West for many centuries, where they were essentially a kind of colony. They lived in ghettos under special laws and were assigned those tasks in society that Europeans did not want to perform, such as peddling and, alas, money-lending. When some of the ghetto walls finally were broken down in the nineteenth century, Jews were offered the choice of entering the majority society if they accepted its values and assimilated to its way of life. Many Jews did exactly this for as long as they could (that is, when anti-Semitism did not intervene against them), but many more felt betrayed and wanted to find a way of entering the modern world *on their own terms.* Zionism was born out of the desire to create a normal environment for Jews in a society of their own in which they could become men of the twentieth century in their own language, in the rhythm of their own calendar, and in the spirit of their own culture.

Here, too, may I recall to your memory some of the recent history of Egypt? Was it so very long ago that Egyptians were performing in their own country those tasks which their recent European masters did not want to perform? What are Third World nationalisms if not assertion by all kinds of peoples, including your own, that they want to enter the twentieth century by modernizing their traditions without being Americanized or Russified? Is it not strange, sad, but perhaps ultimately a seed of peace, that Zionism is the earliest form of the very Third World nationalism with which it is now in conflict?

What does all of this mean to me, writing about it in New York? Because Israel exists it is easier for me now than it was thirty years ago to ask for kosher food even at a White House dinner, or to refuse to attend a meeting, no matter how important, on the Sabbath. It is possible for people like me to send their children for part of their education in Israel so that they can have a sense of themselves which they cannot get in a society, even the freest and the most influenced by Jews such as America, where Jews are forever a minority.

I would be telling you less than the truth if I did not add that Israel's existence gives me every day of my life a bad conscience for not living there, and that for me personally the most essential part of my relationship to it is to keep open that question for myself and for the next generation.

What political meaning does all this have? You can depend on Jews like me to give Israel advice on one or another issue which will be more dovish than its immediate policy. But, please, please do not mistake such action for shallowness in our commitment. The difference between doves and hawks in the American Jewish community is not a difference between weak commitment and strong, or even between bleeding hearts and warmongers. It is an honest difference between people whose fundamental commitment to Israel's safety is equally powerful but who differ, as thoughtful people will, regarding the best way of insuring that security. If some of us are doves it is not that we need Israel less, or care for Israel less; we are doves, if at all, because of a tactical judgment that our policies are better for Israel's safety. And that is why you can never hope to drive a major wedge between Israel and American Jews. We are not spectators sitting in some stadium deciding whether Israel is playing well or badly with the other states on its borders, or most important, with the Palestinians. Israel's existence and fundamental purpose are central to our lives.

I look forward to seeing you again soon precisely because you, or someone like you, will be standing beside President Sadat in his conversations, direct and indirect, with American Jews. You will be wise to address yourself to our fears and concerns. We are crucial to Israel's political strength and, yes, we wield some power in the United States.

The American people as a whole, which has become through its own history hospitable to all kinds of differences, accepts and understands our Jewish fears and our commitments. The American Jewish community (again a paradox) is, in the very midst of its great passion for Israel, perhaps the most patriotic group within America. It is widely accepted as such, no doubt because everyone knows that "only in America" has a Jewish minority had such scope. The ties between the Jewish community and the rest of America are therefore as strong as those between American Jewry and Israel.

Jews like myself are tired of the tension and the threat of war, and we want peace. In fact, in its own way the American Jewish community is in a situation parallel to that of both Israel and Egypt. It has been on a "war footing" for at least two generations: the major energies of American Jewry have been spent (and will continue to be spent, if necessary) on Jewish refugees and on the support of Israel. In large part these labors have held us together as a community and given us practical and tangible common purposes of great power and meaning to us. Nonetheless, a whole host of domestic American Jewish problems are unsolved and waiting for our urgent attention.

In the last two decades the rate of intermarriage and of a general loosening of ties to the Jewish tradition among the young has been growing to alarming proportions. Like Egypt, and like Israel, we too need to turn to our domestic concerns and to our inner selves— provided that all the world understands that such a turn does not mean the displacement of Israel from the very head of our list of priorities, that our continuing and intense connection with Israel is central to the sense of purpose and well-being of American Jews.

All the fields are fertile now, even though the rain of peace falls not gently like the dew but in sudden bursts that sometimes drench. There is a point in our continuing to talk together, my friend of the coffee shops. You, who are so deeply Egyptian, Muslim, and modern, and I, the East European Jew whose "homeland" is Israel but who is deeply an American, we meet not to confront each other. I, for one, have no desire to confront you; what profit is there in that? Nor do I want to be confronted (or seduced). Do not suppose that if you "win" I will do public battle with Begin even on those specific issues where I agree with you more than I do with him—and there are such issues. I will not. Nor have I any interest in simply clarifying the battle lines between us; they are too clear already, and "your side, my side" debate is sterile.

No, the point of our meetings is not to confront *each other,* but —together—the future. For what we both know is that the day will come, sooner or later, when we shall be neighbors in more than history and geography, in living. Our task is to hasten that day, to seize this opportunity to bridge the vast historic and emotional chasms even as the others seek to bridge the political differences. Let us leave those others to their appointed tasks; let us continue to meet, and not only at back tables in obscure coffee shops, and learn not only to talk with one another but to listen to one another. Such a beginning is long, long overdue.

DATE DUE